Formal Approa...
Inform...

FACIT

Springer

London
Berlin
Heidelberg
New York
Barcelona
Budapest
Hong Kong
Milan
Paris
Santa Clara
Singapore
Tokyo

Also in this series:

Proof in VDM: a Practitioner's Guide
J.C. Bicarregui, J.S. Fitzgerald, P.A. Lindsay, R. Moore
and B. Ritchie
ISBN 3-540-19813-X

On the Refinement Calculus
C. Morgan and T. Vickers (eds.)
ISBN 3-540-19931-4

Systems, Models and Measures
A. Kaposi and M. Myers
ISBN 3-540-19753-2

Notations for Software Design
L.M.G. Feijs, H.B.M. Jonkers and C.A. Middelburg
ISBN 3-540-19902-0

Formal Object-Oriented Development
K. Lano
ISBN 3-540-19978-0

K. Lano

The B Language and Method

A Guide to Practical Formal Development

 Springer

Kevin Lano, BSc, MSc, PhD
Department of Computing
Imperial College of Science, Technology and Medicine
180 Queen's Gate
London SW7 2BZ, UK

Series Editor

S.A. Schuman, BSc, DEA, CEng
Department of Mathematical and Computing Sciences
University of Surrey, Guildford, Surrey GU2 5XH, UK

ISBN 3-540-76033-4 Springer-Verlag Berlin Heidelberg New York

British Library Cataloguing in Publication Data
Lano, Kevin
   The B language and method : a guide to practical formal development. - (Formal
   approaches to computing and information technology)
   1.B (Computer program language) 2.Formal languages 3.Computer software
   - Development
   I.Title
   005.1
   ISBN 3540760334

Library of Congress Cataloging-in-Publication Data
A catalog record for this book is available from the Library of Congress

Typesetting: Camera ready by author
Printed and bound at the Athenæum Press Ltd., Gateshead, Tyne and Wear
34/3830-543210 Printed on acid-free paper

Preface

This book provides a comprehensive introduction to the B Abstract Machine Notation, and to the ways in which it can be used to support formal specification and development of high-integrity systems. It aims to be both a text suitable for undergraduate or postgraduate courses, and a practical introduction for industrial users, covering the use of the structuring mechanisms, the use of proof, and the specific issues associated with code generation. Deeper issues of the language semantics are covered in an appendix.

The book discusses the history of B and its relationship with other languages, and successively builds up the description of the notation from the basic mathematical notation for sets, sequences, etc., to the structuring mechanisms of the language and to the ways in which it supports "programming in the large". An emphasis is placed on the use of B in the context of existing software development methods, particularly object-oriented analysis and design.

Chapter 1 gives an overview of B AMN, and its history and position relative to other formal methods.

Chapter 2 gives a rapid guided tour of each of the steps in the B development process.

Chapter 3 gives a more in-depth description of the steps involved in moving from analysis models in diagrammatic notations to a complete formal specification. Systematic translations of OMT notations into outline B AMN specifications are presented, together with a discussion of the validation techniques of internal consistency proof and animation.

Chapter 4 covers the process of refinement, design and implementation, including proofs of refinement, the "layered development" paradigm which forms a basis for compositional development and reuse, and code generation in C.

Chapter 5 gives two extended case studies of the development process.

Each chapter contains graduated exercises in B AMN specification and development, and answers are provided. All exercises have been class tested.

Appendix A gives exercise answers and Appendix B gives more information on the underlying semantics of B AMN. Appendix C introduces some proof techniques suitable for B.

An index of terms and of notation, and a bibliography are provided.

Acknowledgement

My thanks go to Imperial College for their support for the development of this material, which has been used on the MSc course unit "Theory of Specification and Verification", and particularly to Tom Maibaum for encouraging the teaching of formal methods using B. Howard Haughton and Krysia Broda contributed significantly to the technical content, and Steve Schuman and Jeremy Dick, Ib Sørensen and Dave Neilson from B-Core (UK) Ltd. provided valuable guidance on the presentation of the material.

Contents

Chapter 1

Introduction

The B Abstract Machine Notation specification language, originally developed in the early and mid 1980s by J.R. Abrial and by research groups at BP Research, MATRA and GEC Alsthom, is currently attracting increasing interest in both industry and academia. It is one of the few "formal methods" which has robust, commercially available tool support for the entire development lifecycle from specification through to code generation, and it also inherits the advantages of its predecessor, Z, in being based on familiar and well-understood mathematical foundations.

In this chapter we will outline the process of software development using B, and list the applications of the language that have been carried out to date. We also try to justify the claim that B is a more immediately industrially usable language than other formal techniques, by comparing it to some of the most widely used languages and methods.

1.1   Formal Methods

The term "formal method" tends to elicit strong reactions from software engineers and computing academics – either a reaction of enthusiasm extending to the claim that formal techniques will become the new mainstream of software engineering, or a reaction of scepticism about the research bias of much formal methods work.

By calling B AMN a formal method, we simply mean that it uses mathematical notation: predicate logic, symbols denoting sets, sequences, functions and other abstract data types, to describe both the requirements and design of software systems in a precise manner. In addition, it is more than just a notation, as a meaning is provided for this notation which supports mathematical reasoning about properties of B AMN specifications, including verification of the internal consistency of specifications (that the axioms they include can be satisfied by an implementable system) and of refinement (design steps).

Although the notation supports proof and fully formal development, it is also possible to use it in a graduated fashion with existing development methods. In Chapter 3 we give links between diagrammatic notations (entity-relationship-attribute diagrams, and state transition diagrams) and the formal notation: such links allow a developer to use mathematics to make precise the description of complex properties of the required system that cannot be specified on the diagrams. In this case formal methods are being used in a selective manner which do not replace existing skills and methods but supplement them: an approach which has been successfully used in the Fusion and Syntropy object-oriented methods, for example [14, 16].

This book will cover each of the B AMN development steps detailed in Section 1.1.2, but may be used in a selective fashion to provide guidance on only those steps which are required to obtain a particular level of software integrity and quality.

1.1.1   The Role of Specification

Why is specification of a software system useful? There are a number of reasons, which become more significant the larger and more complex the target system is. An important benefit is that a formal specification (a precise and abstract description) provides an intermediate step between requirements (which are abstract and imprecise) and executable code (concrete and precise) (Figure 1.1).

The specification is an abstract but precise description of the required functionality and behaviour of the software, which can then be validated against the customer requirements by techniques such as animation or attempts at proving particular expected properties. *Validation* of a description **D** against a description **C** means checking that **D** satisfies the properties specified in **C**, where **C** is an *informal* or semi-formal description: in the case here it is a check "is the specified system the one that the customer wants", where **C** is the informal set of customer expectations.

A specification can also be used as the basis of *verification* of the developed executable code, via proof of refinement steps. Verification of a description **D** against a description **C** means checking that **D** satisfies the properties specified in **C**, where **C** is a *formal* description. Such a check can be, in principle, a complete guarantee of functional correctness of the code with respect to the specification.

Thus a specification helps to break one (very) difficult development step from requirements to code into two difficult steps. Validation of the specification enables errors in the developer's understanding of the requirements (or inconsistencies and incompleteness in the requirements themselves) to be detected at an early stage, before commitment of effort to coding. It therefore has potential for reducing the cost of error correction. Verification of the code allows a high degree of confidence to be placed in the resulting system.

Testing can still be used as in normal development in order to validate the code against the customer's requirements. Indeed, in the absence of a specification, this is the only form of check that can be performed to identify the

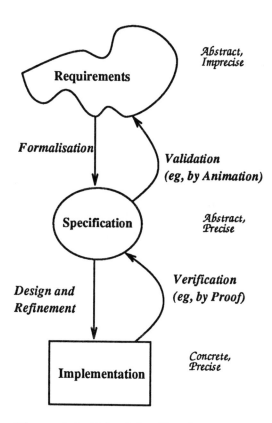

Figure 1.1: Role of Specification in Development

degree of correctness of the developed system. Testing is always an incomplete check however for real systems: it can identify only failures of compliance but cannot prove that the code fully complies with the specification in all cases.

The current state of formal methods technology means that these arguments are only a sufficient motivation for adopting specifications in a restricted number of cases however: to date, security and safety-critical systems, and systems with a very large market where the costs of development can be spread into a small increase in unit cost. The problems are that:

- large systems require large specifications, and hence, good techniques for modularising and decomposing specifications, so that parts of the specification can be analysed in relative isolation from other parts;
- verification becomes infeasible or highly expensive for modules of even moderate complexity.

The B method attempts to solve the first problem by defining a number of ways to break down a large system description into a set of linked subsystem descriptions. This decomposition does *not* imply that the design of the executable system has to follow the same decomposition; it is simply a way of splitting a large specification into a number of smaller and more manageable parts.

It attempts to solve the second problem by using structuring mechanisms which enable proofs about properties of one component to be reused in proving properties about other components: indeed the motivation for B's structuring mechanisms was limitation of the number of proof obligations associated with the internal consistency of a specification. It also allows a series of intermediate specifications to be constructed (Figure 1.2) to break a possibly very difficult verification step into a number of smaller steps.

A central element of the B approach to specification is the *layered development* paradigm, discussed in the following section.

1.1.2   The B Development Process

B supports specification, and all the refinement and design steps subsequent to specification. This is in contrast to the first generation of formal methods (particularly Z) which focussed on the formalisation of requirements and not on construction of correct executable implementations of the specifications. B is termed a *wide-spectrum* language or method, because it includes both executable descriptions and highly abstract mathematical descriptions.

An overview of the complete B development process is given in Figure 1.3. The stages of this life cycle involve the following activities:

1. **Requirements analysis**: creation of informal or structured models of the problem domain and system requirements. The result is a set of **Analysis models** (Chapter 3, Section 1);

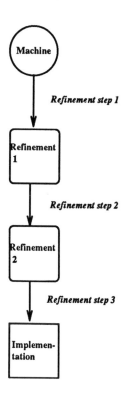

Figure 1.2: Sequence of Specifications in B

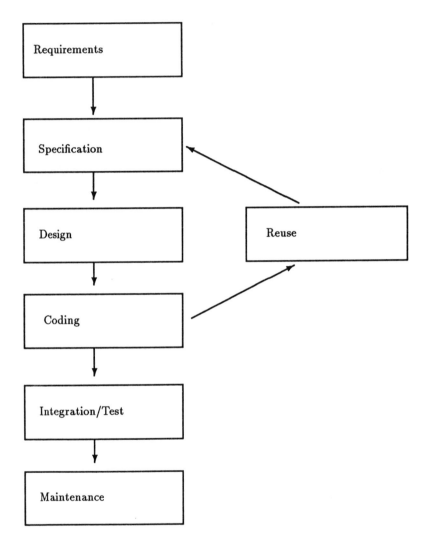

Figure 1.3: B Development Life Cycle

2. **Specification development**:

   (a) formalisation of elements of the analysis models in abstract machines, using the analysis models to decompose the specification into conceptually meaningful components (Chapter 3, Section 2);

   (b) animation to check the specification against selected requirements and test scenarios (Chapter 3, Section 3);

   (c) generation of internal consistency obligations, and proof of internal consistency obligations (Chapter 3, Section 4).

   This stage produces a **Formal specification**;

3. **Design**:

   (a) identification of the decomposition of the implementation of the system, including reusable components from existing developments or specification libraries (Chapter 2, Section 4; Chapter 4, Section 1);

   (b) creation of refinements of selected components of the formal specification (Chapter 2, Section 5; Chapter 4, Section 2);

   (c) refinement proof obligation generation and proof (Chapter 4, Section 3).

   This stage produces a **Formal design**;

4. **Coding/Integration/Test**:

   (a) application of a code generator to the lowest level designs (Chapter 4, Section 5);

   (b) testing of the generated code using test cases based on the requirements.

   This stage produces an **Executable implementation**.

The chapters and sections of the book that relate to a particular development stage are marked after the description of the stage.

If a rapid rigorous development process is required, in which there can be syntax, type-checking and animation of specifications to support the detection of errors at early development stages, then the necessary stages are 1, 2 (a), 2 (b), 3 (a), 3 (b), 4 (a) and 4 (b). In fact, it is possible to also omit stage 3 (b) and proceed directly to a level of B AMN description which is very close to code.

This type of development is close to that which would be performed using a first-generation formal method such as Z or VDM, if proof support was lacking. Such developments can, however, be quite effective in improving software quality, as demonstrated in particular by the CICS development at IBM [15].

Proof can be used at the specification level to increase the possibility of uncovering errors (either errors created by the specifier in misunderstanding the requirements, misunderstanding the notation, or by human error, or errors in the requirements themselves). Automatic proof support is highly effective in discharging most internal consistency obligations, so that if an obligation is not automatically proved, it is worth examining to determine if it is actually true or not. From the failure to prove an obligation, the source of the error can usually be determined, as we discuss in Chapter 3, Section 4.

Finally, if a fully formal development which meets most of the requirements of standards such as MOD DS 00-55 [52] is needed, then proofs of refinement steps can also be attempted and carried out.

There are two current toolkits supporting B which are commercially available. The B-Core (UK) *B Toolkit*[1] provides support for all the above development processes, with syntax and type-checking facilities, animation, proof obligation generation, automatic and interactive proof support, and code generation, in addition to documentation and configuration management facilities.

A toolkit, *Atelier B*,[2] has also been produced by Digilog in collaboration with J.-R. Abrial. This toolkit offers very similar facilities and process support to the B Toolkit, with the omission of animation capabilities. Both the B Toolkit and Atelier B provide a Motif interface.

Specification in B typically decomposes a large system description **S** into a number of linked subsystem descriptions $S_1, \ldots, S_n$. The idea is that each subsystem can be refined separately to code, independent of the design choices made in implementing the other subsystems. A subsystem **D** that makes use of the functionality provided by another subsystem **C** only accesses the abstract *specification* of **C**, and not any of its refinements (Figure 1.4).

Provided that all refinement proofs have been done, **D** can rely on the implementation of **C** obeying the functional and behavioural properties declared in its specification, and so the proof of correctness of **D**'s implementation can make use of the properties of **C** (rather than the probably much more complex properties of **C**'s implementation).

We term each of the separate refinement sequences *subsystem developments*. They are the "layers" in the layered system development. We also talk about the "level" of development that a component belongs to, meaning whether it is in the abstract specification, some intermediate refinement stage, or in the final implementation.

1.2 The History of B

The B-Method and the Abstract Machine Notation (AMN) were developed during a 3-year R & D project within the Programming Research Group (PRG) at Oxford University from 1985 to 1988. The project was initiated and sponsored by British Petroleum International.

The research on the specification language Z in the early 80s formed the background to the B-Method. For Z, J.-R. Abrial originally proposed that a set theoretical notation be used directly to write specifications, and early work on Z also highlighted the desirability of writing computer programs, and modelling their behaviour, using the same set theoretical notation.

---

[1] The B Toolkit is a trademark of B-Core (UK) Ltd.
[2] Atelier B is a trademark of Digilog.

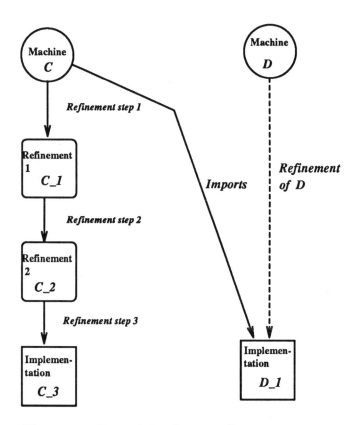

Figure 1.4: Layered Development Concept

The B-Method allows for both programs and specifications of programs to be written in a set theoretical based notation within a uniform mathematical framework. This mathematical framework was provided by using predicate transformers and by extending E.W. Dijkstra's Weakest Precondition Calculus [19].

Work by R-J. Bach, J.M. Morris and C.C. Morgan and others had illustrated how Dijkstra's calculus for programs could be extended to cover abstract specification [55]. The Oxford version of these extensions inspired the development of B's Generalised Substitution Language (GSL) for use within the B-Method. GSL and its associated calculus provides the uniform mathematical framework for reasoning about specification as well as programs. GSL adds the predicate transformers of pre-conditioning and unbounded non-determinism to Dijkstra's notation for guarded commands.

The notion of refinement developed for B is a reformulation of the refinement rules developed for Z, which in turn was an evolution of C.A.R. Hoare's and C.B. Jones's work on this topic [40]. The formulation of the refinement rules used within B's GSL framework were originally proposed by D. Gries, J. Prinz and C.C. Morgan while working in Oxford.

AMN is B's specification and design language. AMN was defined in terms of GSL. During the 3 year research project J-R. Abrial devised most of the features specific to AMN and B-Method, but significant and important contributions also came from C.C. Morgan, P. Gardiner and others working on the BP project and also from other related projects within the PRG. C.C. Morgan and I.H. Sørensen were the principal investigators of the project.

In 1988 all further work on the development of the B-Method, AMN and its supporting tool, the B-Toolkit, was moved from the PRG to the Information Technology Research Unit (ITRU) within BP Research at Sunbury, UK. From 1988 to 1992 I.H. Sørensen led the work in BP to commercialise B. D.S. Neilson led the work on the development of the B-Toolkit. J-R. Abrial was retained as the principal consultant to the development project and played a leading role in the further development of B – most significant was his development of the B-Tool, an interpreter which is at the heart of many of the components of the B-Toolkit. The B-Tool was released by BP in 1991 as part of the commercialisation programme for B. In the period 1988 to 1992 many of the B-Toolkit components were developed, and these were brought together behind a single uniform interface. The development of the B-Toolkit had contributions from D.S. Neilson, J-R. Abrial, I.H. Sørensen, I. McNeil, S. Davies and P. Scharbach. The B-Toolkit was released for alpha-testing in 1992. During this period BP had a collaboration agreement with GEC Alsthom France, and F. Mejia (GEC Alsthom) contributed to the design of some B-Toolkit components.

In 1993 B-Core (UK) Limited took over the further development of B, and in 1994 B-Core were assigned all intellectual rights to the B-Tool, the B-Toolkit and its associated languages. The B-Toolkit was released in 1994.

The use of B has continued in France, with safety critical railway applications being developed by GEC Alsthom and MATRA Transport using B [17, 10]. These included a subway speed control system, of 3000 lines of code, and a further speed control system, of 16000 lines of code.

In 1992 the B User Trials project, involving BP Research, Lloyd's Register, Program Validation Ltd, Rutherford Appleton Laboratories (RAL) and Royal Military College of Science Schrivenham, was initiated under DTI funding. This project aimed to support the industrialisation of B technology via a range of realistic case studies, and through the development of courses and proposals for technology improvement arising from the case studies. The project investigated case studies in the following areas: medical information technology (a patient monitoring system) [47]; ship-loading systems; real-time process control; specification of graphical standards (the GKS system) [61]; integration of B AMN with the SPADE static analyser [64]. A report on the project work is to be published [5]. More recently, there have been two further application case study projects involving B AMN, both funded by the European ESSI programme. The first, MathMeth, including Bull Information Systems and RAL, is investigating B and VDM for the specification of financially critical systems. The second, MIST, involves GEC Avionics. IBM UK are also using B AMN to specify and implement a number of modules of the CICS system, thus extending earlier work at Hursley Park using Z [37]. B has been applied to secure system specification in [7, 8].

1.3   The Relationship of B to Other Formal Methods

There are now a large number of formal, mathematically based, specification and design languages in use. The approach and theoretical foundation for these languages varies quite widely, from the set theory, predicate logic and schema calculus basis of Z [63], which is strongly oriented towards support for the early life cycle phases, particularly specification, to the algebraic, category-theoretic basis of OBJ [38].

An *algebraic* specification uses equational theories to describe the required properties of the software system. For example, the property that the **push(x)** operation on a stack results in a stack with top value **x** could be expressed as:

$$\forall s : Stack; \; x : Item \cdot$$
$$top(push(x, s)) \; == \; x$$

Examples of these languages are OBJ, FOOPS and PLUSS. The restricted logical language used, akin to a functional programming language, results in strong capabilities for animation, via term rewriting (replacing the LHS of a == equation by its RHS until irreducible terms are obtained). Conversely, this restrictiveness reduces the capability for abstraction in the sense of non-determinacy.

A *logical* specification uses a logic language such as general first order logic or temporal logic to express the required properties. For example:

$$push(x) \; \Rightarrow \; \bigcirc top = x$$

asserts that if **push(x)** occurs, then the value $\bigcirc$**top** of **top** in the next state will be **x**.

The object calculus of [27] is an example of this approach. These forms of specification can express relational properties of the post-state, for instance, that an attribute **var** is incremented by some non-determined amount:

$$\textbf{inc} \ \Rightarrow \ \bigcirc\textbf{var} > \textbf{var}$$

B is within the *model based* category of specification notations. These build a specific mathematical model which has the required properties. For example:

$$\textbf{push(x)} \ \hat{=} \ \textbf{contents} := [\textbf{x}] \ ^\frown \ \textbf{contents};$$
$$\textbf{y} \longleftarrow \textbf{top} \ \hat{=} \ \textbf{y} := \textbf{contents}(1)$$

expresses properties of stacks in terms of the sequence data type of B.

As such, a model based formalism is somewhat more design-oriented and less "pure" than an algebraic or logical approach. It is, however, also the most popular in industry and has been the most successful to date. Examples of such languages are Z, VDM and Object-Z.

There has been a move in recent years towards formal methods which support the entire life cycle, and which support effective specification modularisation. The RAISE specification language [60], whose development has been sponsored by the CEC via the ESPRIT programme, is an example of this approach, and includes techniques for specification, for linking formal and structured methods, and for refinement, design and code generation. Unlike B, it uses a wide variety of specification styles and notations, including algebraic, applicative (functional) and concurrent (process algebra) styles. One path that has been taken by a number of researchers is to attempt to combine object-oriented concepts and structuring mechanisms with formal specification. The Object-Z language [22] is perhaps the best known of these, although object-oriented extensions of VDM have also been proposed and used in practice [24].

B Abstract Machine Notation adopts some object-oriented specification mechanisms, although, like RAISE, it may be better termed "object-based", defining modules which are closer to the packages of the Ada language than to the classes of object-orientation: these modules encapsulate static and variable data, and operations on these data, but are not themselves types.

1.3.1 Summary

Table 1.1 summarises some of the perceived advantages of the B method and language over the currently most widespread formal methods.

The critical advantages of B, enabling its effective uptake and use within industry are:

- the relatively simple and familiar notation (generalised substitutions) used to specify state transformations. The uniform use of this from

Attributes	Z	VDM	B
Basis	Predicate Calculus, Set Theory, Schemas	Partial Functions, Set Theory	Weakest Preconditions, Set Theory
Development Stages	Specification	Specification, Design	Specification, Design, Implementation
Style	Schema Notations, Relations	Pre/Post Conditions, Functions	Rigorous Programming Language
Tool Support	At specification level	At specification level	All development stages
Training Support	books, courses	books, courses	case studies, courses

Table 1.1: Comparison of B AMN with other Formal Methods

specification to code reduces the cost of learning the notation, and the possibility of semantic errors through translations. The notation is a "mathematical programming language" which can encourage an overly concrete specification style, but has advantages in terms of familiarity to software engineers;

- constructs for supporting modularity in specification and implementation, allowing decomposition of the task of verification and specification into more feasible sub-tasks. The unusual nature of these constructs may be an initial problem for those familiar with other specification languages, but represent no greater learning difficulty than the structuring facilities of Ada or C++;

- the existence of robust tool support for all the stages of the software development lifecycle, including animation and document production. This collection of facilities is not currently offered for any other formal method;

- the successful application of the method and language to large industrial systems, in a range of technical areas: real-time, simulation, information processing and engineering.

The language and method seem to have considerable potential as a practical and usable formally-based tool for developing software, and could greatly contribute to bringing formal methods into more widespread use in software engineering.

1.4 Summary

- Formal methods are a useful addition to the repertoire of software development, but need to be integrated with existing practices where possible.

- B AMN provides support for all development stages from the formalisation of requirements to the generation of executable code.
- Extensive, commercially available tool support exists for B.
- B was developed from Z in order to enhance the modularity and capability of tool support for this formal method. It has been industrially applied to safety-critical systems such as train control and protection systems, and to the CICS development.
- B is within the "model-based" family of specification languages.

Chapter 2

The Foundations of B AMN

In this chapter we will give a comprehensive description of the B AMN language, building up from the level of elementary mathematics and "generalised substitutions" (the means by which B AMN specifies state transformations) to the level of machines and the visibility relationships induced between machines by the structuring mechanisms (USES, INCLUDES, EXTENDS, etc.).

A description of refinement and implementation is given in Section 2.5 and Chapter 4.

2.1 Mathematical Notation

2.1.1 The Role of Mathematics

Mathematics is used in "formal" software specification and development in two related but distinct ways:

- discrete mathematics (dealing with properties of sets, sequences, maps, etc.) is useful for modelling requirements or designs in a clear, precise and abstract manner, free from implementation details and (for non-critical systems) space considerations;
- systems of proof and reasoning can support *verification* and *validation* of specifications and development steps – proving the internal consistency of individual specification modules and the correctness of development steps between related modules comes into the category of verification, whilst checking that certain expected properties hold by attempting to prove them from a module description comes into the category of validation.

The second depends on the first (Figure 2.1), but does not need to be carried out for all forms of software development, as we discussed in Chapter 1. Indeed, full application of formal proof for non-trivial systems is still at the limits of feasibility, and is only carried out for highly critical systems such as nuclear reactor protection software.

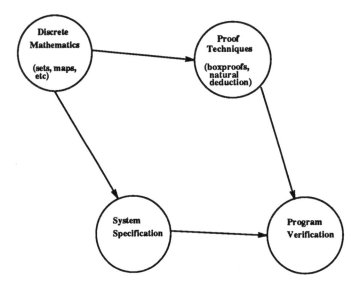

Figure 2.1: Mathematics in System Development

Thus we will focus here on describing the mathematical theories of abstract
data structures (sets, sequences, maps, etc.) and consider proof formalisms in
Appendix C.

2.1.2   Discrete Mathematics

The mathematical notation of B AMN is quite standard. Moreover, a classical
logic is used, that is, with two values, and without the explicit use of "undefined" values. However, there are two variants of the notation which are used
in practice: an ASCII representation which is entered by the developer when
creating machines, refinements, implementations and proof rules via a tool,
and a directly corresponding LaTeX representation. In this book we will use
only the LaTeX representation. The ASCII **NAT** has been given the denotation
$0..\textbf{MAXINT}$ in some work on B, where $\textbf{MAXINT}$ is $2^{31} - 2$. In this book we
will, however, use the mathematical (infinite) set $\mathbb{N}$ of natural numbers, adding
suitable constraints on the values of variables where necessary to ensure that
their types are implementable.

The B notations are mostly identical to the corresponding Z symbols. Set
subtraction − is denoted by \ in Z, and relational image r[S] is denoted by
r⦇ S ⦈ in Z. A literal sequence $[s1, \ldots, sn]$ is denoted by $\langle s1, \ldots, sn \rangle$ in Z. B
somewhat excessively overloads the [ ] and . symbols − this is in part due to
a desire to reduce the gap between the ASCII and mathematical presentation
of notations. The B notations are explained in more detail in the following
sections.

Sets   A set is the most primitive kind of structured data-type: it simply records the presence $x \in S$ or absence $x \notin S$ of an element x in a collection of elements S of the same type as x.

$\mathbb{F}(S)$ denotes the type of sets s all of whose elements are in S, and which are *finite*. $\mathbb{P}(S)$ also includes infinite subsets of S (of course, if S is finite, these two types have the same members).

The $\cup$ (union) operation allows elements to be added to a set ($S \cup T$ contains exactly those elements which are either in S or in T or in both), whilst the $-$ operation allows elements to be removed ($S - T$ contains exactly those elements which are in S but not in T).

A set S is a *subset* of set T if every element of S is also in T. This relation (including the case that $S = T$) is denoted by $\subseteq$:

$$S \subseteq T \equiv \forall x.(x \in S \Rightarrow x \in T)$$

Of key importance is the ability to define sets of elements which satisfy particular properties. If $\varphi(x)$ is a predicate with free variable x of type T, then the notation

$$\{x \mid x \in T \wedge \varphi\}$$

denotes the set of all $x \in T$ which satisfy φ. A list of variables x may be used here – the resulting set is then a relation. This corresponds to the notation $\{x : T \mid \varphi \bullet x\}$ in Z.

Thus

$$\{x \mid x \in \mathbb{N} \wedge \exists y.(y \in \mathbb{N} \wedge x = y * y)\}$$

denotes the (infinite) set $\{0, 1, 4, 9, 16, 25, \ldots\}$ of natural numbers which are perfect squares.

If we had instead written

$$\{y, x \mid x \in \mathbb{N} \wedge y \in \mathbb{N} \wedge x = y * y\}$$

then the result would be the relation

$$\{0 \mapsto 0,\ 1 \mapsto 1,\ 2 \mapsto 4,\ 3 \mapsto 9, \ldots\}$$

which gives for each number its corresponding square (note the order of the identifiers in the set comprehension here).

It is usual to use $\mathbb{F}$ rather than $\mathbb{P}$ to define the types of variables, and most constants, because actually infinite data items will not exist in executable programs.

Relations   A relation $r \in X \leftrightarrow Y$ is a set of pairs $x \mapsto y$ of elements $x \in X$ and $y \in Y$.

For relations, there is a notion of relational image (this also exists for functions, because functions are a special form of relation). This is denoted by $r[\,]$ and has the type:

$$r[\,] \in \mathbb{P}(X) \rightarrow \mathbb{P}(Y)$$

It is defined by:

$$r[S] = \{y \mid y \in Y \land \exists x.(x \in S \land (x \mapsto y) \in r)\}$$

That is, $r[S]$ consists of all those elements in Y which are related by r to some element of S. Thus for the perfect square relation, $r[\{2, 3\}] = \{4, 9\}$.

The *domain* of a relation r is the set of elements

$$\text{dom}(r) = \{x \mid x \in X \land \exists y.(y \in Y \land (x \mapsto y) \in r)\}$$

whilst the *range* is the set

$$\text{ran}(r) = \{y \mid y \in Y \land \exists x.(x \in X \land (x \mapsto y) \in r)\}$$

r is then also a relation between these sets:

$$r \in \text{dom}(r) \leftrightarrow \text{ran}(r)$$

Relational overriding $\oplus$ is an important operator that will be used in many specifications involving functions. Informally, if

$$f \in X \leftrightarrow Y \land$$
$$g \in X \leftrightarrow Y$$

then $f \oplus g$ denotes the set of pairs $x \mapsto y$ which are either in g, or which are in f and for which there is no pair of the form $x \mapsto z$ in g.

Thus g "overrides" the relations between elements given by f. Formally, overriding is defined by:

$$f \oplus g = \{x, y \mid x \in \text{dom}(f) \cup \text{dom}(g) \land$$
$$(x \in \text{dom}(g) \land (x \mapsto y) \in g) \lor$$
$$(x \notin \text{dom}(g) \land (x \mapsto y) \in f)\}$$

Relations can be composed by the operators ; and $\circ$. If $r : X \leftrightarrow Y$ and $s : Y \leftrightarrow Z$, then $r; s : X \leftrightarrow Z$ and

$$r; s = \{x, z \mid x \in X \land z \in Z \land$$
$$\exists y.(y \in Y \land (x \mapsto y) \in r \land (y \mapsto z) \in s)\}$$

$\circ$ is defined by $r \circ s = s; r$.

Functions   A relation $r \in X \leftrightarrow Y$ is a function if for every $x \in X$ there is at most one $y \in Y$ such that $(x \mapsto y) \in r$. Formally:

$$\forall x.(x \in X \Rightarrow \text{card}(r[\{x\}]) \leq 1)$$

Its typing can then be given as

$$r \in X \nrightarrow Y$$

Such a general form of function is called a *partial* function (on **X**) since its domain dom(**r**) may not contain all the elements of **X**.

If in addition we know that

$$\forall \mathbf{x}.(\mathbf{x} \in \mathbf{X} \Rightarrow \mathbf{card}(\mathbf{r}[\{\mathbf{x}\}]) = 1)$$

(for every **x** in **X** there is a *unique* **y** in **Y** such that **x** $\mapsto$ **y** is in **r**) then we can write

$$\mathbf{r} \in \mathbf{X} \rightarrow \mathbf{Y}$$

Such **r** are termed *total* functions, and have dom(**r**) = **X**.

All set and relation operators apply to functions as special cases. Set comprehensions which produce functions may alternatively be written using the λ notation.

Consider the function

$$\mathbf{f} = \{1 \mapsto 2, 2 \mapsto 3, 3 \mapsto 5\}$$

This could be part of an explicit enumeration of the prime numbers.

f is a set (of pairs) and **card(f)** = 3. **f** is also a partial function of the type

$$\mathbb{N} \nrightarrow \mathbb{N}$$

with domain

$$\mathrm{dom}(\mathbf{f}) = \{1, 2, 3\}$$

and range

$$\mathrm{ran}(\mathbf{f}) = \{2, 3, 5\}$$

It is a relation between natural numbers:

$$\mathbf{f} \in \mathbb{N} \leftrightarrow \mathbb{N}$$

f is a total function on its domain:

$$\mathbf{f} \in 1\,.\,.\,3 \rightarrow \mathbb{N}$$

where a $.\,.$ b for **a**, **b** $\in \mathbb{N}$ denotes the contiguous interval of natural numbers **a**, **a** + 1, ..., **b** between **a** and **b**.

A general λ expression has the form

$$\lambda(\mathbf{ind}).(\mathbf{ind} \in \mathbf{Type} \wedge \mathbf{P}(\mathbf{ind}) \mid \mathbf{E}(\mathbf{ind}))$$

and denotes

$$\{\mathbf{ind}, \mathbf{ee} \mid \mathbf{ind} \in \mathbf{Type} \wedge \mathbf{P}(\mathbf{ind}) \wedge \mathbf{ee} = \mathbf{E}(\mathbf{ind})\}$$

For example, $\lambda\,\mathbf{ii}.(\mathbf{ii} \in \mathbb{N} \wedge \mathbf{ii} \leq 5 \mid \mathbf{ii} * \mathbf{ii})$ has the value $\{0 \mapsto 0, 1 \mapsto 1, \ldots, 5 \mapsto 25\}$.

Sequences In B and Z, sequences are regarded as finite functions whose domain is of the form $1 .. \mathbf{x}$ for some natural number $\mathbf{x}$. Thus:

$$\mathrm{seq}(\mathbf{T}) \;=\; \{\mathbf{f} \mid \mathbf{f} \in \mathbb{N} \nrightarrow \mathbf{T} \wedge \exists \mathbf{n}.(\mathbf{n} \in \mathbb{N} \wedge \mathrm{dom}(\mathbf{f}) = 1 .. \mathbf{n})\}$$

A sequence $\{1 \mapsto \mathbf{s}_1, 2 \mapsto \mathbf{s}_2, \ldots, \mathbf{n} \mapsto \mathbf{s}_\mathbf{n}\}$ is more concisely written as $[\mathbf{s}_1, \mathbf{s}_2, \ldots, \mathbf{s}_\mathbf{n}]$.

An important operation on sequences is concatenation: $\mathbf{s} \frown \mathbf{t}$ is the sequence whose first $\mathrm{size}(\mathbf{s})$ elements are those of $\mathbf{s}$, in the order given in $\mathbf{s}$, and whose last $\mathrm{size}(\mathbf{t})$ elements are those of $\mathbf{t}$ in the order given in $\mathbf{t}$ – these are all the elements of $\mathbf{s} \frown \mathbf{t}$.

Thus $[2,3] \frown [4,6,0]$ is $[2,3,4,6,0]$, for example.

The first element of a non-empty sequence $\mathbf{s}$ is given by $\mathbf{first}(\mathbf{s}) = \mathbf{s}(1)$. The sequence of all elements except the first is given by $\mathbf{tail}(\mathbf{s})$, and $\mathbf{front}(\mathbf{s})$ is the sequence of all elements except the last. The last element $\mathbf{s}(\mathrm{size}(\mathbf{s}))$ is given by $\mathbf{last}(\mathbf{s})$.

Notice that the example function $\mathbf{f}$ given above is a sequence:

$$\mathbf{f} \in \mathrm{seq}(\mathbb{N})$$

and can be written as

$$[2, 3, 5]$$

2.2   Defining Operations

2.2.1   Generalised Substitutions

B AMN is based on a particular variant of classical logic and Zermelo-Frankel set theory. It is thus quite close in its foundation to that of the Z language [63]. However, the means by which AMN specifies state transitions (generalised substitutions) is quite different from that of Z (schemas). The generalised substitution approach was chosen for a number of reasons:

- to simplify proof requirements;
- to provide a uniform notation from abstract specifications down to procedural code;
- to support decomposition of operations in refinement-preserving ways.

For example, an operation to insert an item into an array of maximum length **maxlen**, keeping track of the last place where an insert was done, could be defined by:

insert(item, place) $\;\hat{=}$
       PRE **item** $\in$ **Item** $\wedge$ **place** $\in$ $1 ..$ **maxlen**
       THEN

$$\begin{aligned}
&\textbf{array}(\textbf{place}) \; := \; \textbf{item} \; \| \\
&\textbf{pointer} \; := \; \textbf{place}
\end{aligned}$$
END

Notice that typing constraints on input parameters (**item** and **place**) are presented as part of the precondition – the operation should only be invoked if these constraints hold for the actual parameters. The body of the operation carries out a "simultaneous" update of the **array** and the **pointer**: this is akin to predicate conjunction within a Z schema or in the postcondition of a VDM operation.

A *generalised substitution* is an abstract mathematical programming construct, built up from basic substitutions $\mathbf{x} := \mathbf{e}$, corresponding to assignments to state variables, via the following operators:

SKIP	No-op
$S_1 [] S_2$	Bounded choice: do S_1 or S_2
$P \mid S$	Preconditioning: if P holds, behave as S
$P ==> S$	Guarding: execute only if P holds, then do S
$@\mathbf{v}.S$	Unbounded non-determinism: do S for some $\mathbf{v}$
$S_1; \; S_2$	Sequential composition: do S_1 then S_2
$S_1 \; \| \; S_2$	Multiple generalised substitution: do S_1 and S_2
WHILE E DO S	
INVARIANT I	
VARIANT e END	Looping: do S while E

where S, S_1 and S_2 represent generalised substitutions, e an expression, I, E and P predicates, and $\mathbf{v}$ a variable or list of variables.

The difference between $P \mid S$ and $P ==> S$ can be intuitively understood as being that the first *should not* be invoked when P fails to hold, whilst the second *cannot* be executed when P fails to hold. The first may behave in an arbitrary and unpredictable manner outside of P (including failing to terminate), whilst the second will be entirely predictable (but make no progress towards execution) outside of P. This distinction really refers to the possible implementations of these statements (ie, a valid implementation of $P \mid S$ could enter into an infinite loop if P fails) but we will consider that this also describes what the "execution" of these statements means.

These constructs are used to define the substitutions actually used within machine operations as follows:

- $S_1 [] S_2$:   CHOICE S_1 OR S_2 END;
- $P \mid S$:   PRE P THEN S END;
- $P ==> S$:   SELECT P THEN S END;
- $@\mathbf{v}.(P ==> S)$:   ANY $\mathbf{v}$ WHERE P THEN S END;
- $@\mathbf{v}.S$:   VAR $\mathbf{v}$ IN S END.

The ANY and VAR constructs introduce new local variables $\mathbf{v}$ – in the case of ANY these are constrained to satisfy a predicate P.

Only a subset of these constructs can be used at the various development stages. At the abstract specification level the procedural constructs of sequential composition, WHILE loops and VAR are not allowed. At intermediate refinement stages all constructs except WHILE may be used. At the final implementation stage only procedural constructs can be used (so that PRE, ANY, ||, CHOICE and guarding cannot be used).

Some examples of generalised substitutions are:

- select some element **xx** from a set **ss**:

> ANY **vv**
> WHERE **vv** $\in$ **ss**
> THEN **xx** := **vv**
> END

This is usually abbreviated to **xx** :$\in$ **ss**;
- delete **xx** from **ss**:

> **ss** := **ss** $-$ { **xx** }

- add **xx** to the end of the sequence **sq**:

> **sq** := **sq** $\frown$ [**xx**]

- test if a sequence **sq** is strictly ordered:

> IF
> $\quad \forall$ (**ii**, **jj**).(**ii** $\in$ dom(sq) $\wedge$
> $\qquad\qquad\qquad$ **jj** $\in$ dom(sq) $\wedge$
> $\qquad\qquad\qquad$ **ii** < **jj** $\Rightarrow$
> $\qquad\qquad\qquad\qquad$ sq(**ii**) < sq(**jj**))
> THEN **bb** := **TRUE**
> ELSE **bb** := **FALSE**
> END

An operation definition

y $\longleftarrow$ **op(x)** $\widehat{=}$
$\quad$ PRE **Pre**
$\quad$ THEN
$\qquad$ **S**
$\quad$ END

in a machine **M** can be regarded as expressing a *contract* between **M** (in its role as a *supplier* of functionality) and modules that invoke **op** (*clients*) . It asserts that if a client invokes **op** with **Pre** holding, then **M** will execute some behaviour which obeys the specification **S**.

birthday =
    PRE age + 5 ≤ 200
    THEN
        age :∈ age .. (age + 5)
    END

therefore asserts that if **age** $+ 5 \leq 200$ at operation invocation, then **age** will be incremented by at most 5.

Consequently a specification

useless =
    PRE false
    THEN
        S
    END

never guarantees anything – it is akin to the standard disclaimers for commercial software "no warranty expressed or implied" that no particular behaviour can be expected by the user!

The definition of refinement adopted in B preserves satisfaction of contracts. That is, if a substitution **S** obeys contract **C**, then so does any refinement **T** of **S**.

The semantics of generalised substitutions is defined by means of *predicate transformers* [39]. These describe how the substitution transforms pre-states into post-states by specifying what pre-states are required for a particular post-state to arise.

More precisely, for each predicate **P** in the B mathematical language, with variables from among all the possible B identifiers, and for each generalised substitution **S**, a new predicate "**S** establishes **P**"

$$[S]P$$

is defined which describes the set of states which can lead, after "execution" of **S** in one of these states, to a new state which is within the set of states described by **P**.

The definition of this predicate for simple assignments $x := e$, where **x** is a list of identifiers, and e a list (of the same length) of expressions, is:

$$[x := e]P \equiv P[e/x]$$

where the latter predicate stands for the textual substitution of each of the expressions $e_1, \ldots, e_n$ for the corresponding $x_1, \ldots, x_n$. If there is a variable in some e_i which would become bound as a result of the substitution in the resulting predicate, then the quantified variable which would bind this variable is renamed to avoid the variables in the e_i.

In addition, if a variable on the left hand side is of the form **a(i)**, where $a : D \nrightarrow R$ for a partial function type $D \nrightarrow R$ (or for any other function type), then the simple substitution

$$a(i) := e$$

is converted to

$$a := a \oplus \{i \mapsto e\}$$

and so forth, recursively, until all the variables on the left hand side of the simple substitution are identifiers. This process is known as "normalisation". More details are given in Appendix B.

As some simple examples, we have:

$$[\mathbf{xx} := \mathbf{yy}](\mathbf{xx} > \mathbf{yy}) \quad \equiv \quad (\mathbf{yy} > \mathbf{yy})$$
$$[\mathbf{xx}, \mathbf{yy} := \mathbf{xx} + 1, \mathbf{xx} * \mathbf{xx}](\mathbf{xx} > \mathbf{yy}) \quad \equiv \quad (\mathbf{xx} + 1 > \mathbf{xx} * \mathbf{xx})$$
$$[\mathbf{xx}, \mathbf{yy}, \mathbf{zz} := \mathbf{ee}, 2, \mathbf{zz} - \mathbf{xx}](\mathbf{xx} > \mathbf{yy} \wedge \mathbf{zz} \in \mathbb{N}) \quad \equiv$$
$$(\mathbf{ee} > 2 \wedge \mathbf{zz} - \mathbf{xx} \in \mathbb{N})$$
$$[\mathbf{aa}(\mathbf{ii})(\mathbf{jj}) := 12](\mathbf{aa} \neq \mathbf{bb}) \quad \equiv$$
$$\mathbf{aa} \oplus \{\mathbf{ii} \mapsto (\mathbf{aa}(\mathbf{ii}) \oplus \{\mathbf{jj} \mapsto 12\})\} \neq \mathbf{bb}$$
$$[\mathbf{xx} := \mathbf{yy} + \mathbf{zz}] \forall \mathbf{zz}.(\mathbf{zz} \in \mathbf{ss} \Rightarrow \mathbf{xx} > \mathbf{zz}) \quad \equiv$$
$$\forall \mathbf{tt}.(\mathbf{tt} \in \mathbf{ss} \Rightarrow \mathbf{yy} + \mathbf{zz} > \mathbf{tt})$$

The last example illustrates what happens when a "clash of bound variables" occurs.

Intuitively, $[\mathbf{S}]\mathbf{P}$ is the weakest predicate which implies that every (feasible) execution of $\mathbf{S}$ in any state satisfying this predicate leads to a terminating execution of $\mathbf{S}$ in which $\mathbf{P}$ holds in the post-state. Thus the implication

$$\mathbf{R} \Rightarrow [\mathbf{S}]\mathbf{P}$$

states, informally:

> "For every state s, if $\mathbf{R}$ holds in s, then every accepted execution of $\mathbf{S}$ starting from s terminates in a state satisfying $\mathbf{P}$."

The word "accepted" indicates that certain specifications (substitutions) cannot be feasibly executed (accepted for execution) by any physical computational device. The notion of termination is given a formal definition below, as is the distinct concept of "feasibility" of a substitution.

The predicate $[\mathbf{S}]\mathbf{P}$ corresponds to the weakest (total) precondition of [39, 19]. For a machine operation definition $\mathbf{S}$ it is a predicate over the attributes of the machine and the input parameters to the operation. It, therefore, describes the set of states $\mathbf{t}$ such that

$$\forall(\mathbf{t}', \mathbf{e}).(\mathbf{t} \frac{\mathbf{S}}{\mathbf{e}} \mathbf{t}' \quad \Rightarrow \quad \mathbf{t}' \models \mathbf{P})$$

"every execution e of $\mathbf{S}$ from t yields a post-state satisfying $\mathbf{P}$".

Notice that $[\mathbf{S}]\mathbf{true}$, therefore, denotes the set of starting states from which $\mathbf{S}$ is guaranteed to terminate, whilst $\neg [\mathbf{S}]\mathbf{false}$ which is

$$\exists(\mathbf{t}', \mathbf{e}).(\mathbf{t} \frac{\mathbf{S}}{\mathbf{e}} \mathbf{t}' \wedge \neg (\mathbf{t}' \models \mathbf{false}))$$

ie:

$$\exists(\mathbf{t}', \mathbf{e}).(\mathbf{t} \frac{\mathbf{S}}{\mathbf{e}} \mathbf{t}')$$

denotes the set of starting states from which there is a feasible execution (not necessarily terminating, since t' may represent an undefined state, which satisfies no predicate).

2.2.2 Semantics of Generalised Substitutions

The definition of $[S]P$ for other generalised substitutions is given by structural induction.

$$
\begin{aligned}
[\text{SKIP}]P &\equiv P \\
[S_1 [] S_2]P &\equiv [S_1]P \wedge [S_2]P \\
[E \mid S]P &\equiv E \wedge [S]P \\
[E ==> S]P &\equiv E \Rightarrow [S]P \\
[@v.S]P &\equiv \forall v.[S]P \\
[S_1; S_2]P &\equiv [S_1][S_2]P
\end{aligned}
$$

$$
\begin{aligned}
[\text{WHILE } E \text{ DO } S \\
\text{INVARIANT } I \\
\text{VARIANT } v \text{ END}]P &\Leftarrow I \wedge \\
1 &: \forall l.(I \wedge E \Rightarrow [S]I) \wedge \\
2 &: \forall l.(I \wedge \neg E \Rightarrow P) \wedge \\
3 &: \forall l.(I \wedge E \Rightarrow v \in \mathbb{N}) \wedge \\
4 &: \forall l.(I \wedge E \wedge v = \gamma \Rightarrow [S](v < \gamma))
\end{aligned}
$$

In the case of $[@v.S]P$ v is not free in P, and in the last case, γ is a new variable not free in the WHILE substitution or the predicates concerned, and l is the list of variables modified within the loop.

The intuition behind these definitions is as follows:

SKIP is always feasible, always terminates, and always leaves the state unchanged. Thus the post-state satisfies P exactly when the pre-state does.

$S_1 [] S_2$ is the substitution which, for any pre-state, either executes according to S_1, or to S_2, and there is no way to control this choice. Thus, to be certain that every terminating execution of $S_1 [] S_2$ establishes P, we need this to hold for both substitutions separately.

$E \mid S$ is the substitution which is guaranteed to terminate or have a well-defined behaviour only for those pre-states which satisfy E, and which then behaves as S. Thus in order to guarantee that P holds after $E \mid S$ we must ensure that E holds, and then that S establishes P, ie, that $[S]P$.

$E ==> S$ is the substitution which is only required to be feasible for those pre-states satisfying E, and which is infeasible outside this set of pre-states. The intuition we have is that a computer will refuse to execute such a statement outside of its domain of feasibility. Considering $[\text{Def}]P$ as an implicit universal quantification over executions of **Def**, it is clear that it places no constraint on the pre-state if this does not satisfy E, since then there are no executions of $E ==> S$. On the other hand, if E is true, the possible executions of $E ==> S$ are exactly those of S.

@v.S is the substitution which makes a non-deterministic choice between members of a family of substitutions indexed by **v**. Thus, as with bounded choice, we must ensure termination in a post-state satisfying **P** for every member of this family to ensure that the choice itself terminates in a state satisfying **P**.

S_1; S_2 is conventional sequential composition: do S_1 and then S_2. Thus we can break up the overall "execution" of the substitution into these two components.

WHILE **E** DO **S** INVARIANT **I** VARIANT **v** END is the standard 'while' loop construct. It is actually not a primitive construct in [2], but, for simplicity, we will treat it as such. The obligations have the following meanings:

1. The loop invariant **I** is maintained by the loop substitution, provided the loop is entered: this acts like an induction step in a proof that **I** is always true at the 'beginning' of each loop body execution, and at termination of the loop;
2. The invariant, together with the negation of the loop test, implies the post-condition;
3. During loop execution, the variant is always a natural number: it will usually be an expression involving some of the variables modified within the loop;
4. The variant is always strictly decreased by each loop body execution.

Conditions 3 and 4 together imply that the loop terminates in a finite number of iterations.

The generalised substitutions [] and ==> arose from consideration of the nature of programming language statements such as

```
IF E THEN S1 ELSE S2 END
```

It was realised that this statement is in fact a composite of more primitive constructs: bounded choice ([]) and guarding (==>). In B AMN we define the semantics of primitive constructs directly, as above, and then define composite constructs in terms of these. Thus, in particular:

$$\text{IF } \mathbf{E} \text{ THEN } S_1 \text{ ELSE } S_2 \text{ END } = \\ (\mathbf{E} ==> S_1)[](\neg \mathbf{E} ==> S_2)$$

This means that:

$$[\text{IF } \mathbf{E} \text{ THEN } S_1 \text{ ELSE } S_2 \text{ END}]\mathbf{P} \equiv \\ (\mathbf{E} \Rightarrow [S_1]\mathbf{P}) \wedge (\neg \mathbf{E} \Rightarrow [S_2]\mathbf{P})$$

for every **P**, as usual.

We say that two generalised substitutions S_1 and S_2 are equivalent if they establish the same post-conditions under all circumstances:

$$\forall \mathbf{P}.([S_1]\mathbf{P} \equiv [S_2]\mathbf{P})$$

Other constructs may be defined as 'syntactic sugar' for the basic language elements:

```
LET  v
BE  P
IN
    S
END                =    @v.(P    ==>   S)
```

for instance (where **P** must be a conjunction of equalities $x = E_x$ for each identifier **x** in the list **v**, where none of the **x** are free in any of the E_x).

In addition, the *multiple generalised substitution* operator || is defined partly by the requirement:

$$\mathbf{prd}_{x,y}(S_1 \parallel S_2) \equiv \mathbf{prd}_x(S_1) \wedge \mathbf{prd}_y(S_2)$$

where **x** is the list of variables updated in S_1, and **y** those in S_2. $\mathbf{prd}_v$ converts a generalised substitution **S** on variables **v** into a predicate on **v** and **v'** which expresses the effect of the substitution as a relation between initial states **x** and final states **x'**:

$$\mathbf{prd}_x(S) \equiv \neg [S] \neg (x' = x)$$

For example, $(x > 0) ==> ((x > 1) \mid x := 2)$ has the relational interpretation

$$\mathbf{prd}_x(S) \equiv x > 0 \wedge (x > 1 \Rightarrow x' = 2)$$

which is the set of pairs

$$\{x, x' \mid x = 1 \vee (x > 1 \wedge x' = 2)\}$$

so this relation excludes $0 \mapsto \mathbf{v}$ and allows any $1 \mapsto \mathbf{v}$.

More details of **prd** are given in Appendix B. || acts like schema conjunction in Z, and means "do S_1 and S_2". It is only sensibly defined in the case that the lists of variables **x** and **y** are disjoint. The precondition of $S_1 \parallel S_2$ is the conjunction of the preconditions of the separate substitutions.

Examples of the meaning of || are:

$$\mathbf{v} := \mathbf{e} \parallel \mathbf{w} := \mathbf{f} \quad = \quad \mathbf{v}, \mathbf{w} := \mathbf{e}, \mathbf{f}$$

in the case that **v** and **w** are disjoint lists of identifiers, and:

```
v  :=  e  ||  IF  E  THEN  S1  ELSE  S2  END    =
           IF  E  THEN  v  :=  e  ||  S1  ELSE  v  :=  e  ||  S2  END
```

Further laws for || and more detailed properties of weakest preconditions are given in Appendix B.

2.2.3   Examples of Generalised Substitutions

An elementary example of a deterministic and program-like generalised substitution is the following:

```
PRE
   nn ∈ ℕ ∧
   vv ≥ nn
THEN
   vv := vv - nn
END
```

This substitution decrements the variable **vv**, assumed to be a natural number (in practice this substitution would occur within an abstract machine, in which **vv** would be in scope for writing). The decrement is only required to occur if the state **vv, nn** satisfies the precondition at the point where the substitution is invoked. The precondition guarantees that, after the operation is executed, **vv** is still a natural number:

$$[vv := vv - nn](vv \geq 0)$$

is:

$$(vv - nn) \geq 0$$

A second example involves a dynamically varying set of objects **entities**, and the non-deterministic selection of a new 'unallocated' object from a superset **ENTITY** of entities. This object, **oo**, is added to **entities**, and is returned in the variable **new**.

This substitution has the form:

```
PRE ENTITY ≠ entities
THEN
   ANY oo
   WHERE oo ∈ ENTITY - entities
   THEN
      entities := entities ∪ { oo } ||
      new := oo
   END
END
```

The precondition ensures that the non-deterministic selection (ANY **oo**) is only performed if the set **ENTITY** − entities is non-empty. This selection would be an infeasible (and un-implementable) operation otherwise.

The updates to **new** and **entities** are performed, conceptually at least, simultaneously.

2.3   Abstract Machines

The concept of an abstract machine is quite close to that of an object class in Eiffel (except that there are not concepts of inheritance, dynamic binding, operation polymorphism or the equating of modules to types in B), or an Ada package: it serves to encapsulate a set of mathematical items, constants, sets, variables and a set of operations on these variables, into a named module which can then be selectively viewed by, and incorporated into, other modules. A key property is that the variables of a machine can only be modified by the operations of that machine, and not by operations of other machines (except where these operations invoke the operations of the original machine, of course). This has significant implications for the simplification of proof of internal consistency of machines, described below. It also makes conceptual sense – each machine "owns" some local data and provides the essential operations needed to manipulate and access this data.

A general specification-level machine (without inclusion clauses) can be written in the form:

```
MACHINE   N(p)
CONSTRAINTS   C
SETS   St
CONSTANTS   k
PROPERTIES   B
VARIABLES   v
DEFINITIONS   D
INVARIANT   I
ASSERTIONS   A
INITIALISATION   T
OPERATIONS
    y  ←  op(x) =
        PRE   P
        THEN
          S
        END
    . . . .
END
```

We will defer till later detailed discussion of the DEFINITIONS and ASSERTIONS clauses. An elementary example of a machine, involving an array with a distinguished pointer, is:

```
MACHINE  PlacedArray(maxlen, ITEM)
VARIABLES
    pointer, array
INVARIANT
    pointer ∈ 0..maxlen  ∧
    array ∈ 1..maxlen  ⇸  ITEM
```

INITIALISATION
    pointer := 0 ‖ **array** := ∅
OPERATIONS
    insert(item, place) ≙
        PRE **item** ∈ **ITEM** ∧ **place** ∈ 1 .. **maxlen**
        THEN
            array(place) := **item** ‖
            pointer := **place**
        END

⋮   *Other operations*

END

Similarly in the case of operation preconditions, the INVARIANT will contain the typing constraints for the variables of the machine – in this case it consists entirely of such constraints. **maxlen** is implicitly of type $\mathbb{N}$ and **maxlen** > 0 is assumed. **ITEM** is implicitly a non-empty set (to be instantiated by systems which make use of this machine).

The machine clauses have the following syntax and semantics:

- *parameters*: the machine **N** can be parameterised by a list **p** of set-valued (written in capital letters) or scalar-valued parameters (written in small letters). The logical properties of these parameters are specified in the CONSTRAINTS of the machine. These constraints should not connect the various set parameters, since these parameters are assumed to be *independent* of each other. They can, however, assert properties defining the size of such sets, or membership of a scalar parameter in a set parameter. Set-valued parameters can be used to provide types for variables within the machine. For example, if **ENTITY** was a parameter, we could define a variable **parent** with the type **parent** ∈ **ENTITY** ⇸ **ENTITY**. Scalar-valued parameters are typically used to provide a generic size constraint on variables.
  Every set parameter is assumed to be non-empty, and this assumption becomes a requirement which must be established when the machine is instantiated;
- *sets*: If the SETS keyword is present, this clause will have the form

    setdef$_1$;
    . . .
    setdef$_n$

Each **setdef**$_i$ will correspond to a definition of given or enumerated sets in Z. These definitions must either be of the form:

    SS = { **val**$_1$, . . ., **val**$_n$ }

which defines **SS** as a set of the **n** elements (given by distinct identifiers) **val**$_1$, ..., **val**$_n$; or of the form:

SS

which defines **SS** abstractly, with no internal structure, except that it is finite (in contrast to given sets in Z) and non-empty;

- *constants*: the contents of the CONSTANTS clause is a list **con**$_1$, ..., **con**$_n$ of identifiers declaring these **n** items as data which can be referred to in a read-only fashion within the operations of the machine. That is, the **con**$_i$ cannot appear on the left hand side of a (normalised) generalised substitution **v** := **e**, or on the left of an operation invocation **v** ⟵ **op(e)**. In Z terms constants correspond to *axiomatic definitions*, and can denote values of structured types (eg, a factorial function), in addition to elementary values;

- *properties*: logical properties of sets and constants are given in the PROPERTIES clause. This contains a predicate, usually a conjunction of formulae, involving only the constants and sets, and those constant, set and parameter identifiers currently in scope. A typing constraint **constant** ∈ **TYPE** or **constant** = **value** must be provided, for each **constant** listed in the CONSTANTS clause, where the type of **value** should be mechanically determinable. As an example, we could write:

CONSTANTS
  fact
PROPERTIES
  fact ∈ ℕ → ℕ   ∧
  fact(0) = 1   ∧
  ∀ **nn**.(**nn** ∈ ℕ ∧ **nn** > 0 ⇒
      fact(**nn**) = **nn** ∗ **fact**(**nn** − 1))

- *variables*: variables of the machine are listed in the VARIABLES clause. This consists of a list of comma-separated identifiers **var**$_1$, ..., **var**$_n$. This declares these identifiers as denoting writable data within the machine (they are not directly writable in any other machine, that is, they cannot appear on the left hand side of a normalised assignment or invocation);

- *invariant*: constraints on the variables, including the typing of the variables, are specified in the INVARIANT of the machine. This consists of a predicate, usually a conjunction of predicates, which involves identifiers from among the variables, constants, sets and parameters of the machine, and from those data items which are in scope within the machine. We denote the invariant predicate of machine **M** by **Inv**$_\mathbf{M}$: this does not include invariants inherited from machines accessed by **M**.

As an example we can declare a variable **vv** to be a subset of a locally declared set **TT** of a machine by:

  vv ⊆ **TT**

Because **TT** is assumed to be finite this is the same as writing

$$\mathbf{vv} \in \mathbb{F}(\mathbf{TT})$$

- *definitions*: this clause consists of a list

  abbdef$_1$;
  . . . .
  abbdef$_n$

  of mathematical abbreviation definitions of the form **data$_i$** == **val$_i$**, where **data$_i$** is an identifier or a parameterised function name **f(params)**, and **val$_i$** involves the in-scope variables and constants and function parameters. These equations act like macro definitions in the remainder of the machine. For example we could use

  $$\mathbf{sqr(p)} \ == \ ((\mathbf{p}) * (\mathbf{p}))$$

  to define a squaring function. These equations are used as rewrite rules (applied in a left to right direction). == is read as "rewrites to";
- *initialisation*: The initialisation operation of the machine is specified in the INITIALISATION clause of the machine. It is a single generalised substitution which should define the possible ranges of initial values for each variable declared in the VARIABLES clause;
- *operations*: operations of the machine are listed in the OPERATIONS section. This section is a list:

  opheader$_1$ $\ \widehat{=}\ $ **opdef$_1$** ;
  . . . .
  opheader$_n$ $\ \widehat{=}\ $ **opdef$_n$**

  of operation definitions. An **opheader** is of the general form

  $$\mathbf{y} \ \longleftarrow \ \mathbf{opname(x)}$$

  Input parameters **x** are listed after the name of the operation in its header, and output parameters **y** are listed to the left of an arrow from the operation name. Both the **y** $\longleftarrow$ and **(x)** can be omitted if the operation has no outputs or inputs. An **opdef** is a generalised substitution: the variables of the machine, and the variables in the list **y** can appear on the left hand sides of assignments or operation calls within **opdef**, any data in scope in the machine, together with the variables **x**, can appear elsewhere in the substitution.

An elementary example of an abstract machine is:

MACHINE **minimal**
VARIABLES
   xx
INVARIANT
   xx $\in \mathbb{N}$
INITIALISATION
   xx $:\in \mathbb{N}$
OPERATIONS
  up(vv) $\widehat{=}$
      PRE **vv** $\in \mathbb{N}$
      THEN
         xx $:=$ **xx** $+$ **vv**
      END
END

This encapsulates a single scalar variable **xx** and an operation **up** to increment this variable by an input value. The initialisation **xx** $:\in \mathbb{N}$ abbreviates the substitution ANY **vv** WHERE **vv** $\in \mathbb{N}$ THEN **xx** $:=$ **vv** END. This is **xx** :: **NAT** in ASCII notation and represents an unbounded non-deterministic choice of an element of $\mathbb{N}$.

The Z equivalent of this specification is simply:

```
┌─ minimal_state ──────────────────────────
│ xx : ℕ
└──────────────────────────────────────────
```

```
┌─ minimal_init ───────────────────────────
│ minimal_state'
│ ─────────────
│ xx' ∈ ℕ
└──────────────────────────────────────────
```

```
┌─ up ─────────────────────────────────────
│ Δminimal_state
│ vv? : ℕ
│ ──────────────
│ xx' = xx + vv?
└──────────────────────────────────────────
```

Notice that, in contrast to the B machine, there is nothing which ties together these three schemas as belonging to the same module: the specifier has to assert this by using natural language.

More complex examples are:

MACHINE **SortSeq**
CONSTANTS
    is_ordered
PROPERTIES

$$is\_ordered \ \in \ \mathbb{P}(seq(\mathbb{N})) \ \wedge$$
$$\forall \ ss.(ss \ \in \ seq(\mathbb{N}) \ \Rightarrow$$
$$(ss \ \in \ is\_ordered \ \equiv$$
$$\forall \ (ii,jj).(ii \ \in \ dom(ss) \ \wedge$$
$$jj \ \in \ dom(ss) \ \wedge$$
$$ii \ < \ jj \ \Rightarrow$$
$$ss(ii) \ < \ ss(jj)) \ ) \ )$$

VARIABLES sq
INVARIANT
   sq $\in$ is_ordered
INITIALISATION
   sq := [ ]
OPERATIONS
   ordered_insert(xx) $\widehat{=}$
      PRE xx $\in \mathbb{N}$
      THEN
         ANY newsq
         WHERE newsq $\in$ is_ordered $\wedge$
           ran(newsq) = ran(sq) $\cup$ { xx }
         THEN
           sq := newsq
         END
      END

END

This machine provides an operation which is to be used as part of an insertion
sort. Its invariant states that the sequence of elements it contains is always
sorted. Intuitively we can see that this is true because the empty sequence []
given as the initial state is sorted, and the operation **ordered_insert** produces
a sorted sequence **sq** (regardless of whether **sq** is sorted before execution of the
operation) if it is executed within its precondition.

   Similarly we could have a machine which manages a set of elements:

MACHINE **SortSet**
SEES **Bool_TYPE**
VARIABLES ss
INVARIANT
     ss $\in \mathbb{F}(\mathbb{N})$
INITIALISATION
     ss := $\varnothing$
OPERATIONS
  xx $\longleftarrow$ choose $\widehat{=}$
     PRE ss $\neq \varnothing$
     THEN xx :$\in$ ss
     END ;

  remove(xx) $\widehat{=}$
     PRE xx $\in \mathbb{N}$
     THEN ss := ss $-$ { xx }

```
    END;

add(xx)  ≙
    PRE xx ∈ ℕ
    THEN ss := ss ∪ { xx }
    END;

bb  ⟵  is_empty  ≙
    IF ss = ∅
    THEN
           bb := TRUE
    ELSE
           bb := FALSE
    END

END
```

The clause SEES BooL_TYPE is explained in Section 2.4 below.

The following forms of generalised substitutions can be used within the initialisation and operations of an abstract machine:

- x := e;
- PRE P THEN S END;
- BEGIN S END: this is a simple 'bracketing' of S and is semantically equivalent to S;
- IF P THEN S_1 ELSE S_2 END;
- ANY v WHERE P THEN S END;
- LET v BE P IN S END;
- SELECT P THEN S END: this is more often used implicitly within a case statement or IF-THEN-ELSE than as an isolated substitution;
- $S_1 || S_2$;
- CHOICE S_1 OR S_2 END;
- y ⟵ op(x): where op is an operation from an included or extended machine (this case will be covered in Section 2.4 below).

There are two significant omissions from this list:

- ; – sequential composition;
- WHILE v DO S VARIANT v INVARIANT I END – loops.

The reason for omitting these is that we wish the explicit definition of an operation to correspond very closely to the state transition which it is intended to achieve. The abstract specification should be directly comprehensible and should not require the analysis of intermediate states that could arise through the use of ; or WHILE – Figure 2.2 gives an illustration of this. In this case it is easier to reason that $x = a+1$ and $y = 2a$ after execution of the || substitution than for the sequential composition, because of the close connection between the form of the parallel composition and the post-state it establishes.

There are situations, however, where the use of ; in an abstract specification would lead to a more natural problem representation. The use of ; is allowed by Z for this reason.

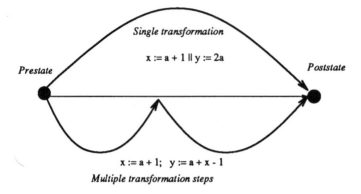

Figure 2.2: Single Versus Successive State Transitions

In order to check that an abstract machine specification is mathematically well-founded, a number of proof obligations are defined for each machine. These obligations can be automatically generated. For a fully formal development (eg, for a system being developed in accordance with Interim Defence Standard 00-55 [52]) it would be required that each of these obligations be discharged before the machine can be accepted into a development.

These proof obligations also arise from the particular approach which B AMN takes to the specification of state transitions via operations and a state invariant. In contrast to the Z notation, for example, the explicit definition of a B AMN operation is expected to preserve the invariant of the machine. This requirement is formalised in a set of internal consistency proof obligations, which also involve checks that the formal model represented by a machine is non-contradictory or non-vacuous. One advantage of the B approach is that identity state transformations ($\mathbf{v}' = \mathbf{v}$ in Z) do not need to be explicitly written in operation definitions: if $\mathbf{v}$ does not occur on the LHS of a normalised assignment or operation invocation in a statement $\mathbf{S}$, then $\mathbf{S}$ cannot modify $\mathbf{v}$. The proof obligations also provide rigorous checks that the model the specifier has created actually can be implemented by an executable system, and hence saves wasted effort during development.

The proof obligations for the general machine given above are (in the absence of DEFINITIONS or ASSERTIONS clauses) shown in Table 2.1. Obligation (5) is required for each operation of the machine.

These check that the following hold:

- (1): "parameter existence" – there are possible machine parameter values satisfying the parameter constraints. If this fails, then the machine can never be validly instantiated and there is no executable system satisfying the specification;

$$
\begin{array}{ll}
(1) & \exists\, p.C \\
(2) & C \;\Rightarrow\; \exists(St, k).B \\
(3) & B \wedge C \;\Rightarrow\; \exists v.I \\
(4) & B \wedge C \;\Rightarrow\; [T]I \\
(5) & B \wedge C \wedge I \wedge P \;\Rightarrow\; [S]I
\end{array}
$$

Table 2.1: Proof Obligations for Internal Consistency

- (2): "constants and sets existence" – assuming the machine constraints, there are sets and constants satisfying the machine properties. Again, if this fails then there is no executable system satisfying the specification;
- (3): "non-emptiness of machine state" – assuming the machine constraints and properties, there is a machine state satisfying the invariant;
- (4): "initialisation" – the initialisation establishes the invariant, under the machine constraints and properties. If this fails it invalidates the base case of the inductive argument that the invariant always holds during the lifetime of the machine implementation;
- (5): "invariant preservation" – each operation maintains the truth of the invariant, provided it is always invoked within its precondition. If this fails there is again no guarantee that the invariant always holds during the lifetime of the implementation.

In the case of the **minimal** machine given above, the non-trivial obligations are:

$$
\begin{array}{ll}
(3) & \exists xx.(xx \in \mathbb{N}) \\
(4) & [xx :\in \mathbb{N}](xx \in \mathbb{N}) \\
    & \text{i.e.: } \forall vv.(vv \in \mathbb{N} \Rightarrow (xx \in \mathbb{N})[vv/xx]) \\
(5) & vv \in \mathbb{N} \wedge xx \in \mathbb{N} \Rightarrow xx + vv \in \mathbb{N}
\end{array}
$$

These obligations are clearly seen to be provable. For the **SortSet** machine we have:

- obligation (3):

$$\exists ss.(ss \in \mathbb{F}(\mathbb{N}))$$

- obligation (5) for **remove**:

$$
ss \in \mathbb{F}(\mathbb{N}) \wedge xx \in \mathbb{N} \Rightarrow \\
ss - \{xx\} \in \mathbb{F}(\mathbb{N})
$$

When machines are composed by means of the structuring mechanisms INCLUDES or EXTENDS, it becomes possible for operations of one machine (the including or extending machine) to use operations of others. In this case, the fact that the precondition of the invoked operation is ensured by the context in which it is invoked, is an additional requirement which is a product of the proof obligation (5). Further discussion of this is included in Appendix B.

2.3.1   Abstract Machine Examples

The following are some basic examples of abstract machines, illustrating the
various clauses and specification elements that can be defined. In the first
example, **Array**1, we have an array of elements **contents**, and a pointer **ptr**
which points to the last index accessed by an update **store** or enquiry **value**
operation.

MACHINE **Array**1(**maxsize**)
CONSTRAINTS
   maxsize $\geq$ 1
VARIABLES
   contents, ptr
INVARIANT
   contents $\in$ 1..**maxsize** $\rightarrow$ $\mathbb{N}$ $\wedge$
   ptr $\in$ 1..**maxsize**
INITIALISATION
   contents := λ **ii**.(**ii** $\in$ $\mathbb{N}$ $\wedge$ **ii** $\in$ 1..**maxsize** | 0) ||
   ptr :$\in$ 1..**maxsize**
OPERATIONS
  store(**ii**, **vv**) $\widehat{=}$
     PRE **vv** $\in$ $\mathbb{N}$ $\wedge$
        ii $\in$ 1..**maxsize**
     THEN
       contents(**ii**) := **vv** ||
       ptr := **ii**
     END;

  vv $\longleftarrow$ **value**(**ii**) $\widehat{=}$
     PRE **ii** $\in$ 1..**maxsize**
     THEN
       vv := **contents**(**ii**) ||
       ptr := **ii**
     END

  END

The initialisation of **contents** involves a function defined by means of the λ
construct.

   The initialisation

$$\text{\textbf{contents}} := \lambda \text{\textbf{ii}}.(\text{\textbf{ii}} \in \mathbb{N} \wedge \text{\textbf{ii}} \in 1..\text{\textbf{maxsize}} \mid 0)$$

sets **contents** to become the value

$$\{\text{\textbf{ii}}, \text{\textbf{jj}} \mid \text{\textbf{ii}} \in \mathbb{N} \wedge \text{\textbf{ii}} \in 1..\text{\textbf{maxsize}} \wedge \text{\textbf{jj}} = 0\}$$

   The parameter of the machine is announced (by putting it in lower case) to
be of natural number type. As a result, the facts:

   maxsize $\in \mathbb{N}$
   $0 \leq$ **maxsize**

are made available to proof tools checking the internal consistency of the specification and specifications that use this machine, regardless of whether the
developer supplies a CONSTRAINTS clause or not. In this case we clearly need
the constraint that **maxsize** $\geq$ 1 in order to render the initialisation of the
machine feasible (if **maxsize** = 0 then **ptr** cannot be assigned a value). Such
an error would not be discovered until we came to generate proof obligations
for refinement, when the appropriate existential obligation would arise (that is:
$\exists$ **ptrx**.(**ptrx** $\in$ 1 .. **maxsize**)).

Since **ptr** is not actually visible to a user of this machine, the machine could
be refined to a component which had no such pointer. However, if **Array**1 was
to be accessed by another machine, via an INCLUDES or EXTENDS clause, it
could be the case that **ptr** was made visible by an operation of this new component. (**ptr** would then somehow need to be implemented in any refinement
of the new component.)

In the second example we specify a dynamically varying set of objects, which
represent rational numbers with a numerator and denominator:

MACHINE
 Rational(RATIONAL, maxrat)
CONSTRAINTS
 card(RATIONAL) = maxrat

> *There are at most* **maxrat** *rationals.*

SEES
 Bool_TYPE
VARIABLES
 rationals, rat_numerator, rat_denominator
INVARIANT
 rationals $\subseteq$ RATIONAL $\wedge$
 rat_numerator $\in$ rationals $\rightarrow$ $\mathbb{N}$ $\wedge$
 rat_denominator $\in$ rationals $\rightarrow$ $\mathbb{N}$

> *The rationals are represented as records with two fields.*

INITIALISATION
 rationals, rat_numerator, rat_denominator := $\varnothing$, $\varnothing$, $\varnothing$
OPERATIONS

> *Initially there are no rationals.*

 ok, rat $\longleftarrow$ create_rational(num, den) $\mathrel{\widehat{=}}$
       PRE num $\in$ $\mathbb{N}$ $\wedge$ den $\in$ $\mathbb{N}$
       THEN
       IF
          rationals $\neq$ RATIONAL
       THEN
          ANY oo
          WHERE
             oo $\in$ RATIONAL $-$ rationals

```
            THEN
              rat := oo ||
              rationals := rationals ∪ {oo} ||
              rat_numerator(oo) := num ||
              rat_denominator(oo) := den ||
              ok := TRUE
            END
          ELSE
            ok := FALSE
          END
          END;

    num ⟵ return_numerator(rat) ≙
          PRE rat ∈ rationals
          THEN
            num := rat_numerator(rat)
          END;

    den ⟵ return_denominator(rat) ≙
          PRE rat ∈ rationals
          THEN
            den := rat_denominator(rat)
          END;

    delete_rational(rat) ≙
          PRE rat ∈ rationals
          THEN
            rationals := rationals − {rat} ||
            rat_denominator := {rat} ◁ rat_denominator ||
            rat_numerator := {rat} ◁ rat_numerator
          END

END
```

To create a rational, we check that there are some possible objects in the abstract set **RATIONAL** which are remaining to be allocated to become actual rationals (elements of **rationals**). If this is so, we select such an element and set its attributes to the values which are given as input parameters to the **create_rational** operation.

We can view the numerator and denominator of selected rationals, and we can delete a rational (to reclaim the space that it uses). The operator ◁ (ASCII <<|) on functions removes all pairs from its second argument whose first elements are within the set given as the first argument to ◁:

$$\{\text{rat}\} \vartriangleleft \text{rat\_denominator} = $$
$$\{\text{rr}, \text{ii} \mid \text{rr} \in \text{rationals} \wedge \text{ii} \in \mathbb{N} \wedge $$
$$(\text{rr} \mapsto \text{ii}) \in \text{rat\_denominator} \wedge \text{rr} \neq \text{rat}\}$$

This specification is appropriate for representing any entity with two natural-number valued attributes, regardless of the names or semantics of these attributes, although additional constraints in the invariant or precondition of the machine may be needed if the attributes are related to each other.

This style of specification is a basic building block for many B developments. A systematic way to create these specifications from domain models is given in Chapter 3.

2.4 Machine Composition Mechanisms

There are a number of additional clauses which may be added to a machine definition in order to declare that this machine makes use of ('accesses') various features of other machines.

The general pattern of access to one or more machines by another is shown in Figure 2.3 below. To represent access relationships we draw suitably labelled arrows from the 'accessed' machines to the 'accessing' machines. Depending on the access relationship, various aspects of the accessed machines may be 'visible' to the accessing machine to various degrees, or may be treated as if they were defined in the accessing machine.

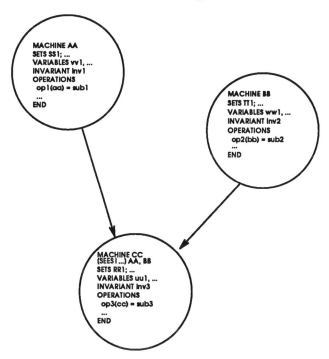

Figure 2.3: General Pattern of Access by one Machine to Others

B provides the following structuring mechanisms as optional clauses in machines, refinements or implementations: SEES, USES, INCLUDES, EXTENDS, REFINES, IMPORTS.

- SEES is valid as a clause in machines, refinements or implementations (with slightly different restrictions: in an implementation variables from seen machines cannot be used in the operations of the seeing implementation, but the enquiry operations of the seen machine can still be used). More than one machine/refinement/implementation can see a particular machine.

  Its principal use is to support separate development of a subsystem which is shared in a read-only fashion between other subsystems within an application. If a machine **A** is seen by a number of implementations then it would usually be IMPORTED in one;

- USES can only be applied in machines. More than one machine can use a particular machine.

  Its principal use is to support shared access to readable data as for SEES, in order to help construct the specification of a subsystem development. If a machine **A** is used in a number of specification components which will all be included or extended by some single specification machine, then it should usually be included in this machine.

  It allows a stronger form of access than SEES – the variables of the USED machine can be used, in a read-manner, within the invariant and operations of the using machine, which is not the case for SEES. This stronger degree of access however prevents the used and using machines from being refined separately to code.

  The used component may have its state changed by operations of the subsystem in which it occurs, because the main machine that gives the specification of the subsystem will typically include or extend this component, and so acquire access to its operations;

- INCLUDES and EXTENDS can only be applied in machines. The PROMOTES clause can be used to selectively promote operations from the included machine. *Promotion* of an operation **op** from **A** to **B** means that it can be regarded as an operation of **B**, and can be promoted and invoked in components that INCLUDE **B**.

  Only one machine can include or extend a specific machine (exclusive access). The principal use of INCLUDES is to support a hierarchical layering of subsystems (subsystem developments), whilst EXTENDS corresponds to inheritance in an object-oriented sense. A group of machines included or extended by a single machine are termed "siblings" – they separately provide related aspects of the machine data and functionality;

- REFINES can be used in refinements and implementations. A machine or refinement can be refined in two or more different ways; however, a refinement or implementation can only be a refinement of one construct;

- IMPORTS can be used in implementations, and only machines can be imported. The PROMOTES clause can be used in this case to promote operations from an imported machine to the importing implementation. Only one implementation within a particular development can import a specific machine.

The restriction of exclusive access on INCLUDES, IMPORTS and EXTENDS can be avoided to an extent by the use of *renaming* of specification constructs. This, and other aspects of the structuring mechanisms, are described in greater detail in Chapter 3 below.

USES, INCLUDES and EXTENDS are referred to as *semi-hiding* mechanisms: they allow variables from the accessed component to be read within operations of the accessing (although they do not allow direct update of these variables within the accessing component). These mechanisms do not, therefore, allow the accessed component to be refined independently of the accessing, because the accessing component depends on a particular data representation (set of variables) being present in the accessed.

REFINES, SEES (in implementations) and IMPORTS are *full-hiding* in the sense that they do not allow even a read access to the variables of the accessed component in the operations of the accessing, outside of loop invariants. These do support independent refinement.

Update operations are not made visible by the mechanisms supporting shared access because no shared write access to the state of a machine is allowed. Such a shared write access (say by **A** and **B** on **C**) would lead, in the case of USES, to a requirement to prove that an invariant linking the state of **A** and **C** is preserved by operations of **B**, and similarly for an invariant linking the state of **B** and **A**. In fact, since only enquiry operations are possible therefore, and since the effect of these can be achieved by accesses to variables or constants of the used or seen machines, access to operations of a seen or used machine in the seeing or using machine is not strictly necessary.

USES and SEES are *intransitive* in the sense that if **A** USES **B** and **B** USES **C**, then **A** does not have access to any of the items defined in **C**. This intransitivity is due to the role of these mechanisms in supporting shared access to a component. Specifically, if we allow two components **A** and **B** to access a third, **C**, via USES or SEES, then if **A** and **B** were included into component **D**, then (in the absence of intransitivity) there would be two copies of the items of **C** in **D**.

To illustrate the above rules, consider the following typical situations:

1. **A** EXTENDS **B** and **B** INCLUDES **C** — then **A** has as its variables all those declared explicitly in **A**, plus those declared in **B** and **C**. Similarly for other data items. However its operations are just those declared explicitly in **A** or in **B**.
2. **A** USES **B** and **C** USES **B**, and **D** EXTENDS **A** and **C** — then **D** has data items just those declared explicitly in **D**, **A** or **C**, but not those of **B**. Its operations are also just those declared explicitly in **D**, **A** or **C** (Figure 2.4).

The structuring mechanisms used in an AMN component are used to construct the proof obligations for that component. In general, a machine constructed by using these mechanisms has fewer and simpler proof obligations than those that would arise had the machine been defined as a single unstructured component.

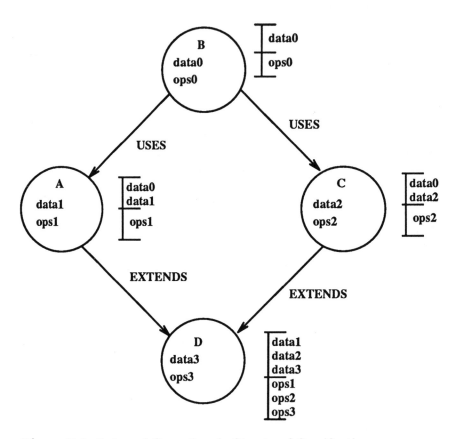

Figure 2.4: Data and Operations in Structured Specifications

In particular, if machine **N** INCLUDES **M**, then the obligation that an operation

$$y \longleftarrow op(x) \;\; \hat{=}$$
$$\text{PRE } P$$
$$\text{THEN}$$
$$S$$
$$\text{END}$$

of **N** preserves the invariant $\text{Inv}_M \wedge \text{Inv}_N$ of **N**:

$$\text{Inv}_M \wedge \text{Inv}_N \wedge P \;\Rightarrow\; [S](\text{Inv}_M \wedge \text{Inv}_N)$$

can be reduced to

$$\text{Inv}_M \wedge \text{Inv}_N \wedge P \;\Rightarrow\; [S]\text{Inv}_N$$

since **S** cannot change the data of **M** except by calls to operations of **M**, and so, if **M** has been proved to be consistent, we therefore know that **S** will preserve the truth of Inv_M.

For instance, consider the following simple example of a machine accessing another:

```
MACHINE  Dispenser
SEES  Vend_data
VARIABLES
    dstate, given
INVARIANT
    dstate ∈ DSTATE ∧
    given ∈ ℕ
INITIALISATION
    dstate := unstocked ||
    given := 0
OPERATIONS
    restock  ≙
        dstate := stocked;

    give_drink  ≙
        PRE dstate = stocked
        THEN
            dstate :∈ DSTATE ||
            given := given + 1
        END

END
```

The proof obligations for this machine are:

1.

$$\text{Constraints} \wedge \text{Context} \;\Rightarrow\; \text{unstocked} \in \text{DSTATE}$$
$$\text{Constraints} \wedge \text{Context} \;\Rightarrow\; 0 \in \mathbb{N}$$

These are the obligations that the initialisation establishes the invariant.

2.

$$\text{Constraints} \wedge \text{Context} \wedge \text{Assertions} \wedge$$
$$\text{Inv} \wedge \text{Pre}_{\text{restock,Dispenser}} \Rightarrow$$
$$\text{stocked} \in \text{DSTATE}$$

This is the obligation that **restock** *preserves the invariant.*

3.

$$\text{Constraints} \wedge \text{Context} \wedge$$
$$\text{Assertions} \wedge \text{Inv} \wedge \text{Pre}_{\text{give\_drink,Dispenser}} \Rightarrow$$
$$(\text{dstatex} \in \text{DSTATE} \Rightarrow \text{given} + 1 \in \mathbb{N})$$

This is the obligation that **give_drink** *preserves the invariant.*

Vend_data is defined in Section 4.2.3.

Constraints gives the facts which can be derived from the parameter declarations and CONSTRAINTS part of a machine and the machines it accesses. Here it is just **true** as neither machine has a parameter.

Context denotes the explicit and implicit facts about the sets and properties of both machines. It is defined by:

$$\text{Context} \equiv \text{Context}_{\text{Dispenser}} \wedge \text{Context}_{\text{Vend\_data}}$$

where

$$\text{Context}_{\text{Vend\_data}} \equiv$$
$$\text{COINS} = \{5, 10\} \wedge$$
$$\text{STATE} = \{0, 5, 10\} \wedge$$
$$\neg (\text{CSTATE} = \varnothing) \wedge$$
$$\neg (\text{DSTATE} = \varnothing) \wedge$$
$$\text{CSTATE} = \{\text{coin\_present}, \text{coin\_absent}\} \wedge$$
$$\text{DSTATE} = \{\text{stocked}, \text{unstocked}\} \wedge$$
$$\text{card}(\text{CSTATE}) = 2 \wedge$$
$$\neg (\text{coin\_present} = \text{coin\_absent}) \wedge$$
$$\text{card}(\text{DSTATE}) = 2 \wedge$$
$$\neg (\text{stocked} = \text{unstocked})$$

$\text{Context}_{\text{Dispenser}}$ is just **true** as there are no local sets or constants defined in **Dispenser**.

Assertions is the conjunction of the explicit assertions of the two machines – in this case both are simply **true**.

Inv is the conjunction of the explicit invariants of the two machines:

$$\text{Inv}_{\text{Vend\_data}} \wedge \text{Inv}_{\text{Dispenser}}$$

In this case only the latter is non-trivial:

$$\text{Inv}_{\text{Dispenser}} \equiv$$
$$\text{dstate} \in \text{DSTATE} \wedge$$
$$\text{given} \in \mathbb{N}$$

Pre$_{op,mach}$ is the precondition of operation **op** as declared in machine **mach**.

Some simplification of the obligations has already been carried out. For example, the trivially true implication **dstatex** $\in$ **DSTATE** $\Rightarrow$ **dstatex** $\in$ **DSTATE** has been omitted from the consequent of the **give_drink** obligation. It should be relatively easy to convince yourself that the above obligations are provable.

A further elementary example of an application of a structuring mechanism is the clause

SEES
    Bool_TYPE

within the **Rational** machine described in Section 2.3.1. **Bool_TYPE** is a library machine which provides a set **BOOL** = {**TRUE, FALSE**} and conventional logical operators on this type. We need to include this clause because we use the values **TRUE** and **FALSE** in the **create_rational** operation.

2.5 Refinement

Refinement is the process of moving from abstract specifications to less abstract specifications, via some data or operation transformation which allows the behaviour of the abstract system to be 'simulated' by the more refined system. The proof of this simulation: that the externally visible behaviour of the refined specification obeys the abstract specification, and is 'at least as good as' the externally visible behaviour of the abstract specification is the core of the obligations generated for refinement.

A refinement step can be from a MACHINE to a REFINEMENT component, from a REFINEMENT component to a REFINEMENT component, or from a REFINEMENT component to an IMPLEMENTATION component (Figure 2.5). A REFINEMENT differs from a machine in that:

- it must possess a REFINES **M** clause immediately after its header, identifying the single component that it refines;
- it must have an identical set of operation headers to the component it refines (ie, same operation and parameter names);
- it has no explicit component parameters (these are given instead by the parameters of the component it refines);
- operations and initiation substitutions can use any generalised substitution constructs except WHILE;
- a conjunct of the invariant identifies how the state of the refinement relates to the state of the component being refined.

Only one component can be refined by a particular component, and no parameters are allowed in the REFINES clause in a refinement or implementation

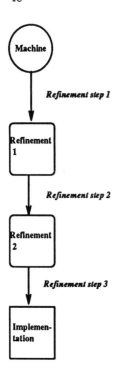

Figure 2.5: Typical Refinement Sequence

N of M. This is because we are really considering that **M** and **N** are two alternative descriptions of the same system, which have the same external interface in terms of parameters, sets of operations and operation signatures, but whose internal implementation of these operations has been modified. The formal definition of refinement also states that the semantics encountered by a user of **N** will be entirely compatible with that encountered by a user of **M**, and that, indeed, it should not be possible to determine if **N** is being used rather than **M**. (After all, eventually a piece of executable code will be used in place of **M**, and must satisfy all the expectations that a user may have of the externally visible functionality of **M**.)

N may provide additional predicates to constrain the sets and constants of **M** (which become visible as sets and constants in **N**).

The states of **N** and **M** must be composed of distinct sets of variables, and these states are linked in **N** by a refinement relation, which expresses the correspondence between the abstract and concrete states. This correspondence must be established as a result of the combined initialisations of the two components, and must be preserved, in a certain sense, by each of the operations.

Specifically, if **u** are the variables of **M**, and **v** the variables of **N**, with values in their declared types:

- to show that an operation **OpN** refines an operation **OpM**, under a refinement relation **R**, we have to show that for every **v** and **u**, with **u**

R-related to **v**, every possible execution of **OpN** starting from a state **v** leads to a state **v'** which is R-related to a state **u'** which can be reached by an execution of **OpM** from **u** (Figure 2.6).

The names and headers of **OpM** and **OpN** must be the same, but the generalised substitutions defining the operations can be different.

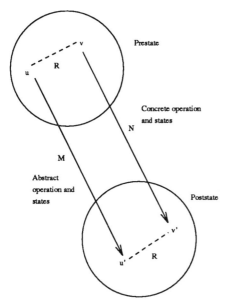

Figure 2.6: Pictorial Representation of Operation Refinement

Formally, the obligations which concern the relationship between two specification components $M(p)$ and **N**, with **N** asserted to be a refinement of $M(p)$ via relation **J** on the variables of the two machines, are given in Table 2.2 below.

Schematically, the components may be described as in Figure 2.7. In this figure **J** is a predicate containing both a typing invariant and other constraints on the local state **w** and the refinement relation, which relates **w** and **v**.

The key proof obligations for refinement are given in Table 2.2. The last

$$
\begin{array}{rl}
(1) & \mathbf{C} \wedge \mathbf{B} \wedge \mathbf{B1} \ \Rightarrow \\
    & \qquad \exists(\mathbf{v}, \mathbf{w}).(\mathbf{I} \wedge \mathbf{J}) \\
(2) & \mathbf{C} \wedge \mathbf{B} \wedge \mathbf{B1} \ \Rightarrow \ [\mathbf{T1}] \neg\, [\mathbf{T}] \neg\, \mathbf{J} \\
(3) & \mathbf{C} \wedge \mathbf{B} \wedge \mathbf{B1} \wedge \mathbf{I} \wedge \mathbf{J} \wedge \mathbf{P} \ \Rightarrow \\
    & \qquad \mathbf{P1} \wedge [\mathbf{S1'}] \neg\, [\mathbf{S}] \neg\, (\mathbf{J} \wedge \mathbf{y'} = \mathbf{y})
\end{array}
$$

Table 2.2: Refinement Proof Obligations

obligation corresponds to the requirement that every execution of **S1** (when **P** holds initially) has a corresponding execution of **S**, as in Figure 2.6. Contained within these obligations are the requirements that the operations of **N** preserve

```
MACHINE  M(p)                    REFINEMENT  N
CONSTRAINTS  C                   REFINES  M
CONSTANTS  k                     CONSTANTS  k1
PROPERTIES  B                    PROPERTIES  B1
VARIABLES  v                     VARIABLES  w
INVARIANT  I                     INVARIANT  J
INITIALISATION  T                INITIALISATION  T1
OPERATIONS                       OPERATIONS
    y  ←  op(x) =                    y  ←  op(x) =
      PRE  P                           PRE  P1
      THEN                             THEN
          S                                S1
      END                              END
    . . . .                          . . . .
END                              END
```

Figure 2.7: Schematic Refinement Step

the local part of the invariant **J**, ie, the part that refers only to the local variables **w**.

Here, **S1'** is **S1** with the output variables **y** renamed to **y'**.

The proof obligations have the following meaning:

- (1): "non-emptiness of joint state" – There is a combined abstract and concrete state which satisfies the refinement relation and abstract machine invariant. If this failed there would not be an executable implementation of the abstract specification via this refinement;
- (2): "initialisation refinement" – The concrete initialisation is a refinement of the abstract one, under the assumptions of the constraints and properties of both machines;
- (3): "operation refinement" – Under the refinement relation and the precondition of the more abstract operation, the precondition of the more concrete operation holds (ie, so that preconditions may be weakened in refinements, or that the operation in the refinement has a wider domain of behaviour) and for every execution of **S1**, there is a corresponding execution from the same initial state (under the relation **J**) which establishes the same external result values (**y' = y**) and which re-establishes the refinement relation between the post-states.

The double negation $\neg [\mathbf{S}]\neg \mathbf{R}$ is used to express the existence of an execution of **S** that establishes **R**. This arises since a predicate transformer assertion [**S**]**R** has the semantic interpretation:

> "For every execution of **S** starting from this state, the execution terminates in a state satisfying **R**".

Thus the assertion $\neg\,[\mathbf{S}]\neg\,\mathbf{R}$ states:

"There exists an execution of $\mathbf{S}$ starting in this state which either fails to terminate or which terminates in a state satisfying $\mathbf{R}$".

Or, symbolically, using the notation of Section 2.2.1

$$\exists(\mathbf{t}',\mathbf{e}).(\mathbf{t}\tfrac{\mathbf{S}}{\mathbf{e}}\mathbf{t}'\,\wedge\,\neg\,(\mathbf{t}'\models\neg\,\mathbf{R}))$$

But either $\mathbf{t}'$ represents the final state of a terminated computation, and $\neg\,(\mathbf{t}'\models\neg\,\mathbf{R})$ implies $\mathbf{t}'\models\mathbf{R}$, or the computation leading to $\mathbf{t}'$ fails to terminate.

As a result, a feasibility condition of the abstract operation will be part of the refinement obligation (3). To see this, recall that the feasibility of an operation $\mathbf{S}$ is the predicate

$$\neg\,[\mathbf{S}]\text{false}$$

For example, the operation $\mathbf{xx}\,:\in\varnothing$ is always infeasible, since its feasibility predicate is:

$$\neg\,\forall\,\mathbf{vv}.(\mathbf{vv}\in\varnothing\Rightarrow\text{false})$$

which is

$$\exists\,\mathbf{vv}.(\mathbf{vv}\in\varnothing)$$

Notice that this substitution is also a counter-example to the implication $[\mathbf{S}]\mathbf{I}\Rightarrow\neg\,[\mathbf{S}]\neg\,\mathbf{I}$ which might be expected to hold: "if every execution of $\mathbf{S}$ establishes $\mathbf{I}$ then there is an execution of $\mathbf{S}$ which establishes $\mathbf{I}$". It fails since "every execution" is a vacuous quantifier here.

Since

$$(\mathbf{P}\Rightarrow\mathbf{R})\Rightarrow$$
$$(\neg\,[\mathbf{S}]\neg\,\mathbf{P}\Rightarrow\neg\,[\mathbf{S}]\neg\,\mathbf{R})$$

we have that the refinement requirement

$$[\mathbf{T}]\neg\,[\mathbf{S}]\neg\,(\mathbf{J}\wedge\mathbf{y}'=\mathbf{y})$$

in general, implies that $\mathbf{T}$ must establish the feasibility of $\mathbf{S}$ (under the relevant preconditions). In Appendix B we show that this actually means that $\mathbf{S}$ must be more feasible than $\mathbf{T}$ (ie, we can only implement an infeasible substitution by a substitution that is at least as infeasible!).

It is useful to informally check that all operations of a specification machine are fully feasible before attempting to refine it to code, as operations which are not cannot be implemented. The cost of a full formal check of feasibility is one reason why the check is not included in internal consistency proofs: it can be equivalent in difficulty to actually providing an implementation of the operation.

In the operations of a refinement, all the constructs which can be used in abstract machines can be used. In addition, sequential composition can be used to combine parts of an operation, and (enquiry) operations from seen machines can be used in an operation. WHILE loops are not allowed.

2.5.1 Refinement Obligations Example

Assuming that the previous machine **minimal.mch** has been analysed, we can define a formal refinement of this machine as follows:

REFINEMENT minimal_ref
REFINES minimal
VARIABLES
    yy
INVARIANT
    $yy \in \mathbb{N} \wedge yy = xx$
INITIALISATION
    $yy := 0$
OPERATIONS
    $up(vv) \;\widehat{=}$
            PRE $vv \in \mathbb{N}$
            THEN
                $yy := yy + vv$
            END
END

The refinement step has simply made the initialisation more determinate, and has changed the name of the variable of the component from **xx** to **yy**. The general proof obligations for refinement are then instantiated as:

$$(1) \quad \exists(xx, yy).(xx \in \mathbb{N} \wedge yy \in \mathbb{N} \wedge xx = yy)$$
$$(2) \quad [yy := 0]\neg\,[xx :\in \mathbb{N}]\neg\,(xx = yy)$$
$$\text{i.e.: } [yy := 0]\,\exists\,vv.(vv \in \mathbb{N} \wedge vv = yy)$$
$$(3) \quad xx = yy \;\Rightarrow$$
$$[yy := yy + vv]\neg\,[xx := xx + vv]$$
$$\neg\,(yy = xx)$$

Because

$$\neg\,[xx := xx + vv]\neg\,P \;\equiv\; [xx := xx + vv]P$$

for any predicate **P**, obligation (3) becomes

$$xx = yy \;\Rightarrow$$
$$[yy := yy + vv][xx := xx + vv](yy = xx)$$

which is trivially true. The other obligations are directly provable.

2.5.2 Examples of Refinement

The following are some simple examples of the forms of transformation that will lead to a refinement in B AMN.

A standard transformation is the weakening of an operation precondition. Obligation (3) above requires that the precondition **P** of the abstract operation must imply the precondition **P1** of the concrete operation. In other words, the refined operation has a larger domain of defined behaviour, or is more robust. Replacing a PRE construct with a corresponding IF is an example of this transformation, where **P1** is just **true**:

PRE **P**
THEN **S** END $\sqsubseteq$

                 IF **P**
                 THEN **S**
                 END

where $\sqsubseteq$ denotes procedural refinement of operations, as defined in Appendix B.

For example, in the following refinement, both operations **store** and **value** of **Array**1 have been refined by weakening their precondition (to omit the test **ii** $\in 1 \mathinner{\ldotp\ldotp} \textbf{maxsize}$):

REFINEMENT
  Array1_1
REFINES
  Array1
CONSTRAINTS
  maxsize $\geq$ 1
VARIABLES
  contents1, **ptr**1
INVARIANT
  contents1 $\in$ 1 $\mathinner{\ldotp\ldotp}$ **maxsize** $\rightarrow \mathbb{N}$ $\wedge$
  ptr1 $\in$ 1 $\mathinner{\ldotp\ldotp}$ **maxsize** $\wedge$

  contents1 = **contents** $\wedge$
  ptr1 = **ptr**
INITIALISATION
  contents1 := λ **ii**.(**ii** $\in \mathbb{N}$ $\wedge$ **ii** $\in$ 1 $\mathinner{\ldotp\ldotp}$ **maxsize** | 0) $\|$
  ptr1 := 1
OPERATIONS

  store(**ii**, **vv**) $\widehat{=}$
      PRE **vv** $\in \mathbb{N}$ $\wedge$
        ii $\in \mathbb{N}$
      THEN
        IF **ii** $\in$ 1 $\mathinner{\ldotp\ldotp}$ **maxsize**
        THEN
           contents1(**ii**) := **vv**;
           ptr1 := **ii**
        END
      END;

  vv $\longleftarrow$ **value**(**ii**) $\widehat{=}$
      PRE **ii** $\in \mathbb{N}$
      THEN

```
IF ii ∈ 1 .. maxsize
THEN
    vv := contents1(ii);
    ptr1 := ii
ELSE
    vv := 0
END
```

```
END
```

```
END
```

Note that in this case there is a trivial (isomorphism) relationship between the refined and unrefined states: **contents** is implemented by **contents1** and **ptr** by **ptr1**. Thus we are specifying a purely *procedural refinement*. All the proof obligations for refinement in this example are automatically resolved.

Another procedural refinement is the reduction of non-determinism in the result of an operation. In general we have

$$
\begin{array}{ll}
\text{CHOICE } S1 & \\
\text{OR } S2 \text{ END} & \sqsubseteq \quad S1
\end{array}
$$

and

$$
vv :\in SS \quad \sqsubseteq \quad vv := ee
$$

where ee is an expression with value in **SS**.

As an example, consider **minimal_ref** and **minimal** above: the effect of the initialisation was made more deterministic in the refinement, and similarly for the initialisations of **Array1** and **Array1_1**. A more general case is the addition of further logical constraints to a WHERE clause of an ANY statement.

An ANY **v** WHERE **P** THEN **S** END construct is typically refined by

```
VAR v
IN
    v := e;
    S1
END
```

where e satisfies the predicate **P**, and S1 refines **S**. Indeed the latter form of statement is the usual way in which a VAR construct is used, whereby the introduced local variables are immediately initialised either by an assignment or by an operation call **v** ⟵ op.

2.6 Implementation

When a new system is to be implemented in executable code using B, it is almost always the case that it is refined to an IMPLEMENTATION which IMPORTS an abstract specification of an existing (coded) development. Certainly this is the case if the system has state variables. This implementation must refine its predecessor, as above, but must also use imported operations within their preconditions (as with INCLUDES, EXTENDS, USES and SEES at the specification level, and SEES at the refinement and implementation levels), and the states of the imported and refined specifications need to be linked.

An IMPLEMENTATION is a particular type of formal B AMN component. It has the following components:

```
IMPLEMENTATION
    Name
REFINES
    component (machine or refinement) being implemented
SEES
    seen machines: S1, S2, ...
IMPORTS
    imported machines: M1, M2, ...
PROMOTES
    operations from imported machines which we wish to use
    without modification to implement operations of identical
    signature from the refined component
SETS
    local sets: fully defined enumerated sets
CONSTANTS
    local constants of scalar or string types
PROPERTIES
    full definitions of local constants,
    linking of imported and local/refined sets and constants
DEFINITIONS
    local definitions
INVARIANT
    implementation of refined state by imported states
OPERATIONS
    implementations of operations from the
    refined component in terms of operations from
    the  SEEN  and  IMPORTED  components
END
```

An ASSERTIONS clause may also be included. Seen machines may be renamed, as at the specification and refinement level. Some versions of B also allow imported machines to be renamed.

Since an implementation is to be used as the basis for translation to executable code, the PROPERTIES clause should ensure that every constant from the component being refined is given a precise value that satisfies its definition. For similar reasons only constants of a basic type can be actually used in the implementation and so need to be defined.

Imported machines must be instantiated by actual set and scalar parameters. These parameters are often based directly on the parameters of the machine being implemented. Examples are given below and in the implementation of the ship-loading system in Section 4.5.

Deferred sets of the component being refined are usually defined by equating them to sets obtained from the imported or seen components.

There are two significant omissions in this template from machine and refinement templates:

- VARIABLES clause: this is absent since it would not be possible to automatically generate executable code for the general case of B AMN variables (eg, for operations on sets or sequences). In future[1] it may be possible to allow scalar valued variables in implementations, with a preprocessor being used to express these variables, and the operations upon them, in terms of library machines. At present, however, any variables required in an implementation must be obtained by importing library machines;
- INITIALISATION clause: this may be absent because there is no local state. Implicitly, the initialisation of the implementation is the sequential combination of the initialisations of the imported machines: this combination must of course refine the initialisation of the component being refined by this implementation. If necessary the initialisation clause may provide more specific initialisations for variables from imported machines.

The proof obligations for an implementation are the same as those for refinement, with the differences being that the variables of imported machines take the place of the local variables of a refinement, with respect to the component being refined. In practical terms, the definition of an operation in an implementation is constructed by using operations of the imported and seen machines, except for trivial assignment statements (of a *basic* value to a variable of a basic type, ie, of STRING, token, enumerated set or scalar type), whereas in a refinement component, such a definition must be constructed using the local state, except for enquiry operations from seen machines.

The following forms of substitution are allowed in operations of an implementation:

- $v := e$, where each of the v are local variables of the operation, or output variables of the operation, and are of basic types. Similarly, each of the e must be of a basic type;
- WHILE E DO S INVARIANT I VARIANT v END;
- IF E THEN S_1 ELSE S_2 END, and other conditional statements which are variants of this or syntactic sugars for more complex combinations of this statement;
- VAR v IN S END;
- operations from imported machines and enquiry operations from seen machines;

---

[1]Extensions to B AMN, allowing a VARIABLES clause in implementations, have been proposed by the French school of B.

• sequential composition.

Only parameters of basic types can be inputs or outputs to operations of an implementation (and hence, of the specifications of these operations in the corresponding abstract machine).

2.6.1 Examples of Implementation

In this section we give five examples of implementation techniques. The first introduces the use of library machines for scalars and arrays to implement new developments. The second introduces the use of library machines for managing dynamically varying collections of "objects", and the final three involve the development of multiple layers of subsystems in order to implement a system.

Consider the **Array1** machine described previously. We can implement this upon two standard library machines for arrays and for variables whose values are a subset of the natural numbers. The structure of the revised system is shown in Figure 2.8.

IMPLEMENTATION
    Array1_2
REFINES
    Array1_1
IMPORTS
    Arr_Varr($\mathbb{N}$, maxsize),
    Arr_Vvar(1 .. maxsize)
SEES
    Bool_TYPE
INVARIANT
    contents1 = **Arr_Varr** $\wedge$
    ptr1 = **Arr_Vvar**

Arr_Varr *is the variable of the library component* **Arr_Varr** *which defines an array of the type* 1 .. maxsize $\rightarrow$ $\mathbb{N}$. **Arr_Vvar** *is the variable of the library component* **Arr_Vvar** *and is of type* 1 .. maxsize.

INITIALISATION

VAR **jj**
IN
    jj := 1;
    WHILE (**jj** $\leq$ maxsize)
    DO
        Arr_STO_ARR(**jj**, 0);
        jj := **jj** + 1
    INVARIANT
        jj $\leq$ maxsize + 1 $\wedge$
        1 $\leq$ **jj** $\wedge$
        $\forall$ ii.(ii $\in$ 1 .. (**jj** - 1) $\Rightarrow$ **Arr_Varr**(ii) = 0)

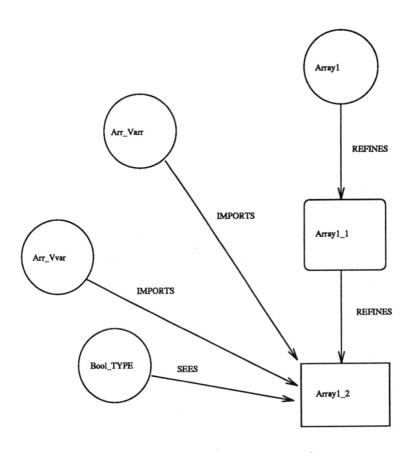

Figure 2.8: Structure of **Array**1 Development

```
        VARIANT
            maxsize + 1 − jj
        END;
    Arr_STO_VAR(1)
END
```

The initialisation is a somewhat complex way of writing a bounded loop which sets each array element of contents1 *(which is also* Arr_Varr, *the variable of* Arr_Varr*) to 0. In practice we would usually not detail loop invariants and variants for such trivial operations.*

OPERATIONS

```
store(ii, vv)    ≙
    VAR bb
    IN
        bb  ⟵  Arr_TST_IDX_ARR(ii);
        IF (bb = TRUE)
        THEN
            Arr_STO_ARR(ii, vv);
            Arr_STO_VAR(ii)
        END
    END;

vv  ⟵  value(ii)    ≙
    VAR bb
    IN
        bb  ⟵  Arr_TST_IDX_ARR(ii);
        IF (bb = TRUE)
        THEN
            vv  ⟵  Arr_VAL_ARR(ii);
            Arr_STO_VAR(ii)
        ELSE
            vv  :=  0
        END
    END
```

END

To implement **store** we test if the index **ii** is in the domain of the array (bb ⟵ Arr_TST_IDX_ARR(ii)), and if it is, store **vv** in the ii-th element of the array, and store **ii** in the data of the Arr_Vvar machine that implements the pointer.

The underlying library machines upon whose developments we are implementing **Array**1 are:

```
MACHINE
    Arr_Varr(VALUE, maxidx)
SEES
    Bool_TYPE
CONSTRAINTS
```

    maxidx $>$ 0
VARIABLES
    Arr_Varr
INVARIANT
    Arr_Varr $\in$ 1 .. maxidx $\rightarrow$ **VALUE**
INITIALISATION
    Arr_Varr $:\in$ 1 .. maxidx $\rightarrow$ **VALUE**
OPERATIONS

  bb $\longleftarrow$ **Arr_TST_IDX_ARR**(ii) $\;\widehat{=}$
    PRE
      ii : $\mathbb{N}$
    THEN
      bb $:=$ bool(ii $\in$ 1 .. maxidx)
    END;

  vv $\longleftarrow$ **Arr_VAL_ARR**(ii) $\;\widehat{=}$
    PRE
      ii $\in$ 1 .. maxidx
    THEN
      vv $:=$ **Arr_Varr**(ii)
    END;

  Arr_STO_ARR(ii, vv) $\;\widehat{=}$
    PRE
      vv : **VALUE** $\wedge$
      ii $\in$ 1 .. maxidx
    THEN
      Arr_Varr(ii) $:=$ vv
    END;

$\vdots$

END

The above machine manages an array variable and provides operations to access and modify this. **bb** := **bool(P)** is an abbreviation for

  IF **P**
  THEN
    bb $:=$ **TRUE**
  ELSE
    bb $:=$ **FALSE**
  END

The library machine **Arr_Vvar** provides a single variable of type **VALUE** and operations to access and update this:

MACHINE
    Arr_Vvar(VALUE)

SEES
    Bool_TYPE
VARIABLES
    Arr_Vvar
INVARIANT
    Arr_Vvar $\in$ **VALUE**
INITIALISATION
    Arr_Vvar $:\in$ **VALUE**
OPERATIONS

   vv $\longleftarrow$ **Arr_VAL_VAR** $\;\widehat{=}$
     BEGIN
       vv := **Arr_Vvar**
     END;

   Arr_STO_VAR(vv) $\;\widehat{=}$
     PRE
       vv $\in$ **VALUE**
     THEN
       Arr_Vvar := vv
     END;

   $\vdots$

END

These and other library machines are reproduced from the distribution directories of Version 3 of the B-Core (UK) B Toolkit. Similar library components are provided by Atelier B.

In contrast, if we have a dynamically varying set of instances of a type, we must use one of the ***_obj.mch library machines, which provide facilities for managing a set of objects with associated set, string, sequence or record values. For example, we can implement **Rational.mch** by the following component:

IMPLEMENTATION
    Rational_1
REFINES
    Rational
SEES
    Bool_TYPE
IMPORTS
    Rati_fnc_obj($\mathbb{N}, 2, \text{maxrat}$)

2 denotes the number of fields in the records managed by **Rati_fnc_obj**, maxrat *the maximum number of tokens.*

CONSTANTS
    numidx, denomidx
PROPERTIES
    RATIONAL = **Rati_FNCOBJ** $\wedge$

    numidx = 1 ∧
    denomidx = 2

INVARIANT
    rationals = Rati_fnctok ∧

    ∀ rr.(rr ∈ rationals ⇒
                numidx ∈ dom(Rati_fncstruct(rr)) ∧
                Rati_fncstruct(rr)(numidx) = rat_numerator(rr)) ∧
    ∀ rr.(rr ∈ rationals ⇒
                denomidx ∈ dom(Rati_fncstruct(rr)) ∧
                Rati_fncstruct(rr)(denomidx) = rat_denominator(rr))

This invariant identifies how the abstract variables **rat_numerator** *and* **rat_denominator** *are implemented by the data of the implementation (imported from the library machine* **Rati_fnc_obj**).

Specifically, each (token for a) rational **rr** *has its numerator value implemented by* **Rati_fncstruct(rr)(numidx)** *and denominator implemented by* **Rati_fncstruct(rr)(denomidx)**.

OPERATIONS

ok, rat ⟵ create_rational(num, den) ≙
        VAR bb, rr1
        IN
            bb, rr1 ⟵ Rati_CRE_FNC_OBJ;
            IF (bb = TRUE)
            THEN
                Rati_STO_FNC_OBJ(rr1, numidx, num);
                Rati_STO_FNC_OBJ(rr1, denomidx, den);
                rat := rr1;
                ok := TRUE
            ELSE
                ok := FALSE
            END
        END;

num ⟵ return_numerator(rat) ≙
        BEGIN
            num ⟵ Rati_VAL_FNC_OBJ(rat, numidx)
        END;

den ⟵ return_denominator(rat) ≙
        BEGIN
            den ⟵ Rati_VAL_FNC_OBJ(rat, denomidx)
        END;

delete_rational(rat) ≙
        BEGIN
            Rati_KIL_FNC_OBJ(rat)
        END

END

In general, a very close correspondence has been maintained between the specification and implementation operations and data, so that it is (relatively) easy to formally prove the implementation against its specification, or to gain a high degree of confidence in this refinement by inspection.

The elements of the library component which are relevant to this implementation are:

MACHINE
 Rati_fnc_obj(VALUE, maxfld, maxobj)
CONSTRAINTS
 maxobj $>$ 0
SEES
 file_dump, Bool_TYPE
SETS
 Rati_FNCOBJ
PROPERTIES
 card(Rati_FNCOBJ) $=$ maxobj
VARIABLES
 Rati_fnctok, Rati_fncstruct, Rati_locate
INVARIANT
 Rati_fnctok $\subseteq$ Rati_FNCOBJ $\wedge$
 Rati_fncstruct $\in$ Rati_fnctok $\rightarrow$ $(1 \,..\, \text{maxfld} \nrightarrow \text{VALUE})$ $\wedge$
 Rati_locate $\in$ $1 \,..\, \text{card}(\text{Rati\_fnctok})$ $\rightarrowtail\!\!\!\!\rightarrow$ Rati_fnctok

This machine manages a set of 'function objects' or records – the currently existing function object identifiers are held in Rati_fnctok, whilst the values of type $1 \,..\, \text{maxfld} \nrightarrow \text{VALUE}$ which these identifiers point to can be obtained by applying the function Rati_fncstruct to these identifiers. The function Rati_locate is a bijection which gives a linear ordering of the Rati_fnctok identifiers, and is used to support iteration over this set.

INITIALISATION
 Rati_fnctok, Rati_fncstruct, Rati_locate := $\varnothing$, $\varnothing$, $\varnothing$
OPERATIONS

This operation checks whether ii denotes a valid field:

 bb $\longleftarrow$ Rati_TST_FLD_FNC_OBJ(ii) $\widehat{=}$
 PRE
  ii $\in$ NAT
 THEN
  bb := bool(ii $\in$ $1 \,..\, \text{maxfld}$)
 END ;

This operation attempts to create a new object, referenced by pp. It returns bb = TRUE if this attempt is successful:

bb, pp ⟵ Rati_CRE_FNC_OBJ ≙
  IF Rati_fnctok ≠ Rati_FNCOBJ THEN
      ANY qq, ll WHERE
          qq ∈ Rati_FNCOBJ − Rati_fnctok ∧
          ll ∈ 1 .. card(Rati_fnctok) + 1 ⤚↠ (Rati_fnctok ∪ {qq})
      THEN
          Rati_fncstruct(qq) := ∅ ||
          Rati_fnctok := Rati_fnctok ∪ {qq} ||
          Rati_locate := ll ||
          pp := qq ||
          bb := TRUE
      END
  ELSE
      bb := FALSE
  END ;

This operation removes the object referenced by ff :

Rati_KIL_FNC_OBJ(ff) ≙
PRE
  ff ∈ Rati_fnctok
THEN
  Rati_fncstruct := {ff} ◁ Rati_fncstruct ||
  Rati_fnctok := Rati_fnctok − {ff} ||
  Rati_locate :∈ (
      1 .. card(Rati_fnctok) − 1 ⤚↠ (Rati_fnctok − {ff})
)
END ;

This operation checks if the ii-th field is defined for ff :

bb ⟵ Rati_DEF_FNC_OBJ(ff, ii) ≙
PRE
    ff ∈ Rati_fnctok ∧
    ii ∈ 1 .. maxfld
THEN
    bb := bool(ii ∈ dom(Rati_fncstruct(ff)))
END ;

This operation obtains the value of the ii-th field of ff :

vv ⟵ Rati_VAL_FNC_OBJ(ff, ii) ≙
PRE
    ff ∈ Rati_fnctok ∧
    ii ∈ dom(Rati_fncstruct(ff))
THEN
    vv := Rati_fncstruct(ff)(ii)
END ;

This operation updates the value of the ii-th field of ff with vv :

Rati_STO_FNC_OBJ(ff, ii, vv) $\hat{=}$
   PRE
      ff $\in$ Rati_fnctok $\wedge$
      ii $\in$ 1..maxfld $\wedge$
      vv $\in$ VALUE
   THEN
      Rati_fncstruct(ff)(ii) := vv
   END;

   $\vdots$

END

For the sorting system introduced above, we could give an abstract specification:

MACHINE **Sorter**
OPERATIONS
  sort $\hat{=}$
         SKIP
END

and a corresponding implementation:

IMPLEMENTATION **Sorter_1**
REFINES **Sorter**
IMPORTS **SortSet, SortSeq**
SEES **Bool_TYPE**
OPERATIONS
  sort $\hat{=}$
    VAR bb, xx
    IN
      bb $\longleftarrow$ is_empty;
      WHILE bb = **FALSE**
      DO
         xx $\longleftarrow$ choose;
         ordered_insert(xx);
         remove(xx);
         bb $\longleftarrow$ is_empty
      INVARIANT (bb = **TRUE**) $\equiv$ (ss = $\varnothing$)
      VARIANT card(ss)
      END
    END

END

This implementation is automatically correct (apart from obligations that **choose, ordered_insert** and **remove** are called within their preconditions – hence our loop invariant) because the initial specification is vacuous: this approach is adopted when developers simply want to use B to formally develop a

few selected components, and to write code without verification for other components. card(ss) is a natural choice for a variant since it is strictly decreased
by each loop iteration, and is bounded below by 0.

The **SortSet** machine could itself be refined in the standard manner by a
sequence-based machine:

REFINEMENT **Seq**
REFINES **SortSet**
SEES **BooLTYPE**
CONSTANTS
  rem
PROPERTIES
  rem $\in$ seq($\mathbb{N}$) $\times$ $\mathbb{N}$ $\rightarrow$ seq($\mathbb{N}$) $\wedge$
  $\forall$ (nn, sq).(nn $\in$ $\mathbb{N}$ $\wedge$ sq $\in$ seq($\mathbb{N}$) $\Rightarrow$
     rem([ ], nn) $=$ [ ] $\wedge$
     rem(sq $\frown$ [nn], nn) $=$
                    rem(sq, nn) $\wedge$
     size(sq) $>$ 1 $\wedge$ **last(sq)** $\neq$ nn $\Rightarrow$
        rem(sq, nn) $=$ **rem(front(sq), nn)**)
VARIABLES
  sq
INVARIANT
  sq $\in$ seq($\mathbb{N}$) $\wedge$

  ss $=$ ran(sq)
INITIALISATION
  sq := [ ]
OPERATIONS
  xx $\longleftarrow$ **choose** $\hat{=}$
    PRE **sq** $\neq$ [ ]
    THEN
       xx := **sq(1)**
    END;

  remove(xx) $\hat{=}$
    PRE **xx** $\in$ $\mathbb{N}$
    THEN
       sq := **rem(sq, xx)**
    END;

  add(xx) $\hat{=}$
    PRE **xx** $\in$ $\mathbb{N}$
    THEN
       sq := **sq** $\frown$ **[xx]**
    END;

  bb $\longleftarrow$ **is_empty** $\hat{=}$
    IF **sq** $=$ [ ]
    THEN
       bb := **TRUE**

ELSE
    bb := FALSE
END

END

The proof of the correctness of this refinement depends upon elementary properties of sets and sequences such as

$$\mathrm{ran}(\mathbf{rem}(\mathbf{sq}, \mathbf{nn})) = \mathrm{ran}(\mathbf{sq}) - \{\mathbf{nn}\}$$

Examples of refinement proof obligations are:

1. Constraints ∧   /∗ Constraints of Seq and SortSet ∗/
   Context ∧   /∗ Properties of Seq and SortSet ∗/
   Assertions ∧   /∗ Assertions of Seq and SortSet ∗/
   Inv ∧   /∗ Both invariants, including ss = ran(sq) ∗/
       $\mathbf{Pre}_{\mathbf{choose,SortSet}}$ /∗ Abstract precondition : ss ≠ ∅ ∗/
           ⇒
               sq ≠ []

   for the **choose** operation – this is the obligation that the precondition
   of **choose** in **Seq** is implied by the precondition of this operation in
   SortSet, under the assumptions of the logical properties of the data of
   Seq and **SortSet**. This implication is clearly valid since ran(sq) ≠ ∅
   implies sq ≠ [];

2.   Constraints ∧
      Context ∧
      Assertions ∧
      Inv ∧
      $\mathbf{Pre}_{\mathbf{add,SortSet}}$
          ⇒
              ss ∪ { xx } = ran(sq ⌢ [xx])

   for the **add** operation – this is the obligation that the effect of the refined
   version of **add** (which concatenates **xx** to the end of the sequence) yields,
   via the refinement relation ss = ran(sq), a state which can be reached by
   an execution of the abstract version.
   Again this is directly seen to be valid.

In turn, **Seq** could be refined to code by using an explicit algorithm to
evaluate **rem**. As a result this recursive function is no longer needed in the
subsystem, and does not need itself to be refined in the following module:

REFINEMENT **Seq_1**
REFINES **Seq**
VARIABLES
    sq1
INVARIANT
    sq1 ∈ seq(ℕ) ∧

```
   sq  =  sq1
INITIALISATION
   sq1  :=  [ ]
OPERATIONS
   xx  ⟵  choose  ≙
      IF sq1  ≠  [ ]
      THEN
          xx  :=  sq1(1)
      ELSE
          xx  :=  0
      END;

   remove(xx)  ≙
      VAR ii, jj, rsq
      IN
          ii  :=  1;
          jj  :=  1;
          rsq  :=  [ ];
          WHILE ii  ≤  size(sq1)
          DO
              IF sq1(ii)  =  xx
              THEN
                  ii  :=  ii + 1
              ELSE
                  rsq(jj)  :=  sq1(ii);
                  jj  :=  jj + 1;
                  ii  :=  ii + 1
              END
          INVARIANT
              rsq↑(jj − 1)  =  rem(sq↑(ii − 1), xx)  ∧
              ii  ≤  size(sq1) + 1
          VARIANT
              size(sq1) + 1 − ii
          END;
          sq1  :=  rsq
      END;

   add(xx)  ≙
      sq1  :=  sq1 ⌢ [xx];

   bb  ⟵  is_empty  ≙
      IF sq1  =  [ ]
      THEN
          bb  :=  TRUE
      ELSE
          bb  :=  FALSE
      END

END
```

Unfortunately the above refinement is not allowed in the present B language because it involves a loop. This means that we are forced to perform data refinement before procedural refinement, and hence cannot express algorithms using loops in an abstract manner.

It is possible to instead go directly to an implementation of **Seq**, however this is likely to be very complex. To avoid this problem we decide to carry out a design step and encapsulate some of the operations needed by this implementation in a new subsystem. The prime candidates for such operations are the initialisation, loop test, finalisation and the body of the while loop needed for **remove**. This approach is taken in the development shown below.

Proving that **Seq_1** is a refinement of **Seq** consists of essentially a code verification exercise. The key part is the proof of the loop invariant in **remove**.

It is clear that $rsq{\uparrow}(jj-1) = rem(sq1{\uparrow}(ii-1), xx)$ is established by the first three statements in the definition of **remove** – both sides of the equation are the empty sequence $[]$.

If the invariant holds before the loop and the loop condition is true, then in the case that $sq1(ii) = xx$ we need to show that

$$rsq{\uparrow}(jj-1) = rem(sq1{\uparrow}ii, xx)$$

which follows from the definition of **rem**, and in the case that $sq1(ii) \neq xx$ we need:

$$(rsq \oplus \{jj \mapsto sq1(ii)\}){\uparrow}jj = rem(sq1{\uparrow}ii, xx)$$

Again this follows from the definition of **rem**, since the LHS is simply

$$rsq{\uparrow}(jj-1) \frown [sq1(ii)]$$

ie:

$$rem(sq1{\uparrow}(ii-1), xx) \frown [sq1(ii)]$$

which is the definition of $rem(sq1{\uparrow}ii, xx)$ in this case.

To implement the system in a valid manner, we introduce a new subsystem which encapsulates the operations used within the above loop for **remove**:

```
MACHINE
    Filter(maxseq)
SEES BooL_TYPE
VARIABLES
    vsq, rsq,
    v_pointer, r_pointer
INVARIANT
    vsq ∈ seq(ℕ) ∧ rsq ∈ seq(ℕ) ∧
    v_pointer ∈ ℕ ∧ r_pointer ∈ ℕ ∧
    size(vsq) ≤ maxseq ∧
    size(rsq) ≤ maxseq ∧
    v_pointer ≤ maxseq + 2 ∧
```

r_pointer $\leq$ maxseq + 2

INITIALISATION
    vsq := [] || rsq := [] ||
    v_pointer := 1 || r_pointer := 1

OPERATIONS

xx ⟵ choose $\hat{=}$
    IF vsq = []
    THEN
        xx := 0
    ELSE
        xx := vsq(1)
    END;

start $\hat{=}$
    BEGIN
        rsq := [] ||
        v_pointer := 1 ||
        r_pointer := 1
    END;

filter(xx) $\hat{=}$
    PRE xx $\in$ $\mathbb{N}$ $\wedge$ v_pointer $\in$ 1..size(vsq)
    THEN
        IF vsq(v_pointer) = xx
        THEN
            v_pointer := v_pointer + 1
        ELSE
            rsq(r_pointer) := vsq(v_pointer) ||
            v_pointer := v_pointer + 1 ||
            r_pointer := r_pointer + 1
        END
    END;

copy $\hat{=}$
    vsq := rsq;

add(xx) $\hat{=}$
    PRE xx $\in$ $\mathbb{N}$ $\wedge$ size(vsq) < maxseq
    THEN
        vsq := vsq $^\frown$ [xx]
    END;

bb ⟵ has_finished $\hat{=}$
    bb := bool(v_pointer > size(vsq));

bb ⟵ is_empty $\hat{=}$
    bb := bool(vsq = []);

END

This is then used to provide an implementation for **Seq**:

IMPLEMENTATION
    DualSeq
REFINES
    Seq
SEES
    Bool_TYPE
IMPORTS
    Filter(1000)
PROMOTES **choose, add, is_empty**
INVARIANT
    sq = vsq
OPERATIONS

  remove(xx) $\hat{=}$
    VAR **fini**
    IN
        start;
        fini $\longleftarrow$ **has_finished**;
       WHILE (**fini** = **FALSE**)
       DO
           filter(xx);
           fini $\longleftarrow$ **has_finished**
       VARIANT size(sq) + 1 − v_pointer
       INVARIANT rsq↑(r_pointer − 1) = rem(sq↑(v_pointer − 1), xx) ∧
             v_pointer ≤ size(sq) + 1
       END;
       copy
    END

END

Filter itself is implemented using four library components:

IMPLEMENTATION
    Filter_1
REFINES
    Filter
SEES
    Bool_TYPE
IMPORTS
    Seq_Vseq($\mathbb{N}$, maxseq),
    Rsq_Vseq($\mathbb{N}$, maxseq),
    Vptr_Nvar(maxseq + 2),
    Rptr_Nvar(maxseq + 2)
INVARIANT
    Seq_Vseq = vsq ∧
    Rsq_Vseq = rsq ∧
    Vptr_Nvar = v_pointer ∧
    Rptr_Nvar = r_pointer

INITIALISATION

```
BEGIN
    Vptr_STO_NVAR(1);
    Rptr_STO_NVAR(1)
END
```

OPERATIONS

```
xx ⟵ choose ≙
    VAR bb
    IN
        bb ⟵ Seq_EMP_SEQ;
        IF bb = FALSE
        THEN
            xx ⟵ Seq_VAL_SEQ(1)
        ELSE
            xx := 0
        END
    END;

start ≙
    BEGIN
        Rsq_CLR_SEQ;
        Vptr_STO_NVAR(1);
        Rptr_STO_NVAR(1)
    END;

filter(xx) ≙
    VAR vv, vptr
    IN
        vptr ⟵ Vptr_VAL_NVAR;
        vv ⟵ Seq_VAL_SEQ(vptr);
        IF vv = xx
        THEN
            Vptr_INC_NVAR
        ELSE
            Rsq_PSH_SEQ(vv);
            Vptr_INC_NVAR;
            Rptr_INC_NVAR
        END
    END;

copy ≙
    VAR bb, vv
    IN
        Seq_CLR_SEQ;
        bb ⟵ Rsq_EMP_SEQ;
        WHILE bb = FALSE
        DO
```

```
            vv  ⟵  Rsq_FST_SEQ;
            Rsq_POP_SEQ;
            Seq_PSH_SEQ(vv);
            bb  ⟵  Rsq_EMP_SEQ
        INVARIANT ((bb  =  TRUE)  ≡  (Rsq_Vseq  =  []))
        VARIANT size(Rsq_Vseq)
        END
    END;

  add(xx)  ≘
    Seq_PSH_SEQ(xx);

  bb  ⟵  has_finished  ≘
    VAR ll
    IN
        ll  ⟵  Seq_LEN_SEQ;
        bb  ⟵  Vptr_GTR_NVAR(ll)
    END;

  bb  ⟵  is_empty  ≘
    bb  ⟵  Seq_EMP_SEQ

END
```

In **DualSeq** we have chosen an arbitrary upper bound of 1000 on the size of the sequences at the implementation level: for a fully formally proved development we would need to also assert this bound at the specification level of **SortSet**, and, in addition, use only a bounded set of possible values for elements of these sequences.

Rename_Vseq(**VALUE, maxsize**) is a library machine that encapsulates a variable Rename_Vseq : seq(**VALUE**) of maximum size **maxsize**, and operations to query and update this variable.

2.7 Summary

- Mathematics is used in software specification in order to support abstract expression of requirements, and in order to support verification and validation of software.
- B uses classical logic and notations for sets, sequences, maps, etc, adapted from those for Z.
- Operations modify or access the state of a module. They are defined by using an abstract programming language termed the "generalised substitution notation". In addition to conventional assignment, conditional, sequencing and loop statements, this provides more abstract statements for non-deterministic choice of actions and for expressing preconditions and blocking guards.
- A weakest precondition semantics is given for generalised substitutions.

- A module in B is termed an *abstract machine.* These contain data and operations on that data. They are akin to Ada packages but provide a mathematical specification of the effect and results of operations in place of a type specification or code implementation. Machines come in three flavours: specification level MACHINEs; REFINEMENTs and IMPLEMENTA-TIONs. Different restrictions apply on the constructs that can be used at each of these levels.

- Internal consistency obligations can be generated for each B machine.

- Machines can access the operations and data of other machines via the inclusion mechanisms SEES, USES, INCLUDES, EXTENDS and IMPORTS. Each has a particular role in development.

- Refinement in B is based on the concept of data refinement of model-based specifications. Proof obligations can be generated for a refinement step.

- Implementations of a system make use of pre-defined library components which provide executable support for data structures such as sets and sequences.

2.8   Exercises 1

(1)   Define B AMN operations to do the following:

1. take as input a natural number **nn** and return the maximum of this and a state variable **val** $\in \mathbb{N}$;

2. test if an input element **xx** is in a set **ss** of natural numbers, returning **TRUE** if so and **FALSE** otherwise;

3. to non-deterministically choose between: adding an input element **xx** to a set **ss** of natural numbers, returning a result **TRUE**, or leaving the state unchanged, returning the result **FALSE**.

(2)   Define a machine to manage a single state variable **val** $\in 0 \mathinner{\ldotp\ldotp} \mathbf{maxval}$ and operations of: replace its value by a new input value; output the value; increment by an input value (provided the bound is not exceeded); decrement by an input value, output the maximum of **val** and an input value. Use the approach of (1) 3. above to report exceptions that may arise from these operations (eg, attempting to set **val** to a number greater than **maxval**, or less than 0). The outline of the machine is:

```
MACHINE  Scalar(maxval)
CONSTRAINTS maxval > 0
SEES BooL_TYPE
VARIABLES
      val
INVARIANT
      val ∈ ℕ ∧ val ≤ maxval
INITIALISATION
      val := 0
```

OPERATIONS

$$\vdots$$

END

(3) Calculate the following weakest preconditions:

   1.

$$[\text{PRE } \mathbf{x} > 0 \text{ THEN } \mathbf{y} := \mathbf{y}/\mathbf{x} \text{ END}](\mathbf{y} > 1)$$

   2.

[CHOICE
     $\mathbf{ss} := \mathbf{ss} \cup \{\mathbf{xx}\} \;||$
     $\mathbf{bb} := \mathbf{TRUE}$ OR
     $\mathbf{bb} := \mathbf{FALSE}$ END]$(\mathbf{xx} \in \mathbf{ss})$

   3.

$$[\mathbf{x} := \mathbf{a} + 1 \;||\; \mathbf{y} := \mathbf{x} + \mathbf{a}](\mathbf{x} = \mathbf{new\_x} \wedge \mathbf{y} = \mathbf{new\_y})$$

   4.

$$[\mathbf{x} := \mathbf{a} + 1;\; \mathbf{y} := \mathbf{x} + \mathbf{a}](\mathbf{x} = \mathbf{new\_x} \wedge \mathbf{y} = \mathbf{new\_y})$$

   5.

[ANY $\mathbf{vv}$
     WHERE $\mathbf{vv} > \mathbf{xx} \wedge \mathbf{vv} \in \mathbb{N}$
     THEN $\mathbf{xx} := \mathbf{vv}$
     END]$(\mathbf{xx} \in \mathbf{ss})$

   6.

$$[\mathbf{ww} := \mathbf{vv} + 1](\mathbf{ww} = \mathbf{vv})$$

(4) Identify and prove the internal consistency obligations for the following machine:

MACHINE **Set**
VARIABLES $\mathbf{ss}$
INVARIANT
     $\mathbf{ss} \in \mathbb{F}(\mathbb{N})$
INITIALISATION
     $\mathbf{ss} := \varnothing$
OPERATIONS
   $\mathbf{xx} \longleftarrow \mathbf{choose} \;\widehat{=}$
     $\mathbf{xx} :\in \mathbf{ss};$

add(xx) $\hat{=}$
    PRE **xx** $\in$ $\mathbb{N}$
    THEN **ss** := **ss** $\cup$ { **xx** }
    END

END

Is it internally consistent?

Identify the feasibility conditions of both operations. Is the machine in a suitable form for refinement towards code?

Chapter 3

Analysis and Specification

In this chapter we will examine each of the life cycle stages of B AMN development from requirements analysis through to the creation of a complete specification. A number of case studies and examples are used to illustrate these stages and the choices that can be made in expressing the semantics of a system using B. We will emphasise a particular approach using translation from diagrammatic models to inspire the choice of features of the formal specification, however it is quite feasible to directly write formal specifications without prior analysis or such a translation process (people have been writing Z or VDM specifications this way for years). For complex systems a loss of quality is nevertheless likely to result from omitting analysis.

Section 3.1 briefly discusses the process of requirements analysis, Section 3.2 describes the formalisation of data and dynamic models, and various choices that may be made in the style of a specification. Section 3.3 describes the process of animation in B. Section 3.4 describes some aspects of internal consistency proof, whilst sections 3.6 and 3.7 describe the renaming facility of B, and some applications of this.

3.1 Requirements Analysis

Requirements analysis proceeds from stated requirements about a system, and information about the domain of the system, to a series of models in a semi-formal notation, or a structured textual representation of the requirements. Many diagrammatic methods are based on three complementary views of a system:

- *static data models*: representing the entities present in the domain and requirements, together with relationships between these entities, and attributes of these entities;
- *dynamic models*: representing the sets of states which an entity may pass through in its 'lifetime', together with transitions between these states;

- *functional models*: representing the operations which the system is designed to support.

The notation we will use in this book is that of OMT [62], which has the following models:

- *static data models*: object model diagrams;
- *dynamic models*: Harel statecharts;
- *functional models*: an extended data flow diagram notation.

Formalisation of the first two of these models will be discussed in the following section. Care must be taken to distinguish models of a domain or situation in the world (*essential models* in the terms of Syntropy [16]) from models of the required software (*specification models* in Syntropy). The task of progressing from an essential to a specification model is not really a part of the B method, although B could be used to animate essential models in order to explore their properties. In the following we assume that we are starting from analysis models which describe the required software.

3.2   Specification Development

This stage takes the analysis models produced from the previous stage and creates formalised expressions of these models using sets of abstract machines. It is usually the case that more than one analysis model form will be used to create a single machine. For example, the transitions on a statechart can form the basis for operations in a machine, and the static data model can contribute to the definitions of the state of that machine. The structure of the formal specification will reflect the structure of the analysis models, and in this way, the comprehensibility and maintainability of the formal specification will be enhanced.

In the following sections we give an overview of how object models and statecharts can be formalised in abstract machines, and how specifications can be structured for improved comprehension.

3.2.1   Formalising Data Models

Object models consist of named boxes for entities or object classes, in which all non-object valued attributes of the class are listed, together with their types. Relationships between entities are represented by lines. The number of participants in a relationship is indicated by means of circles or numeric annotations: a filled circle at the end of a line indicates that there may be many (zero or more) instances of the adjacent entity in this relationship with one instance of the entity at the other end of the line. An unfilled circle indicates zero or one occurrence. A line with no circles indicates a 1:1 relationship.

Inheritance and specialisation can also be explicitly signalled on an object model diagram. An example of an object model, of a set of nodes in a communication network (eg, telephones) and channels denoting direct connections between them, is shown in Figure 3.1.

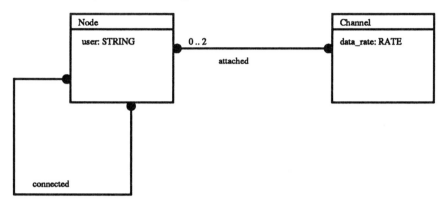

Figure 3.1: Object Model of Nodes and Channels

In this system, each node may be **connected** to many (zero or more) other nodes and may be **attached** to many channels. However a channel may only be attached to at most two nodes. Each node has a variable **user** holding a string value.

Approximately, entity types in a OMT object model will be expressed as B machines, encapsulating the sets of possible and existing instances of the entity type, and a set of functions representing attributes of the type. Links between entity types are represented using the B inclusion mechanisms for machines.

The following process can be used to map analysis models expressed in OMT object model notation into systems of B machines:

1. identify the *families* of entity types in the data model – that is, the sets of entity types which are subtypes of a given type T which has itself no supertypes;
2. identify the *access paths* which are needed by operations and attributes of the types within each family to types in other families;
3. on this basis, produce a directed acyclic graph, whose nodes are the families, and whose edges are inclusion relationships USES or SEES between the nodes;
4. define machines for each family, following the procedure outlined below, and include machines in other machines using the relationships identified in the previous step.

Note that step 3 may not always be possible. Cycles **A → A** are allowed in the graph, but cycles **A → B, B → A** or longer cycles are not allowed (they would lead to cycles in the machine inclusion relations, which are not allowed). If such cycles are required in the system (rather than being a feature of the general domain), then the entities concerned must all be placed in a single abstract machine.

The simple case of an entity without subtypes (that is, of a family containing a single type) will be considered first. In step 4 in this case, each concept Entity with attributes or links att1 : T1, att2 : T2, ..., attn : Tn will have a corresponding machine **Entity**.mch of the form

```
MACHINE  Entity
SETS
    ENTITY
VARIABLES
    entities,
    att1, att2, ..., attn
INVARIANT
    entities ⊆ ENTITY   ∧

    att1 ∈ entities → T1   ∧
    att2 ∈ entities → T2   ∧
    ...
    attn ∈ entities → Tn
    ...
END
```

This machine models a collection of Entity instances, rather than a single entity. If only one instance of the Entity was required, we would omit the declaration of **entities** and have instead a declaration of a machine **Entity**, together with variables att1 : T1, att2 : T2, etc.

The set **ENTITY** represents the set of all *possible* object identities of instances of Entity, **entities** represents the set of object identities of currently existing Entity instances (that are known to the system).

A standard creation operation for **Entity** instances is:

```
ee ⟵  create_entity(att1_val, ..., attn_val)  ≙
       PRE att1_val ∈ T1 ∧ ... ∧ attn_val ∈ Tn ∧
           entities ≠ ENTITY
       THEN
           ANY oo
           WHERE
               oo ∈ ENTITY − entities
           THEN
               ee := oo ||
               entities := entities ∪ { oo } ||
               att1(oo) := att1_val ||
               ...
               attn(oo) := attn_val
           END
       END
```

If there are relationships between entities in the object model, then some of the T1, ..., Tn will themselves involve other entities, say Entity2, Entity3 .... In this case we must SEE or USE the associated machine:

MACHINE **Entity**
SEES **Entity2, Entity3, ...**

   ...

END

We use SEES if we only need to use the object identity sets **ENTITY2**, **ENTITY3**, etc, in the invariant of **Entity** (ie, to provide a range type for a link of Entity), and we use USES if we need to be more specific and use the set of existing entities **entities2**, etc, as range types in the invariant. If there is a 1-1 link for example, such a stronger typing constraint would be needed. Relation types may be used in place of function types, for example:

attached $\in$ **nodes** $\leftrightarrow$ **channels**

if this provides a more flexible model (eg, if many channels can be attached to the same node, and many nodes to the same channel).

We may also use a parameter to place a bound on the maximum number of instances of a given entity which we will allow (in order to account for the finiteness of all types in B):

MACHINE **Entity(maxEntity)**
CONSTRAINTS
   maxEntity $\geq$ 1
   ...
PROPERTIES
   card(ENTITY) = **maxEntity**
INVARIANT
   entities $\subseteq$ **ENTITY** $\wedge$
   ...
END

If we have Entity2 inheriting Entity1, then we need to place the constraint **entities2** $\subseteq$ **entities1** in the invariant of the machine representing the supertype (most abstract entity).

MACHINE **Entity1**
SETS
   ENTITY1
VARIABLES
   entities1, entities2
INVARIANT
   entities1 $\subseteq$ **ENTITY1** $\wedge$
   entities2 $\subseteq$ **entities1**

. . .

END

Similarly with exclusive subtypes Entity1 and Entity2, the constraint **entities1**∩ **entities2** = ∅ is added to the invariant.

When we use machines to model single instances of an entity, rather than a variable set **entities** of instances, we can use the EXTENDS structuring mechanism to express inheritance (see Section 3.2.3 for an example of this).

Aggregation (containment of objects within others) can be modelled by using *constants* of an entity type, or by including a fixed set of (renamed) instances of a machine representing a typical element of an entity type.

3.2.2 Example: Communication System Specification

Using the above approach, the object model for this system can be formalised as follows:

```
MACHINE  Channel(maxChannel, RATE)
CONSTRAINTS
    maxChannel  >  0
SETS CHANNEL
PROPERTIES   card(CHANNEL)  =  maxChannel
VARIABLES
    channels,  data_rate
INVARIANT
    channels  ⊆  CHANNEL  ∧
    data_rate  ∈  channels  →  RATE
INITIALISATION
    channels  :=  ∅  ||  data_rate  :=  ∅
OPERATIONS
    cc  ⟵  create_channel(rate)  ≙
        PRE channels  ≠  CHANNEL  ∧
            rate  ∈  RATE
        THEN
          ANY newc
          WHERE  newc  ∈  CHANNEL  −  channels
          THEN
              cc  :=  newc  ||
              data_rate(newc)  :=  rate  ||
              channels  :=  channels  ∪  { newc }
          END
        END ;

  change_rate(cc, rate)  ≙
        PRE cc  ∈  channels  ∧
            rate  ∈  RATE
        THEN
            data_rate(cc)  :=  rate
```

END

END

We have identified that we need access from a node to its associated channels, but not from a channel to its attached nodes. There would usually typically be additional operations to access attributes of a channel and node.

MACHINE **Node(maxNode)**
USES **Channel**
SETS **NODE**
PROPERTIES
    card(NODE) = **maxNode**
VARIABLES
    nodes, attached, connected
INVARIANT
    nodes $\subseteq$ NODE $\wedge$
    attached $\in$ nodes $\leftrightarrow$ channels $\wedge$
    connected $\in$ nodes $\leftrightarrow$ nodes $\wedge$

    connected = closure(attached; attached^{-1}) $-$ id(nodes) $\wedge$
    $\forall$ **cc.(cc $\in$ channels** $\Rightarrow$
                card(attached^{-1}[{ cc }]) $\leq$ 2)
INITIALISATION
    nodes, attached, connected := $\varnothing$, $\varnothing$, $\varnothing$
OPERATIONS
    / * *operations updating or accessing*
        attributes or links from Node * /
END

The conjunct **connected = closure(attached; attached^{-1}) $-$ id(nodes)** in the invariant indicates that **connected** is the non-reflexive transitive closure of **attached** composed with its inverse – ie, two distinct nodes are connected if and only if there is a non-empty sequence of channels connecting them, via 0 or more intermediate nodes. This constraint could not be expressed in the diagram. In B, **closure(rel)** is the reflexive transitive closure of a relation **rel**, and **id(s)** is the identity relation on the set s. The inverse **rel^{-1}** of a relation has the ASCII notation `rel˜`

The final conjunct expresses the cardinality constraint of Figure 3.1: ie., that each channel has at most 2 attached nodes. We have used relations to express attributes in this machine in order to simplify the statement of the invariant.

3.2.3   Example: Personnel System

This is a further example of the way that the structure of an object model can be interpreted as a collection of B AMN machines and inclusion mechanisms between them.

It shows that the EXTENDS construct represents inheritance in the sense of an 'is a' relationship between a supertype (here **Person**) and a subtype (**Employed_Person**).

The concepts to be specified are shown in Figure 3.2. An identifier preceded

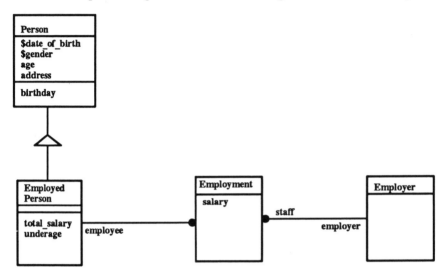

Figure 3.2: Object Model of Personnel System

by a $ symbol denotes a constant.

They have the following requirements:

- **Person:**
    - *constant data*: **date_of_birth, gender**, etc
    - *varying data*: **age, address**, etc;
    - *operations*: **birthday**, etc.
- **Employed_Person** (as for person, but with):
    - a (varying) sequence of current employments;
    - operations to add a job, determine total salary, etc.

The specifications are:

MACHINE **Person**
SETS
   STRING;
   GENDER = { female, male }
CONSTANTS
   date_of_birth, gender
PROPERTIES
   date_of_birth $\in$ $\mathbb{N}$ $\wedge$ **gender** $\in$ **GENDER**
VARIABLES

   age, address
INVARIANT
  age $\in$ 0 .. 200 $\wedge$
  address $\in$ **STRING**
INITIALISATION
  age := 0 $\|$ **address** :$\in$ **STRING**
OPERATIONS

  birthday $\widehat{=}$
    PRE **age** < 200
    THEN
      age := **age** + 1
    END;

 ca $\longleftarrow$ **current_age** $\widehat{=}$
   ca := **age**;

 change_address(addr) $\widehat{=}$
    PRE **addr** $\in$ **STRING**
    THEN
      address := **addr**
    ND

No.... hat we have chosen to only represent a single person – in general a dynamically varying set of people would need to be defined. In this case the distinction between constant and varying data of each person could not be so clearly made.

MACHINE **Employed_Person**
EXTENDS **Person**
USES **Employment**
VARIABLES
    current_jobs
INVARIANT
  current_jobs $\in$ seq(employments)
INITIALISATION
  current_jobs := [ ]
OPERATIONS
  add_job(jb) $\widehat{=}$
    PRE **jb** $\in$ **employments**
    THEN
      current_jobs := **current_jobs** $\frown$ [jb]
    END;

 sal $\longleftarrow$ **total_salary** $\widehat{=}$
   sal := Σ ii.(ii $\in$ dom(current_jobs) $|$
                       salary(current_jobs(ii)))

END

where we have:

MACHINE **Employment**
SETS
   EMPLOYMENT
VARIABLES
   employments, salary
INVARIANT
   employments $\subseteq$ **EMPLOYMENT** $\wedge$
   salary $\in$ **employments** $\rightarrow$ $\mathbb{N}$
INITIALISATION
   employments, salary := $\varnothing$, $\varnothing$
OPERATIONS

  jb $\longleftarrow$ **create_employment(sal)** $\widehat{=}$
   PRE **employments** $\neq$ **EMPLOYMENT** $\wedge$
    sal $\in$ $\mathbb{N}$
   THEN
    ANY **oo**
    WHERE
     oo $\in$ **EMPLOYMENT** $-$ **employments**
    THEN
     jb := **oo** $\|$
     employments :=
      employments $\cup$ { **oo** } $\|$
     salary(oo) := **sal**
    END
   END

END

- **Employed_Person** EXTENDS **Person** as every feature of a person is a feature of an employed person;
- **Employed_Person** USES **Employment** as variables of **Employment** are needed in the invariant and operations of **Employed_Person** – but an **Employed_Person** is not a 'kind of' **Employment**;
- SEES would be too weak in the latter case – we need the set **employments** in the invariant of **Employed_Person**.

The resulting specification structure is shown in Figure 3.3.
A way of avoiding the problem of cyclic reference structures between entities discussed above is to parameterise one of the machines (representing entities) involved with a set representing the set of object identities of the other entity, and to instantiate this appropriately when both machines are combined into a larger system. This works because if we have a clause

INCLUDES **A**(P1), **B**(P2), ...

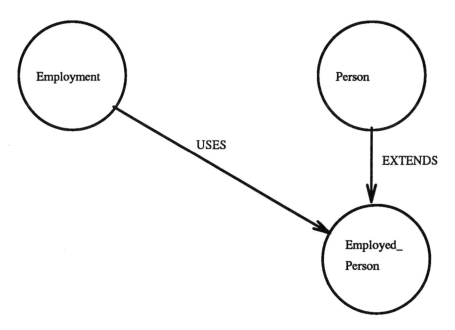

Figure 3.3: Specification Structure of Personnel System

then sets defined locally in **B** can be used in the parameter list **P**1 and similarly local sets of **A** can be used in **P**2.

In this case, if we really wanted references in both directions between an employment and its associated employer we would change **Employment** to:

```
MACHINE  Employment(EMR)
SETS  EMPLOYMENT
VARIABLES
    employments, salary, employer
INVARIANT
    employments ⊆ EMPLOYMENT  ∧
    salary ∈ employments → ℕ  ∧
    employer ∈ employments ↠ EMR
INITIALISATION
    employments := ∅ ‖
    salary := ∅ ‖
    employer := ∅
OPERATIONS
  ee ⟵ create_employment(sal) ≙
      PRE sal ∈ ℕ ∧
          employments ≠ EMPLOYMENT
      THEN
        ANY oo
        WHERE oo ∈ EMPLOYMENT – employments
        THEN
          employments := employments ∪ { oo } ‖
```

```
            ee := oo ||
            salary(oo) := sal
        END
    END;

set_boss(ee, boss) ≙
    PRE ee ∈ employments ∧ boss ∈ EMR
    THEN
        employer(ee) := boss
    END

END
```

where **Employer** is represented by:

```
MACHINE Employer
USES Employment
SETS
    EMPLOYER
VARIABLES
    employers, staff
INVARIANT
    employers ⊆ EMPLOYER ∧
    staff ∈ employers → seq(employments)
INITIALISATION
    employers := ∅ || staff := ∅
OPERATIONS
    ee ⟵ create_employer ≙
        PRE employers ≠ EMPLOYER
        THEN
            ANY oo
            WHERE oo ∈ EMPLOYER − employers
            THEN
                ee := oo ||
                employers := employers ∪ { oo } ||
                staff(oo) := []
            END
        END;

    hire(ee, job) ≙
        PRE ee ∈ employers ∧ job ∈ employments
        THEN
            staff(ee) := staff(ee) ⌢ [ job ]
        END

END
```

Each of the above machines is then included in a single machine which represents the personnel system (ie, the set of operations and data which a user of this system will expect to have available):

MACHINE **System**
EXTENDS
    Employed_Person
INCLUDES
    Employment(EMPLOYER), **Employer**
PROMOTES
    create_employment, **create_employer**
INVARIANT
    $\forall$ (job, company).(job $\in$ employments $\wedge$
                  company $\in$ employers $\Rightarrow$
                         (job $\in$ ran(staff(company)) $\equiv$
                                company = employer(job)))
OPERATIONS
    add_job_to_company(job, company) $\widehat{=}$
        PRE job $\in$ employments $\wedge$
           company $\in$ employers $\wedge$
           job $\notin$ dom(employer)
        THEN
           hire(company, job) $\parallel$
           set_boss(job, company)
        END

END

The complete specification structure is shown in Figure 3.4. This system has been enhanced to reflect the fact that the **staff** and **employer** relationships are mutually inverse – ie, rather than having separate operations to add an employment to the **staff** sequence of an employer and to set the **employer** of an employment, we have hidden these individual operations at the **System** level by using INCLUDES to access **Employment** and **Employer**, and defined a single operation **add_job_to_company** in **System** which performs both updates simultaneously. Unfortunately this means that the **employer** attribute cannot be set on creation of an employment, and we must let this attribute be represented by a partial function in **Employment**. As a result the **System** really represents a diagram where the **Employer** end of the association has cardinality 0 .. 1 rather than 1 as in the original diagram.

3.2.4 Formalisation of Dynamic Models

Dynamic models for systems are often expressed in the form of *statecharts*, which define a set of states that an object can be in, and a set of transitions between states. Typical notations are those of Harel [31] and Moore [54]. Transitions can depend upon the state of other instances of the type whose dynamic model is expressed in the chart, and can involve requests for transitions in other statecharts.

One technique that can be used for formal modelling of such systems is to create a machine encapsulating a set of instances of each object type, and

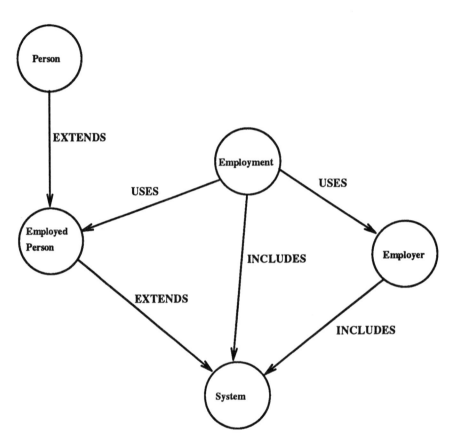

Figure 3.4: Complete Structure of Personnel System

the sets of instances of this object type that are in a given state. This representation regards such states as defining a 'transitory subtype' of the object type whose instances have such states. Transitions from one state to another are modelled by B AMN operations, with suitable preconditions and cases to express the different situations that can arise. One advantage of this scheme is that modularisation of the specification follows the structure of the problem domain, making it easier to trace the location of required changes to a system as a result of changes in the domain. Synchronisation between subsystems is expressed by means of operations which call operations from subsystem machines using the 'multiple generalised substitution' operator ||. The semantics of this operator is similar to that of ∧ in Z operation schemas: it specifies that the state transitions defined by its operands should both be performed, but does not specify any procedural order by which these transitions can be achieved. Naturally, the sets of variables updated by the two operands should be disjoint.

The associated process extends that for transforming static data models into machines described in Section 3.2.1. Steps of recognition of families of entity types and the creation of associated machines are still performed. However, each entity type E may now have an associated dynamic behaviour description given by a statechart. For each state S in this model, a new 'transitory subtype' S of E is considered to exist, and an associated variable ss is added to the machine representing the family of types to which the entity type E belongs.

Each transition between states in this model becomes an operation in the associated machine. Figure 3.5 shows the general form of a transition t from state **State1** to **State2**. The guard of the transition can be expressed either

Figure 3.5: General Form of Statechart Transition

as a precondition of the corresponding operation:

$$t(e, p) \;\; \hat{=}$$
PRE **Guard** ∧ e ∈ state1 ∧ p ∈ **T**
THEN
    state1 := state1 − { e } ||
    state2 := state2 ∪ { e } ||
    actions of the transition
END

where **state1** represents the source state of t, **state2** the target state, and **Guard** is the guard of t; or by a SELECT guard:

t(e, p) $\hat{=}$
    PRE e $\in$ es $\wedge$ p $\in$ **T**
    THEN
        SELECT **Guard** $\wedge$ e $\in$ state1
        THEN
            state1 := state1 $-$ { e } ||
            state2 := state2 $\cup$ { e } ||
            actions of the transition
        END
    END

The second interpretation is more accurate in that it asserts that the transition
cannot take place unless the entity instance e is in the correct source state, and
the guard holds. However it is not implementable via the usual B refinement
process with C as the target language. This interpretation is more appropriate
for a concurrent environment and target languages such as Ada and OCCAM
which support (non-busy) waiting of this form.

Activities within states also become operations of the associated machine.
Synchronisation between instances of entities from different families is ex-
pressed using || combination of transitions from the individual machines, in
a machine which includes all the sibling machines in the development. At this
level, or at the level of systems which use the set of machines, any required
ordering of operations can be imposed (such as that an activity performed in
a state is executed immediately after an instance arrives in that state).

The general steps are therefore:

- create machine **Entity.mch** for each entity type family Entity in the data
  model, and a variable **states** $\subseteq$ **entities** for each state in the chart for
  Entity;
- create operations of **Entity.mch** for each transition and activity;
- express synchronisation between subsystems by means of operations which
  call operations from subsystem machines using the 'multiple generalised
  substitution' operator ||.

In more detail:

- **states become sets of instances;**
- state sets are disjoint;
- state sets make up the entire set of entities;
- **attributes and links become functions;**
- the domain of an attribute may be a proper subset of the instance set of
  the entity (it may only make sense in certain states of the entity);
- **initial states become creation operations;**
- the creation operation of the **Entity.mch** specification initialises an instance to have the initial state (to be in the variable representing the set
  of instances in the initial state);

- **transitions between states become operations moving an instance from one state set to another;**
- transition preconditions become operation preconditions (in a concurrent environment they become operation guards);
- transition preconditions depending on the state of other instances of Entity can be expressed;
- **activities in a state become operations that do not change the state** (and which are preconditioned by membership of the state of which they are activities).

3.2.5 Alternative State Representation

It is clear that the above approach becomes infeasible once the number of states of an entity to be handled climbs above 8 to 10. As an alternative, we have the following process:

- create a machine **Entity.mch** for each entity type family Entity in the data model, and a variable $\text{status}_i\text{\_flag}$: entities $\rightarrow$ **STATUS_SET$_i$** to record the state of the i-th statechart factor for Entity. **STATUS_SET$_i$** is the set of state representatives for the states in the i-th factor;
- create operations of **Entity.mch** for each transition and activity in each statechart. Transitions which occur in more than one statechart require that two or more of the **status$_i$_flag** variables are simultaneously updated;
- synchronisation between subsystems is expressed as in the previous approach.

The overall process is thus quite similar to the previous approach, however:

- **states become sets of instances** defined by the inverse images of elements of the **STATUS_SET$_i$** sets under the **status$_i$_flag** functions;
- these state sets are, therefore, disjoint and exhaustive of **entities**;
- the creation operation of **Entity.mch** initialises each **status$_i$_flag** to the initial state of each statechart factor;
- transitions between states become operations updating the **status$_i$_flag** variables of the affected factors.

Thus the general transition shown in Figure 3.5 is now expressed as:

$t(e, p)$ $\widehat{=}$
    PRE **Guard** $\land$ **status_flag**(e) $=$ state1 $\land$
        $p \in T \land e \in es$
    THEN
        status_flag$(e) := $ state2 $\|$
        actions of the transition
    END

in the PRE interpretation of a guard, and similarly for the SELECT interpretation.

If each factor is itself complex, we may attempt to separate out the definition of different factors into different machines. DEFINITIONS may be used to define the state sets as the inverse images of certain **STATUS_SET$_i$** sets under the **status$_i$_flag** functions.

An example of the second process is given in the following section.

3.2.6   Example: Station Control System

An object model describing railway stations which consist of sets of track sections, is shown in Figure 3.6. The textual requirements corresponding to this

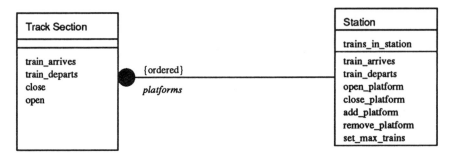

Figure 3.6: Object Model of Station

description are:

- a *track section* is a defined contiguous segment of track which can be occupied by at most one train at any time. In addition, it may be closed (eg, for engineering work) so that no trains may enter the section. A train will take a minimum of 60 seconds to clear a track section, and a closed track section will be closed for a minimum of 120 seconds;

- a *station* consists of a set of track sections, called *platforms*. There is an upper bound on the number of trains which may be in the station at any time, and this upper bound is at most the number of platforms. There are operations to allow the entry of a train to a specified platform of the station, to allow departure of a train, and to close and open a specified platform. In addition there are operations to add and remove platforms, which must occur in mutual exclusion with themselves and all other operations on platforms.

The statechart of track sections is shown in Figure 3.7.

An initial model of a track section, ignoring the timing constraints, is:

MACHINE **TrackSection**
SETS

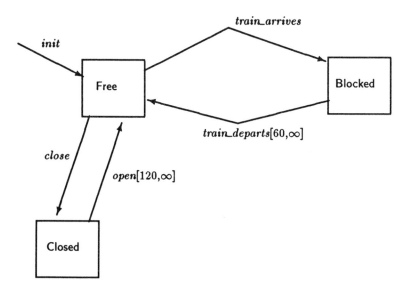

Figure 3.7: Statechart of TrackSection

```
SECTION;
TSTATE = { closed, free, blocked }
VARIABLES
   sections, tstate
INVARIANT
   sections ∈ 𝔽(SECTION) ∧
   tstate ∈ sections → TSTATE
INITIALISATION
   tstate := ∅ ‖ sections := ∅
OPERATIONS
   ts ⟵ newsection ≙
         PRE sections ≠ SECTION
         THEN
               ANY oo
               WHERE oo ∈ SECTION − sections
               THEN
                  sections := sections ∪ { oo } ‖
                  tstate(oo) := free ‖
                  ts := oo
               END
         END;

   arrival(ts) ≙
         PRE ts ∈ sections ∧ tstate(ts) = free
         THEN
               tstate(ts) := blocked
         END;
```

$departure(ts) \; \widehat{=}$
      PRE $ts \in sections \; \wedge \; tstate(ts) \; = \;$ blocked
      THEN
           $tstate(ts) \; := \;$ free
      END ;

$open(ts) \; \widehat{=}$
      PRE $ts \in sections \; \wedge \; tstate(ts) \; = \;$ closed
      THEN
           $tstate(ts) \; := \;$ free
      END ;

$close(ts) \; \widehat{=}$
      PRE $ts \in sections \; \wedge \; tstate(ts) \; = \;$ free
      THEN
           $tstate(ts) \; := \;$ closed
      END

END

The station entity is specified by:

MACHINE **Station**
INCLUDES **TrackSection**
VARIABLES
   platforms, max_trains, trains_in_station
INVARIANT
   $trains\_in\_station \in \mathbb{N} \; \wedge$
   $max\_trains \in \mathbb{N} \; \wedge \; trains\_in\_station \leq max\_trains \; \wedge$

   $platforms \in seq(sections) \; \wedge$

   $size(platforms) \; = \; card(ran(platforms)) \; \wedge$

   $max\_trains \leq size(platforms)$
INITIALISATION
   $platforms, max\_trains, trains\_in\_station \; := \; [\;], \; 0, \; 0$
OPERATIONS
  $train\_arrives(ts) \; \widehat{=}$
      PRE $trains\_in\_station < max\_trains \; \wedge \; ts \in ran(platforms) \; \wedge$
           $tstate(ts) \; = \;$ free
      THEN
           $arrival(ts) \; \|$
           $trains\_in\_station \; := \; trains\_in\_station + 1$
      END ;

  $train\_departs(ts) \; \widehat{=}$
      PRE $ts \in ran(platforms) \; \wedge$
           $tstate(ts) \; = \;$ blocked
      THEN
           $departure(ts) \; \|$

```
            trains_in_station  :=  trains_in_station  −  1
      END;

open_platform(ts)  ≙
      PRE  ts  ∈  ran(platforms)  ∧
           tstate(ts)  =  closed
      THEN
           open(ts)
      END;

close_platform(ts)  ≙
      PRE  ts  ∈  ran(platforms)  ∧
           tstate(ts)  =  free
      THEN
           close(ts)
      END;

set_max_trains(mt)  ≙
      PRE  mt  ∈  ℕ  ∧  mt  ≤  size(platforms)  ∧
           trains_in_station  ≤  mt
      THEN
           max_trains  :=  mt
      END
```

/* Plus operations to add and remove platforms */

END

We assume that the operations on the station (which correspond to events rather than durative activities) are effectively instantaneous and so can be considered to be executed sequentially.

It may be necessary to provide two actions for activities such as the arrival and departure of trains. For example, if trains are to be counted as in the station if they are in the process of departing, then **trains_in_station** would be decremented in a **complete_departure** operation, rather than in **train_departs**.

The formalism has helped to identify preconditions for operations such as **set_max_trains**: this operation must preserve the invariant of the machine, which effectively means that the new value **mt** of **max_trains** must obey the constraints for **max_trains** given in the invariant – this condition then becomes the precondition of the operation.

In order to ensure that the invariant is maintained in the case of the **train_departs** operation, we would need to strengthen the invariant to include the condition:

$$\text{trains\_in\_station} =$$
$$\text{card}(\text{platforms}^{-1}[\{ts \mid ts \in \text{sections} \land \text{tstate}(ts) = \text{blocked}\}])$$

Unlike the **TrackSection** machine, **Station** only encapsulates a single instance of the station entity. This is sufficient provided that there are no operations of the required system which relate to a number of different stations.

3.2.7   Specification Structuring and Decomposition

The correct use of the B AMN specification construction facilities is critical for practical system development, particularly because of the impact of specification decomposition upon proof and upon maintainability of a specification.

The following general guidelines can be formulated:

- decompose state and operations into components which have a strong coherent meaning in domain terms (e.g. bank account, engine);
- do not introduce un-necessary inter-dependencies between specification components: for example if two components each need read access to variables from a third component, then each should USE or SEE this third component, rather than one inheriting these variables from the other;
- use the most restrictive machine inclusion mechanism possible for the given situation (e.g. SEES instead of USES, USES instead of INCLUDES, etc.) − although if it is desired to use the structure of the specification of a system to help decompose its implementation, then INCLUDES or SEES are preferable to USES.

SEES and USES are 'intransitive' in the sense that if **A** USES **B** and **B** USES **C**, then **A** has no access to the components of **C**: if a degree of access is needed then a suitable inclusion relation must be specified between **A** and **C**. Similarly for SEES. The reason for this restriction is that these inclusion mechanisms are intended to support the sharing of information between more than one other construct. In the case of USES, the used construct is shared between two constructs in the same subsystem development, and these two constructs will both be included or extended in a single machine which gathers together all the fragments of the abstract specification of this development, for example, as in Figure 3.8. In this development, the information regarding bulkheads will be referred to in order to define components of a ship and of individual compartments (for example, each ship has a set of bulkheads contained in its structure, and each ship compartment is adjacent to a certain subset of these):

MACHINE **Bulkhead**
SETS **BULKHEAD**
VARIABLES **bulkheads**
INVARIANT **bulkheads** $\subseteq$ **BULKHEAD**
  ...
END

MACHINE **Compartment**
USES **Bulkhead**
  ...
VARIABLES **compartments, adjacent, ...**
INVARIANT **adjacent** $\in$ **compartments** $\rightarrow$ $\mathbb{F}$(**bulkheads**)

```
  ...
END

MACHINE Ship
USES Bulkhead
  ...
VARIABLES s_bulkheads, ...
INVARIANT s_bulkheads ⊆ bulkheads
  ...
END
```

If INCLUDES or EXTENDS had been used in **Ship** or **Compartment**, we would get a duplication of the data **BULKHEAD** and bulkheads in **Loader**.

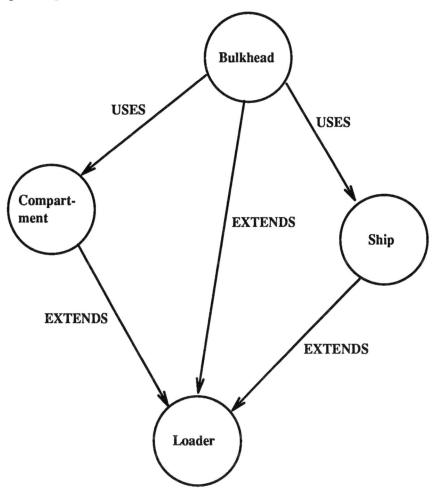

Figure 3.8: Shared Specification Components via USES

In the case of SEES, the intransitivity is required because the seen construct may be shared between different subsystems of the same development, in addition to between different components within one subsystem or 'subsystem development'. The inclusion mechanisms of the B notation may seem somewhat unusual and complex, however they do (mostly) fit together in a consistent and orthogonal manner, and are the result of extensive practical experience.

Sharing of data between machines can also be achieved via the use of common parameters, rather than by the use of a SEES clause. For instance, if we need a set **LMACHINERY** to be available in two machines **Compartment** and **Terminal**, then we could parameterise both machines with this set, and instantiate it in a machine which INCLUDES, EXTENDS or IMPORTS both machines. This approach can be of value in reducing the number of inter-dependencies between specification components, and in the case where external control over the sets of possible objects is required.

3.2.8   Enforcing the Command/Query Distinction

In this section we introduce a specification style which will be used repeatedly in subsequent chapters.

Consider the following very simple specification of a 'random number generator':

MACHINE **RandomNat**
OPERATIONS

    nn ⟵ choose $\mathrel{\widehat{=}}$
        BEGIN
           nn $:\in$ $\mathbb{N}$
        END

END

This appears to achieve the requirements of selecting arbitrary numbers (although the results of applying the operation are not random in a statistical sense, but instead just unpredictable by a user. It would be possible for an implementation of this machine to always return the number 5 for instance).

The problem with the above specification is that the **choose** operation is not a true enquiry operation because it is not guaranteed to give the same answer on successive applications. This violates the principles of the 'command/query' discipline advocated by Meyer [51], whereby the operations of a module should be divided into two kinds:

1. Update operations which do not return an output, but which may change the abstract state of the system (that is, the values returned by enquiry operations);
2. Enquiry operations, which return an output and do not change the abstract state.

Effectively the above machine encapsulates some "hidden state" which should be made visible. In order to overcome this problem the machine should be re-specified as follows:

MACHINE **RandomNat1**
VARIABLES
   rand
INVARIANT
   rand $\in$ $\mathbb{N}$
INITIALISATION
   rand $:\in$ $\mathbb{N}$
OPERATIONS

   new_rand $\;\widehat{=}\;$
      BEGIN
         rand $:\in$ $\mathbb{N}$
      END;

   nn $\longleftarrow$ **choose** $\;\widehat{=}\;$
      nn := **rand**

END

In this specification **new_rand** is the update operation and **choose** is an enquiry operation.

The distinction between enquiry and update operations does not prevent enquiry operations from possessing both inputs and outputs. For example, we could have an operation

  bb $\longleftarrow$ **less_than(nn)** $\;\widehat{=}\;$
     PRE **nn** $\in$ $\mathbb{N}$
     THEN
       IF **nn** $<$ **value**
       THEN
          bb := **TRUE**
       ELSE
          bb := **FALSE**
       END
     END

in a machine encapsulating a variable **value** $\in$ $\mathbb{N}$ and operations on this. **less_than** is an enquiry operation because it does not change the internal state of the machine, and therefore does not change the abstract state: the values returned by any other enquiry operation or by itself.

3.2.9   Testing Preconditions Versus Exception Reporting

There are two alternative styles which may be adopted to handle the occurrence of erroneous situations in B AMN operations. In the first approach, each operation with a non-trivial (ie, not just a typing constraint) precondition has an associated enquiry operation which reports if the condition holds. For example, we could have:

```
ok  ⟵  pre_increment(xx)  ≙
     PRE xx ∈ ℕ
     THEN
             IF xx + val ≤ maxval
             THEN
                   ok := TRUE
             ELSE
                   ok := FALSE
             END
     END;
```

as a test operation for **increment**, where this is defined by:

```
increment(xx)  ≙
     PRE xx ∈ ℕ ∧ xx + val ≤ maxval
     THEN
             val := val + xx
     END
```

A caller would then perform the statements:

```
bb  ⟵  pre_increment(xx);
IF bb = TRUE
THEN
      increment(xx)
ELSE
      /*  Report error to next level  */
END
```

However this approach relies on a user of the operation always applying these tests before trying to use it, and complicates the implementation of the operation. It is also inappropriate in a concurrent context, where the state of a machine that is used by two separate callers can be modified by one whilst the other is between the precondition test and the operation application.

An alternative is to report exceptions as an additional result of the operation. In this case, **increment** would simply be:

```
ok  ⟵  increment(xx)  ≙
     PRE xx ∈ ℕ
     THEN
             IF xx + val ≤ maxval
             THEN
                   val := val + xx ||
                   ok := TRUE
             ELSE
                   ok := FALSE
             END
     END;
```

This approach appears to violate the command/query distinction discussed above. However it is a relatively harmless extension of this categorisation since the **ok** result is not a property of the underlying abstract data type, but an implementation-level mechanism.

3.2.10 Using Object-based Interfaces for Optimisation

An important aspect of the B language and method is the ability it provides to write specifications which are unbiased towards particular implementations or implementation strategies. A familiar concept in the object-oriented world is the decomposition of a complex function (such as sorting or determination of a Hamiltonian path in a graph) into a series of smaller steps that are provided as an object interface. For example, the process of sorting, which would be usually written as a single function in a language such as C, can be decomposed into operations of **insert**ing an element into an object, changing the object to extract mode or to insert mode, and **extract**ing the i-th element in ascending order of size from the object. This interface allows an implementation to carry out the actual sorting process either incrementally during the insertions, in batch mode during the change to extraction, or incrementally during extraction (or a mix of these strategies).

A suitable unbiased specification of this interface is:

MACHINE **SortSpec**
SEES **Sorting**
SETS **SortMode** = { **inserting**, **extracting** }
VARIABLES
    unsorted, sorted, mode
INVARIANT
    unsorted $\in$ $\mathbb{F}(\mathbb{N})$ $\wedge$
    sorted $\in$ seq($\mathbb{N}$) $\wedge$
    mode $\in$ **SortMode** $\wedge$

    (**mode** = **extracting** $\Rightarrow$ **sorted** = sort_of(**unsorted**))

During the extraction process, **sorted** *represents a sort of the* **unsorted** *set.*

INITIALISATION
    unsorted := $\varnothing$ || **sorted** := [] || **mode** := **inserting**
OPERATIONS

  change_to_insert_mode $\hat{=}$
    PRE **mode** = **extracting**
    THEN
        mode := **inserting** ||
        unsorted := $\varnothing$ ||
        sorted :$\in$ seq($\mathbb{N}$)
    END;

insert(xx) $\hat{=}$
    PRE xx $\in$ $\mathbb{N}$ $\wedge$ mode = inserting
    THEN
        unsorted := unsorted $\cup$ {xx} $\|$
        sorted :$\in$ seq($\mathbb{N}$)
    END;

change_to_extract_mode $\hat{=}$
    PRE mode = inserting
    THEN
        mode := extracting $\|$
        sorted := sort_of(unsorted)
    END;

yy $\longleftarrow$ extract(ii) $\hat{=}$
    PRE ii $\in$ dom(sorted) $\wedge$ mode = extracting
    THEN
        yy := sorted(ii)
    END

END

where **sort_of(ss)** obtains the sequence of elements of **ss** (without duplicates) in strictly ascending order:

MACHINE **Sorting**
CONSTANTS
    sort_of
PROPERTIES
    sort_of $\in$ $\mathbb{F}(\mathbb{N})$ $\rightarrow$ seq($\mathbb{N}$) $\wedge$

    $\forall$ ss.(ss $\in$ $\mathbb{F}(\mathbb{N})$ $\Rightarrow$
            (ran(sort_of(ss)) = ss $\wedge$
               $\forall$ (ii,jj).(ii $\in$ dom(sort_of(ss)) $\wedge$
                    jj $\in$ dom(sort_of(ss)) $\wedge$ ii < jj $\Rightarrow$
                      (sort_of(ss))(ii) < (sort_of(ss))(jj))))

END

Although **SortSpec** appears to require the sorting process to be achieved in batch mode by execution of **change_to_extract_mode**, this is in fact not the case. The reason is that an external user of this machine can only access the sorted sequence one item at a time during extraction – there is no way that the user can detect if the sort is being carried out during extraction, was performed "all at once" in **change_to_extract_mode**, or performed incrementally during insertion.

    This is made more clear by the fact that both an insertion sort strategy and an extraction sort strategy can be used to refine **SortSpec**. For the insertion case we only need to retain the sorted sequence:

REFINEMENT **InsertSort**
REFINES
    SortSpec
SEES
    Sorting
VARIABLES
    sq
INVARIANT
    $sq \in seq(\mathbb{N})$ ∧
    $sort\_of(ran(sq)) = sq$ ∧

    $unsorted = ran(sq)$ ∧
    $sorted = sq$
INITIALISATION
    $sq := []$
OPERATIONS

  change_to_insert_mode $\hat{=}$
    BEGIN
      $sq := []$
    END ;

  insert(xx) $\hat{=}$
    PRE **xx** $\in \mathbb{N}$
    THEN
      ANY **newsq**
      WHERE
        $newsq \in seq(\mathbb{N})$ ∧
        $newsq = sort\_of(ran(sq) \cup \{ xx \})$
      THEN
        $sq := newsq$
      END
    END ;

  change_to_extract_mode $\hat{=}$
    skip;

  yy ⟵ **extract(ii)** $\hat{=}$
    PRE **ii** $\in dom(sq)$
    THEN
      $yy := sq(ii)$
    END

END

In this refinement the sort is calculated incrementally by the **insert** operation (we could envisage an implementation which does a single search through the established sorted sequence to determine the right place to insert the new element). Because of this, it is valid to inspect the sort at any stage in the machine execution, so the preconditions referring to the **mode** have been eliminated.

The refinement is directly provable, although we need some auxiliary properties of **sort_of**:

$$\text{sort\_of}(\varnothing) \;==\; [];$$

$$
\begin{aligned}
&n \;=\; \text{sort\_of}(s) \;\wedge \\
&n \;\in\; \text{seq}(\mathbb{N}) \;\wedge \\
&s \;\in\; \mathbb{F}(\mathbb{N}) \;\Rightarrow\; \text{sort\_of}(\text{ran}(n)) \;==\; n;
\end{aligned}
$$

$$
\begin{aligned}
&u \;=\; \text{ran}(s) \;\wedge \\
&n \;=\; \text{sort\_of}(\text{ran}(s) \;\cup\; \{\, x \,\}) \;\wedge \\
&u \;\in\; \mathbb{F}(\mathbb{N}) \;\wedge \\
&s \;\in\; \text{seq}(\mathbb{N}) \;\Rightarrow \\
&\qquad\qquad\quad u \;\cup\; \{x\} \;==\; \text{ran}(n)
\end{aligned}
$$

In the case of an extract sort, we could define:

REFINEMENT ExtractSort
REFINES
    SortSpec
SEES
    Sorting
VARIABLES
    ss
INVARIANT
    ss $\in \mathbb{F}(\mathbb{N})$ $\wedge$

    unsorted $=$ ss $\wedge$
    (mode $=$ extracting $\Rightarrow$ sorted $=$ sort_of(ss))
INITIALISATION
    ss $:=\; \varnothing$
OPERATIONS

  change_to_insert_mode $\;\widehat{=}\;$
      ss $:=\; \varnothing\,;$

  insert(xx) $\;\widehat{=}\;$
    PRE **xx** $\in \mathbb{N}$
    THEN
      ss $:=\;$ ss $\cup\; \{\, \text{xx} \,\}$
    END;

  change_to_extract_mode $\;\widehat{=}\;$
    skip;

  yy $\longleftarrow$ extract(ii) $\;\widehat{=}\;$
    PRE ii $\in$ dom(sort_of(ss))
    THEN
      yy $:=\;$ (sort_of(ss))(ii)
    END

END

Here the sorting is performed on a "as needed" basis in **extract**. This might be a sensible strategy if we knew that only a few enquiries of this form were to be carried out – rather than sorting the whole sequence we might be able to reduce the effort to sorting just the first **ll** elements, where **ll** is the largest value of **ii** needed in an **extract(ii)** enquiry. This could be implemented by a single search of the set **ss**, building up an ordered array of length **ii** of the smallest **ii** elements of **ss**.

This refinement is automatically provable. Notice that it is not a refinement in the sense of VDM [40] because it is not based on a total function from the state space of **ExtractSort** to that of **SortSpec**.

3.2.11   Using Preconditions as Assertions

The PRE construct can be used to achieve the effect of assertions in static analysis tools. That is, it can be used (in refinements) to record the expectations that the developer has about the value of the state at a particular point of execution.

Proof obligations for refinement will then automatically contain the appropriate validation properties as obligations. For example, we could write:

```
mm   ≙
     VAR xx
     IN
         xx  ⟵  op;
         PRE xx  >  1
         THEN
             S
         END
     END
```

The **xx** > 1 condition records the expectation that **op** will set **xx** to such a value. In a procedural language with assertions we might write this as:

```
xx: int;

begin
  op(xx);
  { assert: xx > 1 }
  S
end
```

and an appropriate verification tool would carry out the check that this assertion actually held on each possible program path through the code.

In B the corresponding check becomes part of the proof obligations for the operation **mm**.

3.2.12   Algebraic Specification Styles

B supports some aspects of algebraic specification via the use of functional
constants to represent operation functionality. Such constants can be composed
and equated in a manner similar to that of algebraic languages such as OBJ.

As a simple example, consider a highly abstract specification of rational
numbers:

MACHINE   **ARational**
SETS
  ARATIONAL
CONSTANTS
  den, num
PROPERTIES
  den ∈ **ARATIONAL** → ℕ ∧
  num ∈ **ARATIONAL** → ℕ ∧

  ? * ? ∈ **ARATIONAL** × **ARATIONAL** →
                        ARATIONAL ∧
  ? + ? ∈ **ARATIONAL** × **ARATIONAL** →
                        ARATIONAL ∧
  ? / ? ∈ **ARATIONAL** × **ARATIONAL** →
                        ARATIONAL ∧
  ? // ? ∈ ℕ × ℕ →
                ARATIONAL ∧

  ∀ (aa, bb).(
      aa ∈ ℕ ∧ **bb** ∈ ℕ ⇒
        den(aa//bb) = **bb** ∧
        num(aa//bb) = **aa**) ∧

  ∀ (r1, r2).(
      r1 ∈ **ARATIONAL** ∧
      r2 ∈ **ARATIONAL** ⇒
        den(r1 * r2) = **den(r1) * den(r2)** ∧
        num(r1 * r2) = **num(r1) * num(r2)** ∧

        den(r1 + r2) = **den(r1) * den(r2)** ∧
        num(r1 + r2) =
          den(r1) * num(r2) +
          den(r2) * num(r1) ∧

      */ * Other usual properties of rationals * /*

          r1 = **r2** ≡
            den(r1) * num(r2) = **den(r2) * num(r1)**)

OPERATIONS
  rr ⟵ **add_rats(ss, tt)** =
          PRE **ss** ∈ **ARATIONAL** ∧ **tt** ∈ **ARATIONAL**

THEN
    rr := **ss** + **tt**
END

END

This machine encapsulates an unstructured set **ARATIONAL** and various functions and operations on it: Each element **r** of **ARATIONAL** has a denominator **den(r)** and a numerator **num(r)**, etc. The usual arithmetic operations are extended to **ARATIONAL** by explicitly declaring them as infix operators (the ? notation).

The properties of these operators are then defined by axioms. Ultimately each operator will have a corresponding machine operation, which will allow access to the operator effects from AMN implementations.

3.3   Animation

Animation is a key facility for formal development. It supports validation of a specification by allowing particular scenarios of use of the system to be stepped through. Such animations can identify whether what the specification says about the response of the system to the scenario is what the user actually wants the system to do in that case. Animation is not an alternative to proof; however for complex specifications it should be carried out before any proof effort is expended since it is a waste of time proving (internally) correct an (externally) invalid specification.

Features of animation facilities in the B-Core (UK) Toolkit are:

- animation applies to (abstract) *machines*. Implementations can, of course, be "animated" and tested by execution;
- the user must resolve non-determinacy present in the specification interactively or via animation theory axioms;
- consistency of the animation theories with machine *properties*, the interprover *UserTheory* and the refinement path to code is critical if these tests are to be taken as meaningful for the eventual implementation. It is possible for the user to resolve non-determinacy in a specification via animation in a way that is different from the way the non-determinacy is removed via implementation in the B Toolkit. Thus the results of scenarios at the animation stage need not have a meaning for the results of these scenarios at the code level.

A "batch mode" is also available for simplifying the repeated application of complex scenarios after modifications to specifications.

An example animation, using the **SortSeq** machine defined in Section 2.3 could be as follows (we would actually instantiate **is_ordered** to be some finite set of ordered sequences at the beginning of this animation):

Animating SortSeq

Initialisation:

   sq = [ ]

Which operation? 1: ordered_insert

> ordered_insert(5)

$5 \in \mathbb{N}$ reduces to true

Nondeterminism in: newsq $\in$ is_ordered $\wedge$ ran(newsq) = { 5 }

> newsq == [5]

Guard reduces to true

New state is:

   sq = [5]

Which operation? 1: ordered_insert

> ordered_insert(77)

$77 \in \mathbb{N}$ reduces to true

Nondeterminism in: newsq $\in$ is_ordered $\wedge$ ran(newsq) = { 5, 77 }

> newsq == [5, 77]

Guard reduces to true

New state is:

   sq = [5, 77]

If we had entered [77, 5] in the last case the guard would reduce to **false**.

3.4   Proof of Internal Consistency Obligations

Proof support for automatic and interactive proof of internal consistency obligations is provided by the current toolkits for B AMN. The failure to prove internal consistency can identify the following problems with the specification or requirements:

- empty state space – the specifier has written an inconsistent interpretation of the requirements (or these were inconsistent already), or has misunderstood the meaning of some of the mathematical constructs used;

- initialisation fails to establish the invariant – the initialisation is not strong enough, because of logical constraints of the invariant not being considered. A particular case is when a variable is necessarily an infinite set due to the invariant constraints – it is relatively easy to neglect to define the appropriate value in the initialisation. Alternatively the invariant may be too restrictive;

- operations fail to maintain the invariant – this can be due to an insufficiently strong precondition: in general the precondition

$$(\mathbf{Inv} \Rightarrow [\mathbf{S}]\mathbf{Inv})$$

is necessary for **S** to preserve **Inv**, or to a too weak (non-deterministic) operation definition, or to a too weak invariant (ie, which fails to express some actually invariant property). An example of the last case is given by the **Station** specification of Section 3.2.6.

3.4.1 Assertions

An ASSERTIONS **A** clause is used to declare some additional invariant properties **A** of a B machine, where **A** is expected to be of more use in establishing the proof obligations of the machine than the basic invariant. **A** acts like a useful intermediate theorem in mathematics – its derivation from axioms (the stated invariant and other machine properties) can be quite difficult, but it makes proof of other theorems (machine proof obligations) easier.

Thus if an ASSERTIONS **A** clause is added to a machine, then the machine proof obligations are as given in Table 3.1. As before, (5) is required for each

(1)	$\exists \mathbf{p}.\mathbf{C}$
(2)	$\mathbf{C} \Rightarrow \exists (\mathbf{St}, \mathbf{k}).\mathbf{B}$
(3)	$\mathbf{B} \wedge \mathbf{C} \Rightarrow \exists \mathbf{v}.\mathbf{I}$
(4)	$\mathbf{B} \wedge \mathbf{C} \Rightarrow [\mathbf{T}]\mathbf{I}$
(5)	$\mathbf{B} \wedge \mathbf{C} \wedge \mathbf{I} \wedge \mathbf{P} \wedge \mathbf{A} \Rightarrow [\mathbf{S}]\mathbf{I}$
(6)	$\mathbf{B} \wedge \mathbf{C} \wedge \mathbf{I} \Rightarrow \mathbf{A}$

Table 3.1: Consistency Obligations for Machine with Assertions

operation of the machine – each of these obligations may be easier to prove as a result of adding **A** to the machine (more predicates will be available to support proof of these obligations) whilst the only new obligation is (6).

Assertions can also be used to express validation properties: theorems that we expect to follow from the invariant and other logical features of the machine, if it is a correct representation of the customers requirements. Obligation 6 gives the required obligation that must be proved for this check to succeed.

3.5   Ship Loading Case Study – Specification

This example illustrates the conversion of analysis models into B specifications,
and the congruence of structure which can be maintained between the analysis and specification descriptions. The system is a very simple version of a
ship loading system. It supports monitoring and control of the loading process to ensure that the ship structure is not damaged due to incorrect loading
sequences. The data model of the system is described in Figure 3.9.

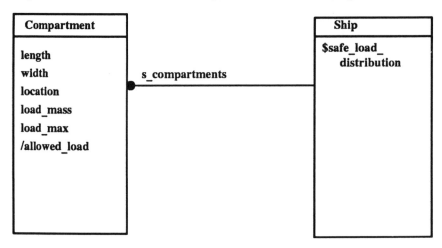

Figure 3.9: Object Model of Ship Loading System

   In this diagram, **allowed_load** is a derived attribute, and is not expected to
be implemented as an actual attribute of the entity, but rather as an operation
or function on the state.
   The formalisation of this system involves creating machines for each of the
entities described in the data model. An overall structure of the system is given
in Figure 3.10.
   The machines which are part of this system are given by:

MACHINE
    Compartment(COMPARTMENT)
CONSTRAINTS
    card(COMPARTMENT) = 100

There are at most 100 compartments under management by the system.

SEES
    Bool_TYPE, Ship_DATA
DEFINITIONS
    CENTIMETERS == 0 . . 10000;
    MASS == 0 . . 10000
VARIABLES
    compartments, c_length, c_width, c_location, c_load_mass,

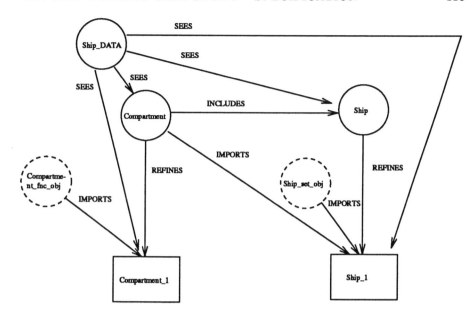

Figure 3.10: General Structure of Ship-loading System

c_load_max
INVARIANT
   compartments $\subseteq$ **COMPARTMENT** $\wedge$
   c_length $\in$ compartments $\rightarrowtail$ **CENTIMETERS** $\wedge$
   c_width $\in$ compartments $\rightarrowtail$ **CENTIMETERS** $\wedge$
   c_location $\in$ compartments $\rightarrowtail$ **C_LOCATION** $\wedge$
   c_load_mass $\in$ compartments $\rightarrowtail$ **MASS** $\wedge$
   c_load_max $\in$ compartments $\rightarrowtail$ **MASS**
INITIALISATION
   compartments := $\varnothing$ $\|$
   c_length := $\varnothing$ $\|$
   c_width := $\varnothing$ $\|$
   c_location := $\varnothing$ $\|$
   c_load_mass := $\varnothing$ $\|$
   c_load_max := $\varnothing$
OPERATIONS

cc $\longleftarrow$ new_compartment(len, wid, loc, lmx) $\hat{=}$
     PRE len $\in$ **CENTIMETERS** $\wedge$ wid $\in$ **CENTIMETERS** $\wedge$
       loc $\in$ **C_LOCATION** $\wedge$ lmx $\in$ **MASS** $\wedge$
       compartments $\neq$ **COMPARTMENT**
     THEN
       ANY oo
       WHERE oo $\in$ **COMPARTMENT** $-$ compartments

```
            THEN
                cc := oo ||
                c_length(oo) := len ||
                c_width(oo) := wid ||
                c_location(oo) := loc ||
                c_load_mass(oo) := 0 ||
                c_load_max(oo) := lmx ||
                compartments := compartments ∪ {oo}
            END
        END;
```

This operation selects an (arbitrary) object identity to add to the set of existing compartments, and returns this identity to the user for the application of further operations.

```
load_compartment(cc, mm) ≙
        PRE cc ∈ compartments ∧
            mm ∈ MASS ∧
            c_load_mass(cc) + mm ≤ c_load_max(cc)
        THEN
            c_load_mass(cc) := c_load_mass(cc) + mm
        END;
```

This operation adds a certain load to a compartment, provided that this load does not lead to a violation of the machine invariant. It is often quite easy to determine what the weakest precondition of an operation must be in order to resolve obligation (5) of internal consistency. Specifically, for $P \land Inv \Rightarrow [S]Inv$ to hold, we must have $P \Rightarrow (Inv \Rightarrow [S]Inv)$.

```
bb ⟵ allowed_load(cc, mm) ≙
        PRE cc ∈ compartments ∧
            mm ∈ MASS
        THEN
            bb := bool(c_load_mass(cc) + mm ≤ c_load_max(cc))
        END;
```

This operation provides a means by which an external user can check to see if the precondition of the load_compartment operation is violated or not.

```
ld ⟵ show_load(cc) ≙
        PRE cc ∈ compartments
        THEN
            ld := c_load_mass(cc)
        END
```

This operation provides a means to examine the value of the c_load_mass attribute of an existing compartment.

END

Ship_DATA encapsulates a set of data which is shared between the components of the development. It is necessary in order to prevent the duplication of these items in the implementation of a specification which includes **Compartment** (and where the implementation imports **Compartment**).

MACHINE
    Ship_DATA
SETS
    C_LOCATION = {forward, aft, mid}
END

The following machine is built on the **Compartment** machine:

MACHINE
    Ship(SHIP,COMPARTMENT)
CONSTRAINTS
    card(SHIP) = 5
INCLUDES
    Compartment(COMPARTMENT)
PROMOTES
    new_compartment, show_load
SEES
    Bool_TYPE, Ship_DATA
DEFINITIONS
    MASS == $0 .. 10000$
CONSTANTS
    safe_load_distribution

This function represents a monitoring process which examines whether the current load distribution is safe or not. In the real system it would also involve monitoring of the state of particular stress sensors within the ship structure.

PROPERTIES
    safe_load_distribution $\in$ **SHIP** $\times$ **COMPARTMENT** $\times$
                                                   MASS $\rightarrow$ **BOOL**
VARIABLES
    ships, s_compartments
INVARIANT
    ships $\subseteq$ **SHIP** $\wedge$
    s_compartments $\in$ **ships** $\rightarrow$ $\mathbb{F}$(**compartments**)
INITIALISATION
   ships := $\varnothing$ ||
   s_compartments := $\varnothing$
OPERATIONS

  ss $\longleftarrow$ **new_ship** $\hat{=}$
        PRE
            ships $\neq$ **SHIP**

```
          THEN
              ANY oo
              WHERE oo ∈ SHIP − ships
              THEN
                  ships := ships ∪ {oo} ||
                  s_compartments(oo) := ∅ ||
                  ss := oo
              END
          END ;
```

add_compartment(ss, cc) $\hat{=}$
```
      PRE
          ss ∈ ships ∧
          cc ∈ compartments ∧
          cc ∉ s_compartments(ss)
      THEN
          s_compartments(ss) := s_compartments(ss) ∪ {cc}
      END ;
```

This operation adds a new compartment to the ship, provided that the compartment is not already within the ship.

load_ship_compartment(ss, cc, mm) $\hat{=}$
```
      PRE ss ∈ ships ∧ cc ∈ s_compartments(ss) ∧
          c_load_mass(cc) + mm ≤ c_load_max(cc) ∧
          mm ∈ MASS ∧
          safe_load_distribution(ss, cc, mm) = TRUE
      THEN
          load_compartment(cc, mm)
      END
```

This operation adds a load to a specified compartment of a ship, provided that the precondition of load_compartment is not violated, and provided that the general ship safety is not compromised.

END

This specification has illustrated the use of domain models in decomposing a specification, and in providing an outline for the data of this specification. In the following chapter we will show how this specification can be refined into an executable system.

3.6   Renaming

Machines can be renamed in some machine inclusion clauses by prefixing their name by an identifier and a '.'. Thus if **M** is a machine, we could define a machine **N** which contains two renamed copies of **M**'s features by the notation:

MACHINE N
EXTENDS aa.M, bb.M

⋮

END

The data items of these copies of **M** are referred to by **aa.att** and **bb.att** respectively, within **N**, where **att** is a set, constant or variable of **M**. In addition, operations of **M** are also renamed in the same manner, so that calls of the form

$$y \longleftarrow aa.m(e)$$

can be included in **N**'s specification, if **m** is an operation of **M**.

At present renaming is supported by the INCLUDES and EXTENDS clauses.

3.7 Aggregation

The concept of *aggregation* in methods such as OMT is not precise – it can mean any one of the following forms of "strong association":

- components have lifetimes that coincide with their containers, and which cannot be shared (eg: cylinders of an engine);
- a component cannot exist except as part of a container (eg: a division of a company);
- as in the previous case, and without sharing being possible;
- no sharing, but with the possibility of components being replaced in the lifetime of the container (eg, wheels of a car);
- possible sharing and separate existence, but with the set of components being constant over the lifetime of each container.

There are a number of ways in which aggregation can be expressed in B AMN. Consider the following example of the first category (Figure 3.11).

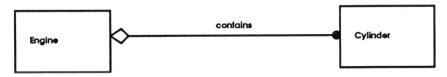

Figure 3.11: Engine as an aggregate of Cylinders

We could express this via renaming. A machine representing a single instance of a **Cylinder** could have the form:

```
MACHINE  Cylinder
SEES  BooLTYPE
VARIABLES
  firing
INVARIANT
  firing ∈ BOOL
INITIALISATION
  firing := FALSE
OPERATIONS
  /* ... */
END
```

and the machine representing the containing entity would INCLUDE a fixed number of copies of this machine:

```
MACHINE   Engine
INCLUDES    c1.Cylinder, c2.Cylinder, c3.Cylinder
VARIABLES
  rotation_rate
INVARIANT
  rotation_rate ∈ ℕ
INITIALISATION
  rotation_rate := 0
OPERATIONS
  /* ... */
END
```

This expresses that instances of the components (**Cylinder**) cannot be shared between **Engine** instances, nor can the cylinders associated with a particular engine be replaced during its lifetime.

A weaker form of aggregation, in which sharing is permitted, would be expressed by using a constant. For example, in the train control example above, we could write

```
CONSTANTS
  platforms
PROPERTIES
  platforms ∈ seq(sections)
```

provided that we allowed **sections** to be non-empty at initialisation. As a result, two stations could share a given platform.

3.8   Summary

- Requirements analysis uses structured textual or diagrammatic models of a domain and system. These models can be mapped into formal B specifications to provide a starting point for formal development, or to assist in animation and validation.

- Data models can be translated into sets of specification-level B machines, one machine representing a "family" of entities closed under inheritance.

- Dynamic models can be formalised by enhancing the initial formal models with a representation of a current "state". State transitions are represented by operations.

- Often there are a number of ways to decompose a B specification or design into sets of machines via USES, SEES and INCLUDES. A number of principles (command/query distinction, abstraction) can assist in making this decomposition.

- Animation is of key importance in obtaining specifications which are correct with respect to the customers true requirements.

3.9   Exercises 2

(1)   Specify the concept of a **Person** as a B AMN machine, where this concept has:

- *constant data*: **date_of_birth**, **gender**, etc;
- *varying data*: **age**, **address**, etc;
- *operations*: **birthday**, etc.

(the specification used in this chapter can be used as a basis; however you should allow for a set of people, rather than just one.)

Specify a **Patient** entity which is a specialisation of **Person**, with additional features:

- (varying data): **body_mass**, and a sequence of **temperature** readings (these can all be assumed to have type $\mathbb{N}$);
- (operations): an operation to extend the sequence of temperature readings with a new value; an operation to calculate and return the difference between the last two temperature readings.

(2)   Consider the collection of machines defined below:

1. What are the variables, constants and operations which are externally visible in the machine **DD**?
2. What are the constants, variables and operations which can be used internally in **DD** (note that operations declared in a machine *cannot* be used within other operations declared in this machine – or in themselves)?
3. Which variables visible in **DD** can be assigned to directly in operations declared in **DD**?

MACHINE **AA**
CONSTANTS

    cc1
PROPERTIES
    $cc1 \in \mathbb{N}$
END

MACHINE **BB**
SEES **AA**
VARIABLES
    vv1, vv2
INVARIANT
    $vv1 \in 12 \;..\; 24 \quad \wedge$
    $vv2 \in \mathbb{N}$
INITIALISATION
    $vv1 := 12 \;\|\; vv2 :\in \mathbb{N}$
OPERATIONS
    correct(val1, val2) $\hat{=}$
        PRE
            $val1 \in 12 \;..\; 24 \quad \wedge$
            $val2 \in \mathbb{N}$
        THEN
            $vv1 := val1 \;\|$
            $vv2 := val2 + cc1$
        END;

  vv $\longleftarrow$ **gtr** $\hat{=}$
    IF $vv1 > vv2$
    THEN
        $vv := vv1$
    ELSE
        $vv := vv2$
    END

END

MACHINE **CC**
SEES **AA**
CONSTANTS **cc2**
PROPERTIES
    $cc2 = 57$
VARIABLES
    ww1
INVARIANT
    $ww1 \in 1 \;..\; cc2$
INITIALISATION
    $ww1 := 1$
OPERATIONS
    set(val) $\hat{=}$
        PRE $val * cc1 \in 1 \;..\; cc2$
          THEN

$$\mathbf{ww1} \;\; := \;\; \mathbf{val} * \mathbf{cc1}$$
      END

END

MACHINE **DD**
INCLUDES **BB**
EXTENDS **CC**
VARIABLES
    uu1
INVARIANT
    $\mathbf{uu1} \in \mathbb{N}$
INITIALISATION
    omitted
OPERATIONS
    redo $\;\widehat{=}$
        definition omitted
END

(3) Consider the **Book** machine partially defined below:

1. calculate the feasibility and termination conditions of the **create_book** operation;
2. is this operation correctly defined? Identify how it should be modified to ensure that its feasibility condition is **true**;
3. complete the operations **change_author** (which takes a book identifier **bk** and new author **newaut** and replaces the author of the book by **newaut**) and **search** (which takes an ISBN and returns any book which has this as its ISBN code). For **search** use the ANY construct and ensure the feasibility of this operation as in part 2.

MACHINE **Book**
SETS **BOOK**
VARIABLES
    books, isbn, author
INVARIANT
    books $\subseteq$ **BOOK** $\wedge$
    isbn $\in$ books $\rightarrow \mathbb{N}$ $\wedge$
    author $\in$ books $\rightarrow$ **STRING**
INITIALISATION
    books, isbn, author $:= \varnothing, \varnothing, \varnothing$
OPERATIONS
    cb $\longleftarrow$ **create_book**(ii, aut) $\;\widehat{=}$
        PRE ii $\in \mathbb{N}$ $\wedge$ aut $\in$ **STRING**
        THEN
            ANY **oo**
            WHERE oo $\in$ **BOOK** $-$ books
            THEN
                books $:=$ books $\cup \{$ oo $\}$ $\|$
                cb $:=$ oo $\|$

$$\textbf{author(oo)} \ := \ \textbf{aut} \ \ \|$$
$$\textbf{isbn(oo)} \ := \ \textbf{ii}$$
            END
        END;

$$\textbf{change\_author(bk, newaut)} \ \ \widehat{=}$$
$$\vdots \ ;$$

$$\textbf{bk} \ \longleftarrow \ \textbf{search(ii)} \ \ \widehat{=}$$
$$\vdots$$

END

(4) Given the following two machines:

MACHINE **Renames_Test1**
VARIABLES **xx, yy**
INVARIANT
   xx ∈ ℕ ∧ **yy** ∈ ℕ
INITIALISATION
   xx := 0 ‖ **yy** := 575
OPERATIONS

up(vv) $\widehat{=}$
            PRE **vv** ∈ ℕ
            THEN
                xx := **yy** * **vv** + **xx**
            END

END

MACHINE **Renames_Test2**
INCLUDES **aa.Renames_Test1, bb.Renames_Test1**
INVARIANT
   aa.xx ≤ **bb.xx**
OPERATIONS

up1(vv) $\widehat{=}$
   PRE **vv** ∈ ℕ
   THEN
      bb.up(vv) ‖
      aa.up(vv/2)
   END

END

show that **Renames_Test2** is internally consistent (with a suitably strength-ened invariant). Would it still be correct if we had EXTENDS as the inclusion mechanism rather than INCLUDES?

(5) Suitable for a term project. Define translation techniques from the Syntropy OO method [16] into B AMN. This translation should enable the animation of Syntropy models, and should also be suitable for further development within B. The object model notation and a useful subset of the (specification level) statechart notation of the method should be covered.

Chapter 4

Design and Implementation

This chapter will cover the stages of development from a complete and validated specification through successive stages of refinement, involving design decisions about how certain specification elements should be expressed in a more code-oriented manner, until a stage is reached which corresponds to an immediately executable system. This process is a key advantage of B over earlier formal methods, particularly Z, which were designed mainly for use at the specification and requirements capture stages.

B supports a number of different development approaches, based on the following essential concepts:

- a development is the set of all specification, design and implementation components involved in the description of a particular application. It can be decomposed into a set of *subsystems* or *subsystem developments*, each subsystem consisting of an abstract specification machine which describes the subsystem functionality to the outside world, and a path of refinement steps down to an executable description which satisfies – ideally – this description (an IMPLEMENTATION);

- the implementation of a subsystem **S** is decomposed by using the specifications of (lower level) subsystems via IMPORTS or SEES clauses. Thus the task of refining **S** is broken down into (presumably simpler) tasks of refining each of the imported subsystems. Indeed, in top-down design we devise a new subsystem to provide part of the functionality of an implementation when this implementation becomes too complex to be manageable;

- specifications of subsystems **S** can be constructed incrementally from a set of machines using the INCLUDES, USES, SEES and EXTENDS mechanisms, but there need be no immediate relationship between this decomposition and that which is used at the implementation level for **S**;

- the final "bottom-level" subsystems are taken, where possible, from previously developed library components, with proven implementations, but they can also be newly defined by the developer for this specific application, in which case the developer must also provide a executable version of the new components in a suitable programming language.

The differences between approaches concern just how the decompositions at the specification and implementation levels are to be achieved. In this book we are mainly using an "object-oriented" approach, ie, identifying machines with entity types and using EXTENDS to imitate class inheritance and INCLUDES and IMPORTS to imitate class composition. This is certainly not the only approach, however, and other ways of developing B specifications are illustrated in many of the references given in the bibliography, including [1, 65, 61, 37].

4.1 The Layered Development Paradigm

The general shape of a formal development using B is shown in Figure 4.1.

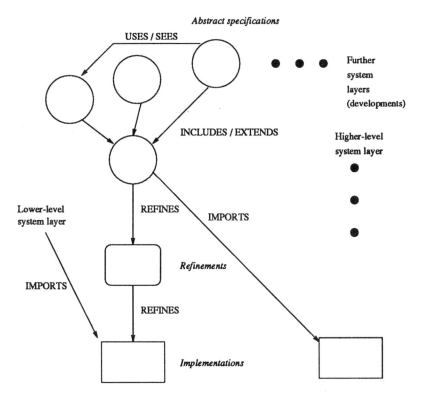

Figure 4.1: General Structure of B Development

As usual, a circle denotes an abstract machine, an oval denotes a refinement, and a rectangle denotes an implementation. An arrow from one construct to another denotes a form of inclusion of the first construct in the second.

The specifications at the top of the diagram can be very abstract state-based or algebraic-style specifications, which will be successively refined towards a procedural implementation. Each refinement path from a set of abstract machines down through a series of refinements to an implementation is termed a "subsystem development". Such developments can use other developments, via the IMPORTS or SEES constructs, to implement some of their functionality and state, and can themselves be used in this fashion by other developments. This implies a layered approach to system development whereby the internal details of the implementation of one layer are hidden from the next higher layer, and only the abstract formal specification of the operations of the lower layer can be assumed by the layer which uses it. Such a structure improves the maintainability of a system because higher system layers are independent of the internal details of lower layers, and rely only on the specifications of these layers.

Figure 4.2 gives a more global view of a typical development structure. In this diagram a subsystem (subsystem development) is identified by a pair of boxes giving just the abstract specification and the implementation of the subsystem, with all intermediate refinement steps elided. We also omit the construction of specifications from other specification-level machines. Subsystems with dashed outlines indicate library components. These are automatically consigned to the bottom layer of the development. Arrows between subsystems indicate the means by which the implementation of the higher layer subsystem makes use of the specification of the lower layer subsystem – either by IMPORTS or SEES. In this case the main subsystem (representing the external interface of the development for users) is implemented on top of subsystems 1 and 2, which in turn are implemented on top of subsystems 3, 6 and 7, and so forth.

Within each subsystem of the system (ie, single development path from specification to implementation) the proof obligations which demonstrate correctness of a more refined stage against the preceding stage of development can be mechanically generated. Correctness of the abstract specification against requirements can be checked by generating internal consistency conditions (which demonstrate that the mathematical model makes internal sense), and by animation, which allows particular scenarios from the requirements to be checked against the specification model.

In the following sections we will show how the structuring mechanisms of B AMN are used to implement the layered development approach.

4.1.1 Structuring Mechanisms for Refinement and Design

There are two aspects of a B development which can be decomposed, or approached by a "divide and conquer" strategy: specification, which we have addressed in the preceding chapter, and refinement and implementation. Decomposition in implementations is achieved via the IMPORTS and SEES structuring mechanisms. These connect B AMN components via the mechanism of *full-hiding*, which only allows direct access to the variables of the (imported) component in the invariants of the importing. Thus, the importing component is independent of changes to the representation of the state of the imported

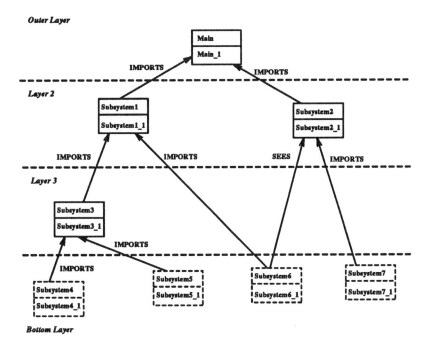

Figure 4.2: Decomposition of Development into Layers

component via data refinements of the latter (such data refinements may be genuine relations in B AMN, so that there may be no way to compute the value of an abstract state variable from the values of variables of the concrete state – as opposed to the functional data refinements of VDM [40]).

Note that refinements and implementations may SEE abstract machines if it is required that a subpart of a system be shared between other parts in a read-only fashion. We may also import a machine into an implementation of an abstract specification which includes or uses the machine: this is part of a general development approach termed "continuity of structure" discussed in Section 4.4.

In more detail, the relevant structuring mechanisms and their properties are as follows:

1. IMPORTS. This is allowed only in implementations, and in this case the imported construct must be an abstract machine, for which, in principle at least, a B implementation or executable code already exists. Within a complete B development, consisting of a number of layered subsystem developments, a given construct can only be imported in one place. The visibility of components of the imported construct are:

    - *parameters*: these must be instantiated in the IMPORTS clause by, for example, using the parameters of the importing development;

    - *sets and constants*: deferred sets of the imported machine are visible in the invariant and properties clauses of the importing implementation, and may be equated to deferred sets of the importing development (for example, see the implementation of the personnel system in the following chapter). However, they are not visible in the operations of the importing machine, since they may not be directly translatable into imperative code. Enumerated sets have the same visibility, however elements of these sets may be referred to freely within the importing construct (although, of course, not updated). Sets and constants are accessible within loop invariants of the importing construct, and can be used to connect the functionality of the construct being refined and the imported machine. Constants of the imported construct are visible in the logical parts of the importing construct (ie, the properties and invariant clauses); however only scalar constants with an explicit numeric value can be referred to within the operations of the importing implementation, apart from in loop invariants;

- *definitions*: these need to be repeated in the importing construct;

- *variables*: the variables of the imported construct are visible in the invariant of the importing, where they are referred to in order to link the states of the refined and imported components – ie., in order to define how the data of the refined component are implemented by that of the imported. They are also visible in the loop invariants of the operations of the importing construct, but are otherwise not visible, for the reasons described above;

- *operations*: the operations of the imported construct are visible in the operations of the importing. They are used to implement the operations of the construct being refined in terms of more primitive and elementary operations of the imported development. In the resulting code, an in-line expansion of operations may be performed for reasons of efficiency, rather than explicit calls;

2. SEES in machines.

- *parameters*: parameters of the seen construct cannot be instantiated in the seeing construct, since if this were allowed it would be possible to instantiate a shared seen machine in inconsistent ways in two different places;

- *sets and constants*: sets and constants, and the elements of enumerated sets, are visible in read-only fashion within the seeing machines. SEES is therefore often used to encapsulate a set of constant and set definitions which must be shared between several machines, refinements and implementations within a complete development, and which in a sense 'parameterise' this development. That is, it is possible that we may wish to change some of these data items in maintenance operations upon the system, and by placing them in a single easily locatable construct, the cost of the maintenance operation is reduced. In the ship-loading case study of Sections 3.5 and 4.5, the set **C_LOCATION** is such a parameter;

- *definitions*: these need to be repeated in the seeing construct. However, care should be taken to not contradict the original definitions or other redefinitions of the items of the DEFINITIONS clause in the seen construct;

- *variables*: these can only be seen in a read-only fashion within the operations of the seeing machines. The reason for not allowing access to the variables within the invariant of the seeing machines is to prevent inconsistent constraints upon the state of the seen machine being imposed from several different locations (and subsystem developments) within a complete development. Intuitively, the references to variables of the seen machine will become, in implementations of the seeing constructs, invocations of enquiry operations which return the value of the variable;

- *Operations*: only enquiry operations that do not change the state of the seen machine can be used in the seeing machine;

3. SEES in refinements. As for the previous case;
4. SEES in implementations.

- *parameters*: as for the previous case;

- *sets and constants*: constants of the seen machine can be referenced within the operations of the seeing implementations only if these constants have an explicit numeric value. Otherwise, constants are fully visible within the logical components of the implementations (loop and implementation invariants, and properties clauses). The visibility of sets is the same as for IMPORTS;

- *definitions*: as for the previous case;

- *variables*: no visibility of the variables of the seen construct within the seeing implementation is allowed, except for their use within the invariant of a loop in the seeing implementation;

- *operations*: as for the previous case.

4.2 Refinement Examples

In this section we illustrate the use of the structuring mechanisms introduced above via a number of small but realistic examples of refinement. The first two are concerned with the situation where a single component is refined by another, with no use of lower-level subsystems. The third illustrates the use of IMPORTS to implement a system on the specification of other subsystems.

4.2.1   Refinement of Sets by Sequences

A standard approach to the refinement of a set-based system is to replace sets
by sequences, and operations on sets by sequence operations, as a progression
towards a more implementation-oriented description.

Consider for example the following extract from such a development.

MACHINE **Set**
VARIABLES
  contents
INVARIANT
  contents $\in$ $\mathbb{F}(\mathbb{N})$
INITIALISATION
  contents $:\in$ $\mathbb{F}(\mathbb{N})$
OPERATIONS

    nn $\longleftarrow$ **choose** $\hat{=}$
      IF **contents** $=$ $\varnothing$
      THEN
          nn $:\in$ $\mathbb{N}$
      ELSE
          nn $:\in$ **contents**
      END

END

The operation **choose** guarantees to select an element of the **contents** variable
of the machine and return it, if **contents** is non-empty.

A refinement using sequences could be:

REFINEMENT **Seq**
REFINES **Set**
VARIABLES
  sq
INVARIANT
  sq $\in$ seq($\mathbb{N}$) $\wedge$
  contents $=$ ran(**sq**)
INITIALISATION
  sq $:\in$ seq($\mathbb{N}$)
OPERATIONS

    nn $\longleftarrow$ **choose** $\hat{=}$
      IF **sq** $=$ [ ]
      THEN
          nn $:=$ 0
      ELSE
          nn $:=$ head(**sq**)
      END

END

This can be proved to be a refinement as follows. The key obligation is that concerning the operation **choose**:

$$\mathbf{Inv_{Set}} \wedge \mathbf{Inv_{Seq}} \Rightarrow$$
$$[\text{IF } \mathbf{sq} = []$$
$$\quad \text{THEN } \mathbf{nn} := 0$$
$$\quad \text{ELSE } \mathbf{nn} := \mathbf{head(sq)}$$
$$\quad \text{END}]$$
$$\qquad \neg [\text{IF } \mathbf{contents} = \varnothing$$
$$\qquad\quad \text{THEN } \mathbf{nn}' :\in \mathbb{N}$$
$$\qquad\quad \text{ELSE } \mathbf{nn}' :\in \mathbf{contents}$$
$$\qquad\quad \text{END}] \neg (\mathbf{nn} = \mathbf{nn}' \wedge \mathbf{R})$$

where **R** is the data refinement relation **contents** = ran(**sq**). **Inv**$_M$ denotes the invariant of machine **M**.

This asserts that for every execution of the concrete operation under the relevant invariants, which returns **nn** as **head(sq)**, there is some possible corresponding execution of the abstract operation (ie, starting from a state **contents** = ran(**sq**)) which returns the same value. This is clear since the abstract operation allows an arbitrary choice of element of **contents** to be given as the result, if ran(**sq**) is non-empty, and certainly the choice of **head(sq)** $\in$ ran(**sq**) satisfies this. Alternatively, if ran(**sq**) is empty it allows any element of $\mathbb{N}$ to be returned, and the choice of 0 by the concrete operation in this case clearly satisfies this specification as well.

The obligation can be broken down into four cases given by the combinations of truth and falsity of the two if-statement tests. We have to check that (given that **R** holds initially):

$$\mathbf{sq} = [] \wedge \mathbf{contents} = \varnothing \Rightarrow$$
$$\exists \mathbf{nn}'.(\mathbf{nn}' \in \mathbb{N} \wedge \mathbf{nn}' = 0)$$

which is clearly true, and:

$$\mathbf{sq} \neq [] \wedge \mathbf{contents} \neq \varnothing \Rightarrow$$
$$\exists \mathbf{nn}'.(\mathbf{nn}' \in \mathbf{contents} \wedge \mathbf{nn}' = \mathbf{head(sq)})$$

which also holds. The other two cases are eliminated because their hypotheses are false.

If instead we had insisted on a *constant* function which performed the randomisation:

MACHINE **Set**
CONSTANTS
   choice
PROPERTIES
   choice $\in$ $\mathbb{F}(\mathbb{N})$ $\rightarrow$ $\mathbb{N}$
VARIABLES
   contents

INVARIANT
   contents $\in$ $\mathbb{F}(\mathbb{N})$
INITIALISATION
   contents $:\in$ $\mathbb{F}(\mathbb{N})$
OPERATIONS

  nn $\longleftarrow$ choose $\hat{=}$
     nn := choice(contents)

END

Then the corresponding proposed refinement would be:

REFINEMENT **Seq**
REFINES **Set**
VARIABLES
  sq
INVARIANT
  sq $\in$ seq($\mathbb{N}$) $\wedge$
  contents $=$ ran(sq)
INITIALISATION
  sq $:\in$ seq($\mathbb{N}$)
OPERATIONS

  nn $\longleftarrow$ choose $\hat{=}$
     nn := choice(ran(sq))

END

It would be wrong to return the head of the sequence because we would have
no guarantee that

$$\text{head(sq)} = \text{choice(ran(sq))}$$

for non-empty sequences, or that $0 = \textbf{choice}(\varnothing)$.

4.2.2   Linked Lists

The following machine defines an abstract concept of a list with operations
to insert and remove elements, to go to a specific point in the list (specified
either by a displacement from the beginning of the list, or by requiring that
the element at that place has a particular value), and to modify and access
elements and determine the current place:

MACHINE **List(ITEM)**
VARIABLES
  contents, pointer
INVARIANT
  contents $\in$ seq(ITEM) $\wedge$

   pointer $\in \mathbb{N} \wedge$
   pointer $\leq$ size(contents)
INITIALISATION
 contents := [ ] ||
 pointer := 0
OPERATIONS

  extend(xx) $\widehat{=}$
     PRE xx $\in$ ITEM
     THEN
       contents := contents $\frown$ [xx]
     END ;

  go(ii) $\widehat{=}$ /* *Move to* ii-th *position in list* */
     PRE ii $\in \mathbb{N} \wedge$ ii $\leq$ size(contents)
     THEN
       pointer := ii
     END ;

  update(xx) $\widehat{=}$ /* *Set value of current list item to* xx */
     PRE xx $\in$ ITEM $\wedge$ pointer $\in$ dom(contents)
     THEN
       contents(pointer) := xx
     END ;

  vv $\longleftarrow$ access $\widehat{=}$
     PRE pointer $\in$ dom(contents)
     THEN
       vv := contents(pointer)
     END ;

  search(xx) $\widehat{=}$ /* *Move to a position whose value is* xx */
     PRE xx $\in$ ran(contents)
     THEN
       ANY pp
       WHERE
          pp $\in \mathbb{N} \wedge$ pp $\leq$ size(contents) $\wedge$
          contents(pp) = xx
       THEN
          pointer := pp
       END
     END ;

  pp $\longleftarrow$ current_pointer $\widehat{=}$
     BEGIN
       pp := pointer
     END ;

  insert_before(xx) $\widehat{=}$
     PRE contents $\neq$ [ ] $\wedge$ xx $\in$ ITEM

THEN
    contents := (contents ↑ (pointer − 1))   ⌢   [xx]   ⌢
                 (contents ↓ (pointer − 1))
END ;

delete $\widehat{=}$
    BEGIN
        contents := contents ↑ (pointer − 1) ⌢ contents ↓ pointer ||
        pointer := 0
    END

END

Notice the orthogonal nature of the operations of this machine − updating of existing elements of the list is performed by a separate operation than is creation of new elements, and is also separated from operations which move the current position in the list. This machine thus provides a collection of indivisible 'primitive' operations which may be combined into more elaborate functionality by other systems which make use of list data.

In this machine the notation **contents** ↑ **ii** denotes the subsequence of **contents** formed by the elements

    [contents(1), . . . , contents(ii)]

and **contents** ↓ **ii** denotes the subsequence of **contents** formed of the elements

    [contents(ii + 1), . . . , contents(size(contents))]

Thus the **delete** operation simply removes the currently pointed at element and resets the pointer.

An implementation of this machine could use a linked list, which provides an efficient implementation of the insert and delete operations. The idea of this design decision is illustrated in Figure 4.3. A doubly linked list is used because we have operations which require access in both directions along the list.

The refinement has the form:

REFINEMENT **LinkedList**
REFINES **List**
SETS
    NODE
VARIABLES
    nodes, back, forward, last_node, first_node, current, value
INVARIANT
    nodes ⊆ NODE ∧
    current ∈ NODE ∧
    value ∈ nodes → ITEM ∧

    back ∈ nodes ↠ nodes ∧
    forward ∈ nodes ↔ nodes ∧

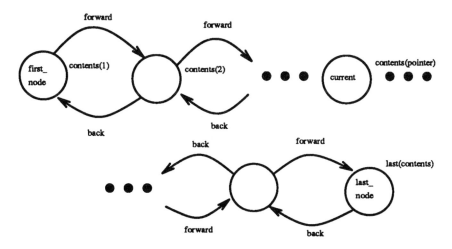

Figure 4.3: List Refinement to Linked List

first_node ∈ NODE ∧
last_node ∈ NODE ∧

nodes ≠ ∅ ⇒
     (current ∈ nodes ∧
     last_node ∈ nodes ∧
     first_node ∈ nodes) ∧

∀ nn.(nn ∈ nodes ⇒
  nn ∉ dom(back) ≡ nn = first_node) ∧

∀ nn.(nn ∈ nodes ⇒
  nn ∉ dom(forward) ≡ nn = last_node) ∧

∀ nn.(nn ∈ nodes ∧ nn ∈ dom(back) ⇒
     (back(nn) ↦ nn) ∈ forward) ∧

∀ (nn, ff).(nn ∈ nodes ∧ ff ∈ nodes ∧
     (nn ↦ ff) ∈ forward ⇒
        back(ff) = nn) ∧

∀ (ii, item).(ii ∈ 1 .. card(nodes) ∧
  item ∈ ITEM ⇒
   (contents(ii) = item ≡
   ∃ node.(node ∈ nodes ∧
     item = value(node) ∧
     ii = card({ ind | ind ∈ nodes ∧
      node ∈ closure(forward)[{ ind }] })))) ∧

pointer = card({ ind | ind ∈ nodes ∧

$$current \ \in \ closure(forward)[\{ \ ind \ \}] \ \})$$

The last two conjuncts express the refinement relation between **List** *and* **LinkedList***:* contents *is implemented as the sequence of node values* [value(node$_1$), ..., value(node$_n$)] *where* node$_1$ *is the* first_node, *and each* node$_i$ $\mapsto$ node$_{i+1}$ *is in* forward.

pointer *is represented by the number of steps needed to go along the* forward *relation from the first node to the current node (plus one).*

INITIALISATION
    nodes, back, forward, value := ∅, ∅, ∅, ∅ ||
    last_node :∈ **NODE** || first_node :∈ **NODE** ||
    current :∈ **NODE**

OPERATIONS

  extend(xx) $\widehat{=}$
     ANY nn
     WHERE nn ∈ **NODE** − nodes
     THEN
       IF nodes = ∅
       THEN
         last_node := nn ||
         first_node := nn ||
         current := nn
       ELSE
         last_node := nn ||
         forward := forward ⊕ { last_node $\mapsto$ nn } ||
         back(nn) := last_node
       END ||
       value(nn) := xx ||
       nodes := nodes ∪ { nn }
     END ;

  go(ii) $\widehat{=}$
     ANY cc
     WHERE cc ∈ nodes ∧
     ii = card({ ind | ind ∈ nodes ∧
                  current ∈ closure(forward)[{ ind }] })
     THEN
       current := cc
     END ;

  update(xx) $\widehat{=}$
     BEGIN
       value(current) := xx
     END ;

  vv ⟵ access $\widehat{=}$
     BEGIN
       vv := value(current)

END;

search(xx) $\hat{=}$
    ANY cc
    WHERE cc $\in$ nodes $\wedge$
        value(cc) = xx
    THEN
        current := cc
    END;

pp $\longleftarrow$ current_pointer $\hat{=}$
    BEGIN
        pp := card({ ind | ind $\in$ nodes $\wedge$
                  current $\in$ closure(forward)[{ ind }] })
    END;

insert_before(xx) $\hat{=}$
    ANY nn
    WHERE nn $\in$ NODE $-$ nodes
    THEN
        nodes := nodes $\cup$ { nn };
        IF current $\in$ dom(back)
        THEN
            forward := forward $\oplus$ { back(current) $\mapsto$ nn };
            back(nn) := back(current)
        ELSE
            first_node := nn
        END;
        forward := forward $\oplus$ { nn $\mapsto$ current };
        back(current) := nn;
        value(nn) := xx
    END;

delete $\hat{=}$
    / * *Exercise for reader* * /

END

The notation **closure(rel)** denotes the reflexive transitive closure of a relation rel; that is, all pairs $x \mapsto y$ such that either $x = y$, $x \mapsto y$ is in r, or for which there is a chain $x_1, \ldots, x_n$ of elements such that $x = x_1$, $y = x_n$ and each $x_i \mapsto x_{i+1}$ is in r.

A possible validation property that can be proved from the above specification is that when there is just one node, this is the first and last node of the list:

$$\text{card(nodes)} = 1 \Rightarrow \text{nodes} = \{\text{last\_node}\} = \{\text{first\_node}\}$$

The preconditions of the abstract version of the component can effectively be assumed to hold when the more concrete operations are executed: any user of the subsystem must obey the specification given in the abstract component, and hence must invoke the operations within their preconditions.

Code based on the following algorithms could be used at the implementation level:

```
go(ii)  ≙
     VAR ind
     IN
       ind := 1;
       current := first_node;
       WHILE ind < ii
       DO
            current := forward(current);
            ind := ind + 1
       INVARIANT
          ind = card({ nn | nn ∈ nodes ∧
                            current ∈ closure(forward)[{ nn }] }) ∧
          ind ≤ ii
       VARIANT ii − ind
       END
     END;

search(xx)  ≙
     BEGIN
       current := first_node;
       WHILE value(current) ≠ xx
       DO
            current := forward(current)
       INVARIANT true
       VARIANT
          card(nodes) −
             card({ nn | nn ∈ nodes ∧
                            current ∈ closure(forward)[{ nn }]})
       END
     END;
```

These definitions would not be valid in the above refinement, since WHILE loops may only be used in implementations.

4.2.3 Example: Vending Machines

This specification concerns a vending machine consisting of three components: a coin slot, a dispenser and a controller. The structure of the specification will follow the decomposition of the system into these three subsystems. The statechart of the controller is shown in Figure 4.4. The controller receives input events from the coin slot (**accept_5** and **accept_10**) and sends output events to the dispenser (**give_drink**) and coin slot (**give_change**). A more detailed treatment of this example is given in Chapter 5. Statecharts are useful

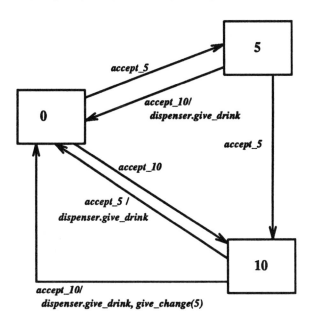

Figure 4.4: Statechart of Vending Machine

to express the functionality of simple finite state systems such as this one. Their use when more complex data (such as a sequence of track sections in the **Station** example) is involved is less straightforward.

The dispenser has operations of **give_drink** and **restock**:

```
MACHINE Dispenser
SEES Vend_data
VARIABLES
   dstate
INVARIANT
   dstate ∈ DSTATE
INITIALISATION
   dstate := unstocked
OPERATIONS
   restock ≙
      dstate := stocked;

   give_drink ≙
      PRE dstate = stocked
      THEN
            dstate :∈ DSTATE
      END

END
```

where:

```
MACHINE Vend_data
SETS
  CSTATE  =  { coin_present, coin_absent };
  DSTATE  =  { stocked, unstocked }
CONSTANTS
  COINS, STATE
PROPERTIES
  COINS  =  { 5, 10 } ∧
  STATE  =  { 0, 5, 10 }
END
```

encapsulates the shared data of the development.

The coin slot provides a sensor to identify the last coin entered, and an operation to give change:

```
MACHINE Coin_slot
SEES Vend_data
VARIABLES
  cstate, current_coin
INVARIANT
  cstate ∈ CSTATE ∧
  current_coin ∈ COINS
INITIALISATION
  cstate := coin_absent ||
  current_coin :∈ COINS
OPERATIONS
  give_change(cc) ≙
      PRE cc ∈ COINS
      THEN
            cstate := coin_absent
      END ;

  cc ⟵ accept_coin ≙
      ANY coin
      WHERE coin ∈ COINS
      THEN
          current_coin := coin ||
          cstate := coin_present ||
          cc := coin
      END

END
```

The controller is then defined in two stages (note that the price of a drink is 15 units):

```
MACHINE BasicController
SEES Vend_data
INCLUDES Dispenser, Coin_slot
```

```
PROMOTES restock, accept_coin
VARIABLES
    state       / *    The current change held by the
                        machine  * /
INVARIANT
    state  ∈  STATE
INITIALISATION
    state  :=  0
OPERATIONS
    accept_10  ≙
        BEGIN
            IF state  =  0
            THEN
                state  :=  10
            ELSE
                state  :=  0
            END ||

            IF state  =  5
            THEN
                give_drink
            ELSE
                IF state  =  10
                THEN
                        give_drink  ||  give_change(5)
                END
            END
        END ;

    accept_5  ≙
        BEGIN
            state  :=  (state  +  5) mod 15  ||
            IF state  =  10
            THEN
                    give_drink
            END
        END

END
```

This machine describes what actions should be taken in each of the two possible cases (entering a 5p coin or a 10p coin). The definitions of these operations abstract away from the order of giving a drink and giving change by using the || operator. Likewise they separate the change of state resulting from a statechart transition from the actions triggered on other components by this transition.

```
MACHINE  Controller
INCLUDES  BasicController
SEES  Vend_data
PROMOTES  restock
```

```
OPERATIONS
    enter_coin ≙
        ANY cc
        WHERE cc ∈ COINS
        THEN
            IF cc = 5
            THEN
                accept_5
            ELSE
                accept_10
            END
        END

END
```

This machine provides the external interface to the user – the only way the user can control the vending machine is by entering a coin, modelled here by a non-deterministic choice (since at the abstract specification level we cannot use sequential composition to apply the **accept_coin** operation of **Coin_slot**).

The refinement of **Controller** can, however, use this operation:

```
IMPLEMENTATION Controller_1
REFINES Controller
IMPORTS BasicController
SEES Vend_data
PROMOTES restock   / * restock is used to implement itself * /
OPERATIONS

    enter_coin ≙
        VAR cc
        IN
            cc ⟵ accept_coin;
            IF cc = 5
            THEN
                accept_5
            ELSE
                accept_10
            END
        END

END
```

Notice that there is no change of state between the abstract specification and its refinement. This form of data refinement is termed 'procedural refinement'.

The architecture of the specification and implementation of the development is shown in Figure 4.5.

The global view of the relationships between the subsystems, including the library components, is given in Figure 4.6.

This describes the structure of the full vending machine development given in Section 5.3.

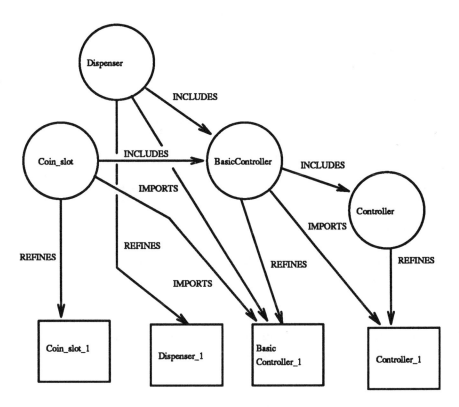

Figure 4.5: Structure of Vending Machine Development

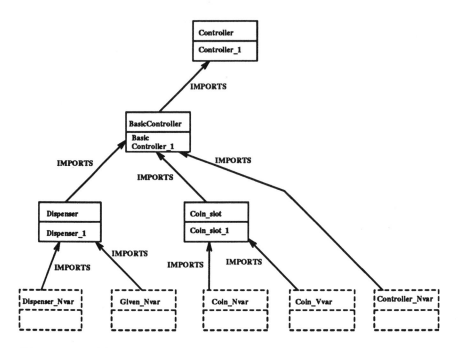

Figure 4.6: Global Structure of Vending Machine Development

4.3   Proofs of Refinement

Proof obligations for refinement are often existential requirements of the form

$$\mathbf{P} \quad \Rightarrow \quad \exists \ \mathbf{v}.\mathbf{Q}$$

These arise **(i)** from the refinement obligation (1) : $\mathbf{C} \wedge \mathbf{B} \wedge \mathbf{B1} \Rightarrow \exists(\mathbf{v}, \mathbf{w}).(\mathbf{I} \wedge \mathbf{J})$ that there are suitable constants and variable state to satisfy the abstract requirements, and **(ii)** from the implicit existential requirements of the obligations

(2) :
$$\mathbf{C} \wedge \mathbf{B} \wedge \mathbf{B1} \Rightarrow [\mathbf{T1}]\neg [\mathbf{T}]\neg \mathbf{J}$$
(3) :
$$\mathbf{C} \wedge \mathbf{B} \wedge \mathbf{B1} \wedge \mathbf{I} \wedge \mathbf{J} \wedge \mathbf{P} \Rightarrow$$
$$\mathbf{P1} \wedge [\mathbf{S1}']\neg [\mathbf{S}]\neg (\mathbf{J} \wedge \mathbf{y}' = \mathbf{y})$$

"For every concrete execution of the operation there is an abstract execution which gives the same results and transition, modulo the refinement relation **J**".

That is, to show that operation **N** refines an operation **M**, under a refinement relation **R**, we need, for every **v** and **u**, with **u** R-related to **v**, that every possible execution of **N** starting from state **v** leads to a state **v**′, R-related to a state **u**′ reachable by an execution of **M** from **u**.

This is an existential assertion $\forall(\mathbf{v}, \mathbf{u}).(\exists \mathbf{u}'.(\ldots))$.

As an example of refinement proof, consider the following well-known example of a dictionary specification. The first machine describes an abstract dictionary mechanism, by which words can be entered in a dictionary and can be tested for membership:

MACHINE **Dictionary_as_set(WORD)**
SEES **Bool_TYPE**
VARIABLES
    contents
INVARIANT
    contents ∈ 𝔽(**WORD**)
INITIALISATION
    contents := ∅
OPERATIONS
  add_word(wd) ≙
      PRE **wd** ∈ **WORD**
      THEN
          contents := **contents** ∪ { **wd** }
      END ;

  bb ⟵ **lookup_word(wd)** ≙
      PRE **wd** ∈ **WORD**
      THEN
          IF **wd** ∈ **contents**
          THEN
              bb := **TRUE**
          ELSE
              bb := **FALSE**
          END
      END

END

Its refinement uses the concept of a hash function to make operations on the dictionary more efficient (this is an example of the use of domain features to inspire the form of refinement – since in the domain there are natural partitions on the set of words, such as distinguishing words with different initial letters):

REFINEMENT **Partitioned_dictionary**
REFINES **Dictionary_as_set**
SEES **Bool_TYPE**
CONSTANTS
    hash
PROPERTIES
    hash ∈ **WORD** → ℕ
VARIABLES
    pcontents
INVARIANT
    pcontents ∈ ran(**hash**) → 𝔽(**WORD**) ∧
    / * *Refinement relation* * /

```
INITIALISATION
    pcontents := λ ii.(ii ∈ ran(hash) | ∅)
OPERATIONS
    add_word(wd)  ≙
        PRE wd ∈ WORD
        THEN
            pcontents(hash(wd)) :=
                    pcontents(hash(wd)) ∪ { wd }
        END;

    bb ⟵ lookup_word(wd)  ≙
        PRE wd ∈ WORD
        THEN
            IF wd ∈ pcontents(hash(wd))
            THEN
                bb := TRUE
            ELSE
                bb := FALSE
            END
        END

END
```

This refinement has the same interface (operation names and signatures) as its more abstract specification, but is intended to be more efficient – if the **hash** function is non-trivial then searches should be less expensive than in the original specification. A suitable hash function would be one that partitions the dictionary into sets of approximately equal size (rather than the simplistic hash function using the initial letter of a word).

The refinement relation **R** is that **contents** is implemented by the union of all the **pcontents(i)** sets, for all **i** ∈ ran(**hash**). More precisely, we have:

$$\forall x.(x \in \textbf{WORD} \Rightarrow$$
$$(x \in \textbf{contents} \equiv x \in \textbf{pcontents}(\textbf{hash}(x))))$$

We need to prove that **R** is true after the initialisation of the two components, and is maintained by every operation. These obligations are (assuming the other logical properties of both components):

$$[\textbf{pcontents} := \{ii, tt \mid ii \in ran(\textbf{hash}) \land tt = \emptyset\}] \neg [$$
$$\textbf{contents} := \emptyset] \neg \textbf{R}$$

for the initialisation, which simplifies to:

$$\textbf{R}[\{ii, tt \mid ii \in ran(\textbf{hash}) \land tt = \emptyset\}/\textbf{pcontents}, \emptyset/\textbf{contents}]$$

ie, that $\{ii, tt \mid ii \in ran(\textbf{hash}) \land tt = \emptyset\}$ and $\emptyset$ are related by **R**:

$$\forall x.(x \in \textbf{WORD} \Rightarrow$$
$$(x \in \emptyset \equiv x \in \{ii, ss \mid ii \in ran(\textbf{hash}) \land ss = \emptyset\}(\textbf{hash}(x))))$$

which is clearly true.

For the **add_word** operation:

$$\mathbf{R} \Rightarrow$$
$$[\text{pcontents} := \text{pcontents} \oplus$$
$$\{\text{hash(wd)} \mapsto \text{pcontents(hash(wd))} \cup \{\text{wd}\}\}] \neg \, [$$
$$\text{contents} := \text{contents} \cup \{\text{wd}\}] \neg \, \mathbf{R}$$

Again this reduces to showing that if **contents** and **pcontents** satisfy **R**, then so do the new values of these variables resulting from the above assignments.

For the **lookup_word** operation we need:

$$\mathbf{R} \Rightarrow$$
[IF **wd** $\in$ **pcontents(hash(wd))**
  THEN
    $\mathbf{bb} := \mathbf{TRUE}$
  ELSE
    $\mathbf{bb} := \mathbf{FALSE}$
  END]$\neg$ [
        IF **wd** $\in$ **contents**
        THEN
          $\mathbf{bb'} := \mathbf{TRUE}$
        ELSE
          $\mathbf{bb'} := \mathbf{FALSE}$
        END]$\neg \, (\mathbf{bb} = \mathbf{bb'} \wedge \mathbf{R})$

There are four cases which arise from this obligation, two from the formula:

$$\mathbf{R} \wedge \mathbf{wd} \in \text{pcontents(hash(wd))} \Rightarrow$$
$$[\mathbf{bb} := \mathbf{TRUE}] \neg \, ((\mathbf{wd} \in \text{contents} \Rightarrow$$
$$\neg \, (\mathbf{R} \wedge \mathbf{TRUE} = \mathbf{bb})) \wedge$$
$$(\mathbf{wd} \notin \text{contents} \Rightarrow$$
$$\neg \, (\mathbf{R} \wedge \mathbf{FALSE} = \mathbf{bb})))$$

and a further two from the **bb** := **FALSE** side of the concrete operation.

The above implication can be simplified to:

$$\mathbf{R} \wedge \mathbf{wd} \in \text{pcontents(hash(wd))} \Rightarrow$$
$$(\mathbf{wd} \in \text{contents} \wedge \mathbf{R}) \vee (\mathbf{wd} \notin \text{contents} \wedge \text{false})$$

which is clearly true. Similarly for the **bb** := **FALSE** case.

The requirements upon **hash** are only that it is a function, and, for the termination of the initialisation, that it has a finite range.

4.4 Decomposing Implementations

As stated above, there need be no direct relationship between the way that the specification of a system is decomposed into specification modules, and the way that the implementation of that system is decomposed into subsystems. Alternatively we can have a close correspondence between these structurings, if the specification components can be separately implemented and are suitable for supporting the definition of the implementation. There are several cases:

- in the case that specification components are linked by the USES construct we cannot separately implement the used and using machines, and import the used machine into the implementation of the using. This is because USES is only a semi-hiding mechanism: there may be too many dependencies between the used and using machines to permit separate refinement.

  Thus we must find another means to implement the functionality and data provided by the used machine. This is an instance of the *separate decomposition* approach, whereby new subsystems are introduced during design, which do not feature in the abstract specification.

  A simple example where such a process is used is in the implementation of a numerical function, where an original abstract recursive definition in a single machine is carried into a loop implemented upon library machines which provide arithmetic operations upon scalar variables. This approach can also be used when the data items in the abstract specification correspond exactly to the specification of a library component (for instance, the machine **Compartment** and its implementation in the example of Sections 3.5 and 4.5);

- if the implementation decomposition consists of importing a set of machines into a single implementation (as opposed to introducing layers of new subsystems to support the implementation) we term this the 'monolithic' approach. Because the resulting implementation contains all the data contributed by each subsystem, this approach can lead to severe difficulties if formal proof is attempted;

- if a specification component **B** INCLUDES a machine **A** then we can use an IMPORTS **A** clause in the implementation **B_1** of **B** to carry out the functionality supplied by **A** in the specification. **A** itself must then be separately implemented. Any sets and constants of **A** will be visible *twice* in **B_1** (once via the IMPORTS clause, and once via the INCLUDES/REFINES path), so these must be factored out into a new machine **C**, which is seen by each of **A**, **B_1** and **B**. An example of this situation is shown in Section 3.5, where **Compartment** plays the role of **A**, **Ship** plays the role of **B**, **Ship_1** plays the role of **B_1**, and **Ship_DATA** the role of **C**. If operations of **A** are promoted to **B** (for example the operations **new_compartment** and **show_load** of the **Ship** development), then these can simply be promoted from **A** to **B_1** (they are actually implemented in **A_1**);

- if a specification component **B** SEES a machine **A** then the implementation **B_1** of **B** can also access **A** via SEES. References in **B** to attributes of **A** are implemented by invocations of corresponding enquiry operations of **A** in **B_1**.

It is important to thoroughly review the structure of a specification before carrying out an implementation, in order that effort is not wasted as a result of mis-matches between the specification structure and a desired implementation structure. This review should look at:

- the location of data and operations in machines – is there always a good conceptual coherence to a machine?;
- can complex operations be factored into calls to operations of other machines?;
- are all operations which are intended to be implemented defined to only input and output simple data (ie, not structured values such as sets, sequences or relations)?;
- can INCLUDES structures in the specification be translated into IMPORTS structures in an implementation? This translation will require that any sets and constants in the included machine are factored out into a new machine that is seen by all the relevant components.

4.5   Ship Loading Case Study – Implementation

In this case we can directly copy the specification structure and decomposition in the implementation of the system. The development is therefore an example of the "continuity of structure" approach.

The implementation of **Compartment** is given by:

IMPLEMENTATION
    Compartment_1
REFINES
    Compartment
IMPORTS
    Compartment_fnc_obj($\mathbb{N}$ $\cup$ **C_LOCATION**, 5, 100)

This library machine manages a set of 100 records, whose 5 attributes have values in the union of $\mathbb{N}$ *and* **C_LOCATION**. *In an* IMPORTS *clause, unlike in* INCLUDES *or* EXTENDS, *we can use such union types as actual parameters because every set at the implementation level is considered to be a subset of the natural numbers.*

Each of the abstract attributes is implemented by a corresponding index of the function values managed by **Compartment_fnc_obj**.

SEES
    Scalar_TYPE, Bool_TYPE, Ship_DATA
DEFINITIONS
    CENTIMETERS == $0..10000$;
    MASS == $0..10000$
CONSTANTS
    length_idx, width_idx, location_idx, load_mass_idx,
    load_max_idx
PROPERTIES
    COMPARTMENT = **Compartment_FNCOBJ** $\wedge$

length_idx = 1 ∧
width_idx = 2 ∧
location_idx = 3 ∧
load_mass_idx = 4 ∧
load_max_idx = 5

These constants represent particular fields of the entity being implemented.

INVARIANT

compartments = Compartment_fnctok ∧
∀ cc.(cc ∈ compartments   ⇒
     Compartment_fncstruct(cc)(length_idx) = c_length(cc)) ∧
∀ cc.(cc ∈ compartments   ⇒
     Compartment_fncstruct(cc)(width_idx) = c_width(cc)) ∧
∀ cc.(cc ∈ compartments   ⇒
     Compartment_fncstruct(cc)(location_idx) = c_location(cc)) ∧
∀ cc.(cc ∈ compartments   ⇒
     Compartment_fncstruct(cc)(load_mass_idx) =
                           c_load_mass(cc)) ∧
∀ cc.(cc ∈ compartments   ⇒
     Compartment_fncstruct(cc)(load_max_idx) = c_load_max(cc))

This invariant states that the records implemented by the library machine variables
Compartment_fnctok *and* Compartment_fncstruct *do serve to implement the*
attributes of compartments *expressed by functions at the abstract level.*

OPERATIONS

cc ⟵ new_compartment(len, wid, loc, lmx)   ≙
     VAR bb, dd
     IN
        bb, dd ⟵ Compartment_CRE_FNC_OBJ;
        IF bb = TRUE
        THEN
           Compartment_STO_FNC_OBJ(dd, length_idx, len);
           Compartment_STO_FNC_OBJ(dd, width_idx, wid);
           Compartment_STO_FNC_OBJ(dd, location_idx, loc);
           Compartment_STO_FNC_OBJ(dd, load_mass_idx, 0);
           Compartment_STO_FNC_OBJ(dd, load_max_idx, lmx);
           cc := dd
        END
     END ;

The STO_FNC_OBJ *operations are update operations from the library machine*
Compartment_fnc_obj, *which is given below. They correspond directly to the ab-*
stract specification statements

    c_length(dd) := len ‖
    c_width(dd) := wid ‖

and so forth.

```
load_compartment(cc, mm)  ≙
        VAR bb, xx, yy, zz
        IN
            xx  ⟵  Compartment_VAL_FNC_OBJ(cc, load_max_idx);
            yy  ⟵  Compartment_VAL_FNC_OBJ(cc, load_mass_idx);
            zz  ⟵  ADD(yy, mm);
            bb  ⟵  LEQ(zz, xx);
            IF bb  =  TRUE
            THEN
                Compartment_STO_FNC_OBJ(cc, load_mass_idx, zz)
            END
        END;

    bb  ⟵  allowed_load(cc, mm)  ≙
        VAR xx, yy, zz
        IN
            xx  ⟵  Compartment_VAL_FNC_OBJ(cc, load_max_idx);
            yy  ⟵  Compartment_VAL_FNC_OBJ(cc, load_mass_idx);
            zz  ⟵  ADD(yy, mm);
            bb  ⟵  LEQ(zz, xx)
        END;

    ld  ⟵  show_load(cc)  ≙
        BEGIN
            ld  ⟵  Compartment_VAL_FNC_OBJ(cc, load_mass_idx)
        END

END
```

Ship_DATA has the trivial implementation:

```
IMPLEMENTATION
    Ship_DATA_1
REFINES
    Ship_DATA
END
```

Compartment_fnc_obj is as follows (we have omitted those parts which are not of interest in this particular specification):

```
MACHINE
    Compartment_fnc_obj(VALUE, maxfld, maxobj)
CONSTRAINTS
    maxobj  >  0
SEES
    file_dump, Bool_TYPE
SETS
    Compartment_FNCOBJ
PROPERTIES
```

card(Compartment_FNCOBJ) = maxobj

VARIABLES
  Compartment_fnctok, Compartment_fncstruct,
  Compartment_locate

INVARIANT
  Compartment_fnctok $\subseteq$ Compartment_FNCOBJ $\wedge$
  Compartment_fncstruct $\in$ Compartment_fnctok $\rightarrow$
$$(1 .. maxfld \nrightarrow VALUE) \wedge$$
  Compartment_locate $\in$ 1.. card(Compartment_fnctok) $\rightarrowtail$
$$Compartment\_fnctok$$

INITIALISATION
  Compartment_fnctok, Compartment_fncstruct,
$$Compartment\_locate := \varnothing,\ \varnothing,\ \varnothing$$

OPERATIONS

  bb $\longleftarrow$ Compartment_TST_FLD_FNC_OBJ(ii) $\hat{=}$
  PRE
    ii $\in$ $\mathbb{N}$
  THEN
    bb := bool(ii $\in$ 1.. maxfld)
  END ;

  bb, pp $\longleftarrow$ Compartment_CRE_FNC_OBJ $\hat{=}$
  IF Compartment_fnctok $\neq$ Compartment_FNCOBJ THEN
    ANY qq, ll WHERE
      qq $\in$ Compartment_FNCOBJ $-$ Compartment_fnctok $\wedge$
      ll $\in$ 1.. card(Compartment_fnctok) $+$ 1 $\rightarrowtail$
$$(Compartment\_fnctok \cup \{qq\})$$
    THEN
      Compartment_fncstruct(qq) := $\varnothing$ $\|$
      Compartment_fnctok := Compartment_fnctok $\cup$ {qq} $\|$
      Compartment_locate := ll $\|$
      pp := qq $\|$
      bb := TRUE
    END
  ELSE
    bb := FALSE
  END ;

  bb $\longleftarrow$ Compartment_XST_FNC_OBJ(pp) $\hat{=}$
  PRE
    pp $\in$ Compartment_FNCOBJ
  THEN
    bb := bool(pp $\in$ Compartment_fnctok)
  END ;

  bb $\longleftarrow$ Compartment_DEF_FNC_OBJ(ff, ii) $\hat{=}$
  PRE
    ff $\in$ Compartment_fnctok $\wedge$
    ii $\in$ 1.. maxfld

THEN
    bb := **bool**(ii $\in$ dom(Compartment_fncstruct(ff)))
END;

vv $\longleftarrow$ **Compartment_VAL_FNC_OBJ**(ff, ii) $\;\widehat{=}\;$
PRE
    ff $\in$ **Compartment_fnctok** $\wedge$
    ii $\in$ dom(Compartment_fncstruct(ff))
THEN
    vv := **Compartment_fncstruct**(ff)(ii)
END;

Compartment_STO_FNC_OBJ(ff, ii, vv) $\;\widehat{=}\;$
PRE
    ff $\in$ **Compartment_fnctok** $\wedge$
    ii $\in$ 1 .. maxfld $\wedge$
    vv $\in$ **VALUE**
THEN
    Compartment_fncstruct(ff)(ii) := **vv**
END;

Compartment_RMV_FNC_OBJ(ff, ii) $\;\widehat{=}\;$
PRE
    ff $\in$ **Compartment_fnctok** $\wedge$
    ii $\in$ 1 .. maxfld
THEN
    Compartment_fncstruct(ff) := {ii} $\lhd\!\!\!-$ **Compartment_fncstruct**(ff)
END;

...

END

In the implementation of **Ship** we make the simple assumption that a load distribution is always safe:

IMPLEMENTATION
    Ship_1
REFINES
    Ship
SEES
    Bool_TYPE, **Ship_DATA**
IMPORTS
    Compartment(COMPARTMENT),
    Ship_set_obj(COMPARTMENT, 5, 100)

This specifies that there can be at most 5 ships, and a maximum memory allocation of 100 compartments.

PROMOTES
    new_compartment, **show_load**

PROPERTIES
    SHIP = Ship_SETOBJ
INVARIANT
    s_compartments = Ship_setstruct ∧
    ships = Ship_settok
OPERATIONS

    ss ⟵ new_ship $\widehat{=}$
            VAR bb
            IN
                bb, ss ⟵ Ship_CRE_SET_OBJ
            END;

    add_compartment(ss, cc) $\widehat{=}$
            VAR bb, bb1
            IN
                bb ⟵ Ship_MBR_SET_OBJ(ss, cc);
                IF bb = FALSE
                THEN
                    bb1 ⟵ Ship_ENT_SET_OBJ(ss, cc)
                END
            END;

This definition ignores any space failure resulting from trying to add too many compartments to the system (signalled by bb1). In a fully formal development we would have to take appropriate action in this case.

    load_ship_compartment(ss, cc, mm) $\widehat{=}$
            VAR bb, bb1
            IN
                bb ⟵ Ship_MBR_SET_OBJ(ss, cc);
                bb1 ⟵ allowed_load(cc, mm);
                IF ((bb = TRUE) ∧ (bb1 = TRUE))
                THEN
                    load_compartment(cc, mm)
                END
            END

END

safe_load_distribution has been assumed to be always true, for simplicity. In a complete system this would involve complex numerical calculations.

4.5.1   Discussion

The decomposition of the specification and implementation in this example is based on the entity types present in the system: we have conceptually coherent **Ship** and **Compartment** entities, and we wish to formalise these entities as separate developments (on the basis that we may wish to use the **Compartment** subsystem development independently of the **Ship** development: this would not be possible if we had adopted the 'monolithic' approach and placed the refinements of the data of both machines in one implementation component). The monolithic approach tends also to result in a larger set of proof obligations, since:

- partitioning an implementation into several developments means that operations of an implementation can use invocations of a specification-level operation in place of its code: this definition will almost always be simpler and more concise than the corresponding code;
- implementation invariants can be simpler, since they need refer only to that part of the structure of the implementation data which is managed by the specific subsystem development, and can defer to lower level developments the management of finer structure;
- there will be fewer variables in the individual implementation components than in the single monolithic implementation.

A partitioned approach will also allow some proof obligations to be generated earlier than with the monolithic approach, since only parts of the implementation of the development need to be created at any one time.

The advantages of the monolithic approach are:

- it may make it easier to comprehend the entire system and the inter-relationships between the layers of data involved, rather than these layers being separated into distinct developments;
- it may improve the efficiency of the resulting code, since the cost of invoking operations between development layers is not present.

4.6 Summary

- The central concept of development in B is *layered development*: the implementation of one subsystem by making use of the specifications of previously implemented subsystems.
- Three separate development strategies are supported by B:
  - using specification decompositions as the basis of implementation decompositions;
  - using no decomposition at the implementation level;
  - using distinct decompositions at the specification and implementation levels.
- A number of standard steps can be used to define refinements of a machine by a refinement or of a refinement by an implementation.

4.7   Exercises 3

(1)   Define a refinement of the **SortSet** machine using a machine which represents strictly (increasing) ordered sequences – ie, as in the **SortSeq** machine. Notice that such sequences do not contain duplicate elements. Write out the refinement proof obligations and prove them.

(2)   Define a refinement of the **Dispenser** machine which uses a state variable **drinks** $\in \mathbb{N}$ to record the number of drinks in stock and decrements and increments this appropriately in the **restock** and **give_drink** operations (assume that each restock results in 10 more new drink containers being available in the machine). Again, generate and prove the obligations.

(3)   *Suitable for term project.* Investigate how graphics libraries (such as the G++ XObj libraries) of C or C++ can be utilised within B-developed implementations. Encapsulate suitable facilities (eg, window creation, drawing of various forms of shape, resizing, moving, etc.) in B machines and provide meaningful abstract specifications of these facilities.

Chapter 5

Case Studies

This chapter will provide three case studies in the B development method. The first gives an example of the refinement of entity-relationship-attribute models, the second is a standard reactive system example, and the third is a detailed development of the vending machine case study. The first is an example of the "monolithic" approach to implementation structuring, the second an example of "separate decomposition" and the third an example of "continuity of structure".

5.1 Personnel System Development

This case study extends the example of a personnel system introduced in Chapter 3 to a full implementation. It illustrates the "monolithic" development approach, and the systematic way in which entity-relationship-attribute models can be implemented using the B libraries for mathematical objects.

5.1.1 Specification

The specification of the system is similar to that given in Chapter 3, with the exception that we wish to model a set of people and employed people, rather than just a single person:

```
MACHINE
    Person(maxper)
SEES String_TYPE
SETS
    PERSON;
    GENDER  =  { female,  male }
PROPERTIES
    card(PERSON)  =  maxper
VARIABLES
    date_of_birth,  gender,  age,  address,  persons
```

INVARIANT
  persons ⊆ **PERSON** ∧
  age ∈ persons → 0 .. 200 ∧
  address ∈ persons → **STRING** ∧
  date_of_birth ∈ persons → ℕ ∧
  gender ∈ persons → **GENDER**
INITIALISATION
  age := ∅ ‖ address := ∅ ‖
  persons := ∅ ‖ date_of_birth := ∅ ‖
  gender := ∅
OPERATIONS

  pp ⟵ create_person(dob, gen, addr) ≙
      PRE persons ≠ **PERSON** ∧
          dob ∈ ℕ ∧ gen ∈ **GENDER** ∧ addr ∈ **STRING**
      THEN
        ANY oo
        WHERE
          oo ∈ **PERSON** − persons
        THEN
          persons := persons ∪ {oo} ‖
          age(oo) := 0 ‖
          date_of_birth(oo) := dob ‖
          address(oo) := addr ‖
          gender(oo) := gen ‖
          pp := oo
        END
      END;

  birthday(pp) ≙
      PRE pp ∈ persons ∧ age(pp) < 200
      THEN
          age(pp) := age(pp) + 1
      END;

  ca ⟵ current_age(pp) ≙
      PRE pp ∈ persons
      THEN
          ca := age(pp)
      END;

  change_address(pp, addr) ≙
      PRE pp ∈ persons ∧ addr ∈ **STRING**
      THEN
          address(pp) := addr
      END

END

The set **STRING** is encapsulated within the **String_TYPE** library component, which defines it as seq(0 .. 255).

MACHINE
    Employed_Person(maxper)
EXTENDS Person(maxper)
SEES **String_TYPE**
USES
    Employment
VARIABLES
    current_jobs
INVARIANT
    current_jobs $\in$ persons $\nrightarrow$ seq(employments)
INITIALISATION
    current_jobs := $\varnothing$
OPERATIONS

  add_job(pp,jb) $\;\widehat{=}\;$
      PRE pp $\in$ persons $\wedge$ jb $\in$ employments
      THEN
        IF pp $\in$ dom(current_jobs)
        THEN current_jobs(pp) := current_jobs(pp) $\frown$ [jb]
        ELSE
           current_jobs(pp) := [jb]
        END
      END ;

  sal $\longleftarrow$ total_salary(pp) $\;\widehat{=}\;$
      PRE pp $\in$ persons
      THEN
        sal := Σ ii.(ii $\in$ dom(current_jobs(pp)) |
                      salary(current_jobs(pp)(ii)))
      END

END

Because **Employed_Person** is a subtype of **Person**, there may be elements of **persons** with no associated employment sequence. Thus **current_jobs** is a partial function, and we need the case analysis of **add_job** in order to determine if we are adding a new job to someone for whom **current_jobs** is defined, or if this is the first job for the person.

    The specifications of **Employer** and **Employment** are unchanged except for additional size bounds:

MACHINE Employer(maxemployer)
USES Employment
SETS
    EMPLOYER
PROPERTIES
    card(EMPLOYER) = maxemployer

VARIABLES
    employers, staff
INVARIANT
    employers $\subseteq$ EMPLOYER $\wedge$
    staff $\in$ employers $\rightarrow$ seq(employments)
INITIALISATION
    employers := $\varnothing$ || staff := $\varnothing$
OPERATIONS
    ee $\longleftarrow$ create_employer $\hat{=}$
        PRE employers $\neq$ EMPLOYER
        THEN
          ANY oo
          WHERE oo $\in$ EMPLOYER $-$ employers
          THEN
             ee := oo ||
             employers := employers $\cup$ { oo } ||
             staff(oo) := []
          END
        END;

    hire(ee, job) $\hat{=}$
        PRE ee $\in$ employers $\wedge$ job $\in$ employments
        THEN
             staff(ee) := staff(ee) $\frown$ [job]
        END

END

MACHINE Employment(EMR, maxemployment)
SETS EMPLOYMENT
PROPERTIES
    card(EMPLOYMENT) = maxemployment
VARIABLES
    employments, salary, employer
INVARIANT
    employments $\subseteq$ EMPLOYMENT $\wedge$
    salary $\in$ employments $\rightarrow$ $\mathbb{N}$ $\wedge$
    employer $\in$ employments $\nrightarrow$ EMR
INITIALISATION
    employments := $\varnothing$ ||
    salary := $\varnothing$ ||
    employer := $\varnothing$
OPERATIONS
    ee $\longleftarrow$ create_employment(sal) $\hat{=}$
        PRE sal : $\mathbb{N}$ $\wedge$
            employments $\neq$ EMPLOYMENT
        THEN
          ANY oo
          WHERE oo $\in$ EMPLOYMENT $-$ employments

```
            THEN
              employments := employments ∪ { oo } ||
              ee := oo ||
              salary(oo) := sal
            END
          END;

  set_boss(ee, boss)  ≙
        PRE ee ∈ employments ∧ boss ∈ EMR
        THEN
            employer(ee) := boss
        END

END
```

Thus the specification of the complete system is now:

```
MACHINE System(maxper, maxemployment, maxemployer)
SEES String_TYPE
EXTENDS
    Employed_Person(maxper)
INCLUDES
    Employment(EMPLOYER, maxemployment),
    Employer(maxemployer)
PROMOTES
    create_employment, create_employer
INVARIANT
    ∀ (job, company).(job ∈ employments ∧
                    company ∈ employers  ⇒
                        (job ∈ ran(staff(company))  ≡
                            company = employer(job) ) )
OPERATIONS
    add_job_to_company(job, company)  ≙
        PRE job ∈ employments ∧
            company ∈ employers ∧
            job ∉ dom(employer)
        THEN
            hire(company, job) ||
            set_boss(job, company)
        END

END
```

Of course, in a real system there would be many more operations required at this level, to remove a job from a company, to remove an employment from a person, etc. We have chosen to define and implement only a selection of these operations in order to focus on the essential issues of how such data structures and typical operations upon them are refined.

Because the specification of the system is built via the USES construct, we cannot, for example, refine **Employer** or **Employed_Person** to code independently of **Employment**.   This is because both **Employer** and **Employed_Person** depend upon the details of the data representation of **Employment**, which cannot be guaranteed to exist in any implementation of **Employment**.

Thus there is no non-trivial decomposition of the implementation that can be made on the basis of the specification (ie, we cannot separately define implementations **Employed_Person_1** of **Employed_Person** and **System_1** of **System**, with **System_1** importing or seeing **Employed_Person**). There are thus two alternatives from the three approaches discussed in Chapter 4: create a separate decomposition, with new specification machines and subsystems to assist in implementing part of the functionality of **System_1**, or to adopt a monolithic approach and import or see all necessary library components directly into **System_1**.

We adopt the latter approach here as it is the quickest way of getting the system up and running, but in terms of long-term quality and maintainability, the former is probably preferable.

The implementation is as follows (omitting the **add_job_to_company** operation):

IMPLEMENTATION
    System_1
REFINES
    System
SEES
    String_TYPE, Bool_TYPE, Scalar_TYPE
IMPORTS
    Pers_str_obj(maxper, maxper ∗ 30),
    Pers_fnc_obj($\mathbb{N}$ ∪ **Pers_STROBJ** ∪ **GENDER** ∪ **Jobs_SEQOBJ**,
            5, maxper),

    Employment_fnc_obj($\mathbb{N}$ ∪ **Employer_FNCOBJ**, 2, maxemployment),
    Employer_fnc_obj(**Staff_SEQOBJ**, 1, maxemployer),

    Staff_seq_obj(**EMPLOYMENT**, maxemployer, 20 ∗ maxemployer),
    Jobs_seq_obj(**EMPLOYMENT**, maxper, maxper ∗ 20)

Pers_fnc_obj *is used to provide records with 5 fields to implement the attributes of an employed person – there are at most* **maxper** *such records allowed in the system. The actual string values of the specification (for addresses) are instead implemented via references to strings (these references belong to the set* **Pers_STROBJ***), which are then dereferenced to actual strings in* **Pers_str_obj***.*

Because **STRING** *is a structured set it cannot be used as a parameter of an imported machine – all such parameters must be sets of tokens or unstructured discrete sets that can be viewed as subsets of* $\mathbb{N}$*.*

The bound **maxper** *here represents the total number of string references we will need at any time – ie, the same as the number of people. The second bound is the sum of the lengths of all the referenced strings. We assume that each string is at most 30 characters long.*

The **Jobs_seq_obj** *component is used to store the sequences of employments associated with each working person. The references to these sequences are contained in the set* **Jobs_SEQOBJ** *used as a parameter for the* **Pers_fnc_obj** *machine. Again at most* **maxper** *references for such sequences are needed, and we place a bound of 20 jobs per person in order to arrive at a total memory usage of* 20 ∗ **maxper**.

Employment_fnc_obj *represents the two fields of the employment objects.* **Employer_fnc_obj** *manages the one field of the employer objects – the contents of this field, a sequence of employments, is separately managed by the* **Staff_seq_obj** *component. We place a bound of 20 on the number of staff associated with an employer.*

CONSTANTS
  age_idx, address_idx, dob_idx, gender_idx,
  staff_idx, salary_idx, employer_idx, currjobs_idx
PROPERTIES
  EMPLOYMENT = Employment_FNCOBJ ∧
  EMPLOYER = Employer_FNCOBJ ∧
  Pers_FNCOBJ = PERSON ∧
  age_idx = 1 ∧
  address_idx = 2 ∧
  dob_idx = 3 ∧
  gender_idx = 4 ∧

  staff_idx = 1 ∧
  salary_idx = 1 ∧
  employer_idx = 2 ∧
  currjobs_idx = 5
INVARIANT
  employments = Employment_fnctok ∧
  employers = Employer_fnctok ∧
  persons = Pers_fnctok ∧
  ∀ pp.(pp ∈ persons ⇒
        age_idx ∈ dom(Pers_fncstruct(pp)) ∧
        Pers_fncstruct(pp)(age_idx) = age(pp) ∧

        address_idx ∈ dom(Pers_fncstruct(pp)) ∧
        Pers_strstruct(
            Pers_fncstruct(pp)(address_idx)) = address(pp) ∧

        dob_idx ∈ dom(Pers_fncstruct(pp)) ∧
        Pers_fncstruct(pp)(dob_idx) = date_of_birth(pp) ∧

        gender_idx ∈ dom(Pers_fncstruct(pp)) ∧
        Pers_fncstruct(pp)(gender_idx) = gender(pp) ∧

        (currjobs_idx ∈ dom(Pers_fncstruct(pp)) ⇒
         Staff_seqstruct(
            Pers_fncstruct(pp)(currjobs_idx)) =
                            current_jobs(pp))) ∧

$$\forall \ ee.(ee \ \in \ \text{employments} \ \Rightarrow$$
$$\text{salary\_idx} \ \in \ \text{dom}(\text{Employment\_fncstruct}(ee)) \ \wedge$$
$$\text{Employment\_fncstruct}(ee)(\text{salary\_idx}) \ = \ \text{salary}(ee))$$

The invariant is used to (partly) demonstrate how the specification data structures are implemented by those imported from the library components. For the address of a person a two-stage dereferencing, first by Pers_fncstruct and then by Pers_strstruct, must be used to get the actual string value in the implementation data that represents the specification data address(pp). *Similarly for the sequence values.*

OPERATIONS

pp ⟵ create_person(dob, gen, addr) ≙
    VAR bb, ss
    IN
        bb, pp ⟵ Pers_CRE_FNC_OBJ;
        IF (bb = TRUE)
        THEN
            Pers_STO_FNC_OBJ(pp, age_idx, 0);
            bb, ss ⟵ Pers_NEW_STR_OBJ(addr);
            Pers_STO_FNC_OBJ(pp, address_idx, ss);
            Pers_STO_FNC_OBJ(pp, dob_idx, dob);
            Pers_STO_FNC_OBJ(pp, gender_idx, gen)
        END
    END;

The Pers_NEW_STR_OBJ *operation creates a new string reference* ss *whose referenced value is the string* addr. *This reference then needs to be stored as the value of the address field of the record referenced by* pp.

birthday(pp) ≙
    VAR currage
    IN
        currage ⟵ Pers_VAL_FNC_OBJ(pp, age_idx);
        IF currage < 200
        THEN
            Pers_STO_FNC_OBJ(pp, age_idx, currage + 1)
        END
    END;

ca ⟵ current_age(pp) ≙
    ca ⟵ Pers_VAL_FNC_OBJ(pp, age_idx);

change_address(pp, addr) ≙
    VAR ss_ref, new_ref, bb
    IN
        ss_ref ⟵ Pers_VAL_FNC_OBJ(pp, address_idx);
        Pers_KIL_STR_OBJ(ss_ref);
        bb, new_ref ⟵ Pers_NEW_STR_OBJ(addr);
        Pers_STO_FNC_OBJ(pp, address_idx, new_ref)
    END;

```
add_job_to_company(job, company)  ≙  ...;

add_job(pp,jb)  ≙
    VAR bb, ss
    IN
        bb  ⟵  Pers_DEF_FNC_OBJ(pp, currjobs_idx);
        IF bb = TRUE
        THEN
            ss  ⟵  Pers_VAL_FNC_OBJ(pp, currjobs_idx);
            bb  ⟵  Jobs_PSH_SEQ_OBJ(ss, jb)
        ELSE
            bb, ss  ⟵  Jobs_CRE_SEQ_OBJ;
            bb  ⟵  Jobs_PSH_SEQ_OBJ(ss, jb);
            Pers_STO_FNC_OBJ(pp, currjobs_idx, ss)
        END
    END;

sal  ⟵  total_salary(pp)  ≙
    VAR bb, ss
    IN
        bb  ⟵  Pers_DEF_FNC_OBJ(pp, currjobs_idx);
        IF bb = TRUE
        THEN
            ss  ⟵  Pers_VAL_FNC_OBJ(pp, currjobs_idx);
            VAR ii, ll, tot, vv, job, uu
            IN
                ii := 1;
                tot := 0;
                ll  ⟵  Jobs_LEN_SEQ_OBJ(ss);
                WHILE (ii ≤ ll)
                DO
                    job  ⟵  Jobs_VAL_SEQ_OBJ(ss, ii);
                    vv  ⟵  Employment_VAL_FNC_OBJ(job, salary_idx);
                    uu  ⟵  SCL(vv);
                    tot := tot + uu;
                    ii := ii + 1
                VARIANT
                    ll + 1 − ii
                INVARIANT
                    ii + 1 ≤ ll
                END;
                sal := tot
            END
        ELSE
            sal := 0
        END
    END;
```

The loop in this operation is a simple iteration along the sequence of employments associated with a person, accumulating the sum of the salaries in the tot variable. The SCL operation is used to cast the value vv returned from an employment object (which is of a union type) to a scalar (numeric) value.

ee ⟵ create_employment(sal) ≙
    VAR bb
    IN
        bb, ee ⟵ Employment_CRE_FNC_OBJ;
        IF bb = TRUE
        THEN
            Employment_STO_FNC_OBJ(ee, salary_idx, sal)
        END
    END;

ee ⟵ create_employer ≙
    VAR bb, ss
    IN
        bb, ss ⟵ Staff_CRE_SEQ_OBJ;
        bb, ee ⟵ Employer_CRE_FNC_OBJ;
        IF bb = TRUE
        THEN
            Employer_STO_FNC_OBJ(ee, staff_idx, ss)
        END
    END

This operation creates an empty staff sequence ss and stores it as the staff attribute of the new employer reference ee.

END

The way this implementation was arrived at was perhaps counter to the ideals of formal methods: systematic rules were used to convert the abstract data model into data structures contained within library machines, and to convert operations on these data structures into calls to operations of these library machines. Once the implementation was written it was tested to ensure it had the expected behaviour (this revealed one minor error of omission) and then finalised. Proof obligations should also be generated and checked, although we would expect there to be unprovable obligations relating to the fact that the implementation places constraints on the length of address strings, number of employments per person and number of employments per company which the abstract specification does not make. To obtain a correct development these constraints would need to be inserted at the specification level in addition, via preconditions on the add_job, hire and add_job_to_company operations. The invariant of the loop in total_salary also needs to be more informative in order that we can prove that this operation does compute the sum.

The rules for transformation of ERA diagram derived data models into implementation data models are as follows (these rules are automated in the base generation tool of the B Toolkit). Assume first that we have an entity type Entity with attributes – possibly also including entity-valued attributes or associations – att_1, ..., att_n of types T_1, ..., T_n respectively. Then we express the sets of existing and possible instances of this entity type by a variable **entities** and set **ENTITY** as usual. To ensure compatibility with the corresponding implementation data, we need to place a size bound **max_entity** on **ENTITY**:

PROPERTIES
    card(ENTITY) = max_entity
VARIABLES
    entities, att_1, ..., att_n
INVARIANT
    entities $\subseteq$ ENTITY $\wedge$
    $att_1 \in$ **entities $\rightarrow$ T_1 $\wedge$**
    ...
    $att_n \in$ **entities $\rightarrow$ T_n**

These data structures will be implemented using a **Entity_fnc_obj** machine:

IMPLEMENTATION **Entity_1**
REFINES **Entity**
IMPORTS
    Entity_fnc_obj($S_1 \cup$ ... $\cup S_n$, n, max_entity)
    $\vdots$
CONSTANTS
    att_1_idx, ..., att_n_idx
    $\vdots$
PROPERTIES
    ENTITY = Entity_FNCOBJ $\wedge$
    att_1_idx = 1 $\wedge$ ... $\wedge$
    att_n_idx = n
    $\vdots$
INVARIANT
    entities = Entity_fnctok $\wedge$
    $\forall$ ee.(ee $\in$ entities $\Rightarrow$
            att_1(ee) = f_1(ee, att_1_idx) $\wedge$
            ...
            att_n(ee) = f_n(ee, att_n_idx))
    $\vdots$

S_i is the implementation equivalent of T_i. The details of the invariant clause depend upon the types T_i and on the nature of the attributes (ie., if they are partial rather than total a slightly different invariant clause is needed in the implementation, as illustrated in **System_1** above for the current jobs attribute).

There are various cases depending on the $\mathbf{T_i}$ (which are the mathematical representations of the $\mathbf{T_i}$). Let $\mathbf{T}$ be one of these attribute types, for the attribute **att**. Then the corresponding implementation elements are given by:

- if $\mathbf{T}$ is another entity type **entities2**, then we simply have that its implementation **S** is the corresponding **Entity2_FNCOBJ** reference set and that

$$\mathbf{att\_idx} \in \text{dom}(\mathbf{Entity\_fncstruct}(ee)) \ \wedge$$
$$\mathbf{att}(ee) = \mathbf{Entity\_fncstruct}(ee)(\mathbf{att\_idx})$$

in the invariant of **Entity_1**. In the "monolithic" approach we import **Entity2_fnc_obj** with suitable parameterisations into **Entity_1** (or into an implementation in which **Entity** is being implemented).

For a partial attribute this invariant clause would be replaced by:

$$(\mathbf{att\_idx} \in \text{dom}(\mathbf{Entity\_fncstruct}(ee)) \ \Rightarrow$$
$$\mathbf{att}(ee) = \mathbf{Entity\_fncstruct}(ee)(\mathbf{att\_idx}))$$

This is the case for **Entity** as **Employment** and **Entity2** as **Employer** in the above example, with **att** as **employer**.

- if $\mathbf{T}$ is a sequence type seq(T0) then its implementation is the set of references **Att_SEQOBJ** for sequences provided by a component **Att_seq_obj(S0, max_entity, k ∗ max_entity)** where S0 is the implementation of T0 and **k** is the maximum length of the **att** sequence values to be stored. In the invariant we need a two-stage dereferencing:

$$\mathbf{att\_idx} \in \text{dom}(\mathbf{Entity\_fncstruct}(ee)) \ \wedge$$
$$\mathbf{att}(ee) = \mathbf{Att\_seqstruct}(\mathbf{Entity\_fncstruct}(ee)(\mathbf{att\_idx}))$$

Similarly if **att** were partial. An example of this case is the attribute **current_jobs** of the **Person** entity.

- if $\mathbf{T}$ is **STRING** then it is implemented by **Att_STROBJ** and the library component **Att_str_obj(max_entity, k∗max_entity)** is imported, where **k** is the maximum length of string needed in the attribute. The invariant clause linking the abstract and implemented data is:

$$\mathbf{att\_idx} \in \text{dom}(\mathbf{Entity\_fncstruct}(ee)) \ \wedge$$
$$\mathbf{att}(ee) = \mathbf{Att\_strstruct}(\mathbf{Entity\_fncstruct}(ee)(\mathbf{att\_idx}))$$

In the case study the **address** attribute is an example of this case.

The case of set-valued attributes is similar, using the **Name_set_obj** machine from the libraries.

More creativity is needed in transcribing operations on the abstract attributes into operations that invoke operations of the library components to manipulate their implementations.

The first significant difference between the two levels is that at the implementation level we must always explicitly *create* new objects (via the **Name_CRE_SEQ_OBJ** or **Name_NEW_STR_OBJ** operations) for items which were just values (sequences or strings) at the specification level.

A creation operation returns a new reference plus a flag which indicates whether the creation was successful or not. All manipulations of the value linked to the reference are subsequently carried out via the reference. Thus the abstract specification statements:

    date_of_birth(oo) := **dob** ‖
    address(oo) := **addr** ‖

in **create_person** at the specification level become:

    Pers_STO_FNC_OBJ(pp, dob_idx, dob);
    bb, ss ⟵ **Pers_NEW_STR_OBJ(addr)**;
    Pers_STO_FNC_OBJ(pp, address_idx, ss);

at the implementation level – where we should probably check **bb** and take suitable reparation action if **bb** = **FALSE**, indicating an error.

Update operations on **att** are implemented by library operations such as **Name_STO_FNC_OBJ, Name_STO_SEQ_OBJ, Name_PSH_SEQ_OBJ, Name_STO_STR_OBJ** or other update operations. The simple case of **FNC** is illustrated above. The key point is that the state change effected at the implementation level must correspond (via the invariant relating the two levels) to a possible effect of the corresponding abstract operation. Thus the abstract transformation

    current_jobs(pp) := **current_jobs(pp)** ⌒ **[jb]**

corresponds to:

    ss ⟵ **Pers_VAL_FNC_OBJ(pp, currjobs_idx)**;
    bb ⟵ **Jobs_PSH_SEQ_OBJ(ss, jb)**

at the implementation level: "get the reference **ss** to **pp**'s sequence of jobs and push **jb** onto the end of the sequence it refers to".

Direct enquiries to aspects of structured data at the specification level need to be turned into (possibly several) enquiry operations at the implementation level. Thus the test

    IF **pp** ∈ dom(**current_jobs**)

in the specification is implemented by

    bb ⟵ **Pers_DEF_FNC_OBJ(pp, currjobs_idx)**;
    IF **bb** = **TRUE**

Finally we need to be aware of space constraints in the implementation, and to utilise **KIL** operations to reclaim space for unused references where possible. Thus we write

> ss_ref ⟵ Pers_VAL_FNC_OBJ(pp, address_idx);
> Pers_KIL_STR_OBJ(ss_ref);
> bb, new_ref ⟵ Pers_NEW_STR_OBJ(addr);
> Pers_STO_FNC_OBJ(pp, address_idx, new_ref)

to first delete the string reference **ss_ref** (and its associated storage) for the string value we are replacing, and then generate a new reference for the new address **addr** in the abstract assignment

> **address(pp) := addr**

An example execution of the resulting C system is:

```
0 System Menu

1 add_job_to_company
2 add_job
3 total_salary
4 create_person
5 birthday
6 current_age
7 change_address
8 create_employment
9 create_employer

10 Quit

System operation number? 4

 Input (NAT) Value for dob: 120566
 Input (GENDER enumerated element) for gen: female
 Input (STRING) Value for addr: "aerraewr"

 Token (PERSON/NAT) returned in pp: 1

System operation number? 8

 Input (NAT) Value for sal: 23000

 Token (EMPLOYMENT/NAT) returned in ee: 1

System operation number? 4

 Input (NAT) Value for dob: 300380
 Input (GENDER enumerated element) for gen: male
 Input (STRING) Value for addr: "aweawerafa"
```

```
Token (PERSON/NAT) returned in pp: 2

System operation number? 2

  Input (PERSON/NAT) Token for pp: 1
  Input (EMPLOYMENT/NAT) Token for jb: 1

System operation number? 3

  Input (PERSON/NAT) Token for pp: 1

  Value (NAT) returned in sal: 23000

System operation number? 3

  Input (PERSON/NAT) Token for pp: 2

  Value (NAT) returned in sal: 0

System operation number? 8

  Input (NAT) Value for sal: 55450

  Token (EMPLOYMENT/NAT) returned in ee: 2

System operation number? 8

  Input (NAT) Value for sal: 120250

  Token (EMPLOYMENT/NAT) returned in ee: 3

System operation number? 2

  Input (PERSON/NAT) Token for pp: 2
  Input (EMPLOYMENT/NAT) Token for jb: 2

System operation number? 2

  Input (PERSON/NAT) Token for pp: 2
  Input (EMPLOYMENT/NAT) Token for jb: 3

System operation number? 3

  Input (PERSON/NAT) Token for pp: 2

  Value (NAT) returned in sal: 175700

System operation number?
```

Here only the salary computation part of the system has been tested. Further test cases would be constructed for the other relationships, entities and operations.

5.2 Mine Pump Control

This is a classic example of a real-time control system. A controller for a mine pumping system is to be devised to pump water out of a coal mine when the water level reaches a critical level. However for safety reasons the pump should only operate when the level of methane is below a critical level. A data and control flow diagram for the system is shown in Figure 5.1 (using the notation of Ward/Mellors RTSA [49]).

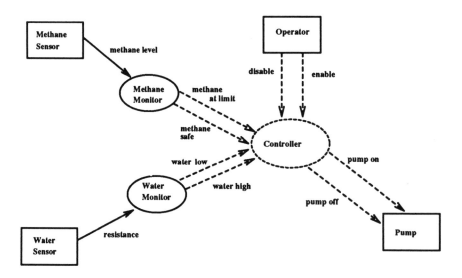

Figure 5.1: Data and Control Flow for Mine System

Data flows such as the level of resistance between two contacts (used to sense the presence of water at a certain location) or in a semiconductor sensor for methane are marked as solid lines. These flows are converted into discrete events by the appropriate monitors (probably implemented in hardware, but this is not a concern of the specification as yet). The main operation of the system is to transform flows of events from the two sensors, and from the user of the system, into a suitable flow of events to the pump (controller). We will show that a B AMN specification of the system can be given which is closely related to the analysis models in RTSA/statechart notation.

5.2.1 Specification

The sensors are represented as follows.

MACHINE **MethaneSensor**
SETS
    MSTATE $=$ { **mok, mnotok** }
VARIABLES
    mstate
INVARIANT
    mstate $\in$ **MSTATE**
INITIALISATION
    mstate $:=$ **mok**
OPERATIONS
    sample_methane $\hat{=}$
        BEGIN
            mstate $:\in$ **MSTATE**
        END;

    ml $\longleftarrow$ **methane_level** $\hat{=}$
        ml $:=$ **mstate**

END

MACHINE **WaterSensor**
SETS
    WSTATE $=$ { **whigh, wlow** }
VARIABLES
    wstate
INVARIANT
    wstate $\in$ **WSTATE**
INITIALISATION
    wstate $:=$ **wlow**
OPERATIONS
    sample_water $\hat{=}$
        BEGIN
            wstate $:\in$ **WSTATE**
        END;

    wl $\longleftarrow$ **water_level** $\hat{=}$
        wl $:=$ **wstate**

END

The **sample_water** and **sample_methane** operations model the non-deterministic (or uncontrolled) behaviour of the real-world objects which this component monitors. We provide separate operations for updating and enquiry in order to conform to the command/query discipline of [51].

The controller of the system has the statechart shown in Figure 5.2. As a

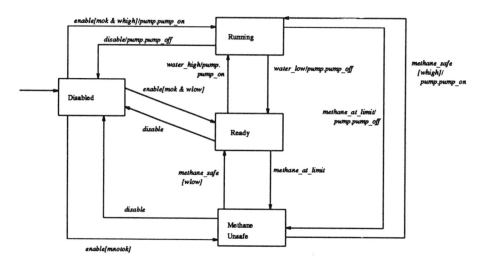

Figure 5.2: Statechart of Controller

result we have the description:

MACHINE **Controller**
SEES **WaterSensor, MethaneSensor**
INCLUDES **Pump**
SETS
   CSTATE = { disabled, running, ready, methane_unsafe }
VARIABLES
   cstate
INVARIANT
   cstate ∈ **CSTATE**
INITIALISATION
   cstate := **disabled**
OPERATIONS
   enable ≙
      IF **wstate** = **whigh** ∧ **mstate** = **mok**
      THEN
         cstate := **running** ||
         pump_on
      ELSE
          IF **mstate** = **mnotok**
          THEN **cstate** := **methane_unsafe**
          ELSE **cstate** := **ready**
          END
      END;

   methane_at_limit ≙
      BEGIN
         cstate := **methane_unsafe** ||
         IF **cstate** = **running**

```
                THEN
                    pump_off
                END
          END ;

   methane_safe  ≙
       IF wstate  =  whigh
       THEN
              cstate  :=  running  ||
              pump_on
       ELSE
              cstate  :=  ready
       END ;

   water_high  ≙
       IF cstate  =  ready
       THEN
              cstate  :=  running  ||
              pump_on
       END ;

    water_low  ≙
         BEGIN
              cstate  :=  ready  ||
              IF cstate  =  running
              THEN
                     pump_off
              END
          END ;

   disable  ≙
         BEGIN
              cstate  :=  disabled  ||
              IF cstate  =  running
              THEN
                     pump_off
              END
         END

END
```

Notice the use of the || operator here to avoid premature decisions regarding
the order of execution of state updates. **Pump** is a machine that provides
two operations **pump_on** and **pump_off**. As with the sensor machines it will
be implemented by hardware in the actual system, so does not need to be
developed to code. Indeed, if we wrote **Pump** as:

```
MACHINE  Pump
OPERATIONS
    pump_on  ≙  skip ;
```

        pump_off $\hat{=}$ skip
END

then it would be valid to use SEES **Pump** in place of INCLUDES **Pump** in
Controller, because no state would be modified by the operation calls on
Pump.

        The operation **methane_at_limit** should only be performed if **cstate** $\neq$
disabled. This condition could, therefore, be added as a precondition for the
operation, in order to provide formal documentation to assist in later maintenance activities, although strictly these conditions are *guards* rather than
preconditions. Similarly for other operations.

MACHINE **System**
OPERATIONS
    operate(bound) $\hat{=}$
            PRE **bound** $\in$ $\mathbb{N}$
            THEN
                    SKIP
            END
END

The **System** machine coordinates the interaction between the user, sensors
and controller, regularly sampling the sensors and requesting the controller to
take appropriate action. It plays the role of the input processes on Figure 5.1.

5.2.2   Design and Implementation

The implementation of the system uses a 'polling loop' to repeatedly monitor
the sensor states and take appropriate action on changes of state. Detailed
analysis of the timing properties of the resulting code would be needed in order
to prove that required responsiveness properties hold.

IMPLEMENTATION **System_1**
REFINES **System**
IMPORTS
    Controller, WaterSensor, MethaneSensor, Interface
OPERATIONS
    operate(bound) $\hat{=}$
            VAR **ii, ml, wl, com, old_ml, old_wl**
            IN
                ii := 0;
                old_wl := **wlow**;
                old_ml := **mok**;
                set_command;
                com $\longleftarrow$ **get_user_command**;
                IF **com** = **enable_com**
                THEN **enable**
                ELSE **disable**

```
END;
WHILE ii ≤ bound ∧ com ≠ disable_com
DO
    sample_water;
    wl ⟵ water_level;
    sample_methane;
    ml ⟵ methane_level;
    IF ml ≠ old_ml
    THEN
        IF ml = mnotok
        THEN
            methane_at_limit
        ELSE
            methane_safe
        END
    END;
    IF wl ≠ old_wl
    THEN
        IF wl = whigh
        THEN
            water_high
        ELSE
            water_low
        END
    END;
    old_ml := ml;
    old_wl := wl;
    ii := ii + 1;
    set_command;
    com ⟵ get_user_command
    INVARIANT ii ≤ bound + 1 ∧ ii ∈ ℕ
    VARIANT bound + 1 − ii
    END
END

END
```

set_command and get_user_command are operations of the interface to the user, defined below. In the final production system, the interface would be executing in a separate task, concurrently with the controller, which would simply enquire about the most recent user command received by the interface using the get_user_command call. The use of set_command here is simply to assist in testing the controller implementation.

Notice that the methane level is accessed after the water level, since the system must react more rapidly to dangerous levels of methane than to high water levels.

Interface simply consists of:

MACHINE Interface
SETS

USERCOMMAND = { enable_com, disable_com }
VARIABLES
   istate
INVARIANT
   istate ∈ **USERCOMMAND**
INITIALISATION
   istate := **enable_com**
OPERATIONS
  set_command $\widehat{=}$
       ANY **com**
       WHERE **com** ∈ **USERCOMMAND**
       THEN
          istate := **com**
       END;

  com ⟵ **get_user_command** $\widehat{=}$
      com := **istate**
END

Controller can itself be implemented as follows (for the B Toolkit, **cstate** needs to be encapsulated in a library machine **Mines_Vvar(CSTATE)**):

IMPLEMENTATION **Controller_1**
REFINES
   Controller
SEES
   WaterSensor,
   MethaneSensor
IMPORTS
   Pump, Mines_Vvar(CSTATE)
INVARIANT
   Mines_Vvar = **cstate**
INITIALISATION
   Mines_STO_VAR(disabled)
OPERATIONS

enable $\widehat{=}$
   VAR **ws, ms**
   IN
      ws ⟵ **water_level**;
      ms ⟵ **methane_level**;
     IF **ws** = **whigh** ∧ **ms** = **mok**
     THEN
        pump_on;
        Mines_STO_VAR(running)
     ELSE
       IF **ms** = **mnotok**
       THEN
          Mines_STO_VAR(methane_unsafe)
       ELSE
          Mines_STO_VAR(ready)

```
                  END
              END
          END;

   methane_at_limit  ≙
       VAR cs
       IN
           cs  ⟵  Mines_VAL_VAR;
           IF cs = running
           THEN
               pump_off
           END;
           Mines_STO_VAR(methane_unsafe)
       END;

   methane_safe  ≙
       VAR ws
       IN
           ws  ⟵  water_level;
           IF ws = whigh
           THEN
               pump_on;
               Mines_STO_VAR(running)
           ELSE
               Mines_STO_VAR(ready)
           END
       END;

   water_high  ≙
       VAR cs
       IN
           cs  ⟵  Mines_VAL_VAR;
           IF cs = ready
           THEN
               pump_on;
               Mines_STO_VAR(running)
           END
       END;

   water_low  ≙
       VAR cs
       IN
           cs  ⟵  Mines_VAL_VAR;
           IF cs = running
           THEN
               pump_off
           END;
           Mines_STO_VAR(ready)
       END;
```

disable $\hat{=}$
   VAR **cs**
   IN
      cs $\longleftarrow$ Mines_VAL_VAR;
      IF **cs** = **running**
      THEN
         pump_off
      END;
      Mines_STO_VAR(disabled)
   END

END

The structure of the development is shown in Figure 5.3. Notice that because no update operations are applied to the sensors by the **Controller**, the implementation **Controller_1** only needs to use the SEES inclusion mechanism, rather than IMPORTS. This provides a formal documentation of the degree of coupling between these modules, which can be of assistance during maintenance.

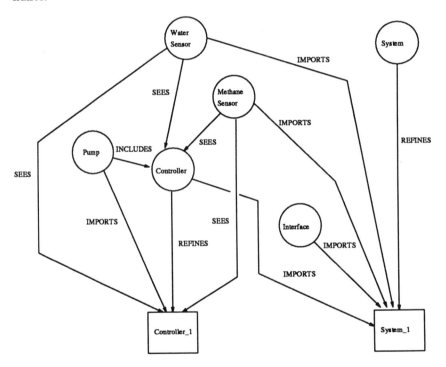

Figure 5.3: Structure of Mine Controller Development

For the purpose of a prototype, we could implement **WaterSensor** by a machine which queries the user for the sensor readings:

IMPLEMENTATION **WaterSensor_1**

REFINES
    WaterSensor
SEES **basic_io**
IMPORTS
    Water_Vvar(WSTATE)
INVARIANT
    Water_Vvar = wstate
INITIALISATION
    Water_STO_VAR(wlow)
OPERATIONS

  sample_water $\widehat{=}$
    VAR **ws**
    IN
        ws ⟵ GET_PROMPT_NBR("Enter Water Monitor State :
                                          0 (low), 1 (high): ", 2);

        IF **ws = 0**
        THEN
            Water_STO_VAR(wlow)
        ELSE
            Water_STO_VAR(whigh)
        END
    END;

  wl ⟵ water_level $\widehat{=}$
      wl ⟵ Water_VAL_VAR

END

Similarly for the **MethaneSensor**. For the **Pump**, we simply report the action
being undertaken:

IMPLEMENTATION **Pump_1**
REFINES
    Pump
SEES
    basic_io
OPERATIONS

pump_on $\widehat{=}$
    BEGIN
        PUT_STR("Activating pump");
        NWL(1)
    END;

pump_off $\widehat{=}$
    BEGIN
        PUT_STR("Deactivating pump");
        NWL(1)
    END

END

Interface_1 is similarly constructed (although we must IMPORT **basic_io** in just one implementation in a development that uses it, and we choose to do this in **Interface_1**):

IMPLEMENTATION
    Interface_1
REFINES
    Interface
IMPORTS
    basic_io, Interface_Vvar(USERCOMMAND)
INITIALISATION
    Interface_STO_VAR(enable_com)
OPERATIONS

  set_command $\widehat{=}$
     VAR cc
     IN
      cc ⟵ GET_PROMPT_NBR("Enter command (0 to enable,
                               1 to disable): ", 2);
      IF cc = 0
      THEN
        Interface_STO_VAR(enable_com)
      ELSE
        Interface_STO_VAR(disable_com)
      END
     END;

  com ⟵ get_user_command $\widehat{=}$
    com ⟵ Interface_VAL_VAR

END

Thus we obtain execution runs as follows:

```
Input (NAT) Value for bound: 3
Enter command (0 to enable, 1 to disable): 0
Enter Water Monitor State: 0 (low), 1 (high): 1
Enter Methane Monitor State: 0 (ok), 1 (notok): 0
Activating pump
Enter command (0 to enable, 1 to disable): 0
Enter Water Monitor State: 0 (low), 1 (high): 0
Enter Methane Monitor State: 0 (ok), 1 (notok): 0
Deactivating pump
Enter command (0 to enable, 1 to disable): 0
Enter Water Monitor State: 0 (low), 1 (high): 1
Enter Methane Monitor State: 0 (ok), 1 (notok): 1
Enter command (0 to enable, 1 to disable): 0
```

5.3 Vending Machine

This development is an example of the "continuity of structure" approach. It will also be used to illustrate the steps which are taken to develop systems using a toolkit for B.

5.3.1 Specification

The structure of this development is shown in Figure 5.4. Library machines are not shown, nor are the relationships between **Vend_data** and the implementation components (it is SEEN by each of these). Notice that we have factored

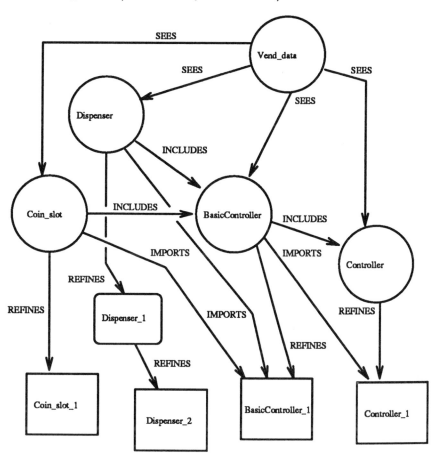

Figure 5.4: Development Architecture of Vending Machine Development

out all type and constant declarations into the shared component **Vend_data**. The rationale for this decision is that there would otherwise be duplication of these data items (declared in **C.mch**, say) in implementations **B_1.imp** where

B.mch INCLUDES **C.mch** and **B_1.imp** IMPORTS **C.mch**. Such situations arise when a continuity of structure approach is taken.

The machine encapsulating shared data is:

MACHINE **Vend_data**
SETS
  CSTATE = { coin_present, coin_absent };
  DSTATE = { stocked, unstocked }
CONSTANTS
  COINS, STATE
PROPERTIES
  COINS = { 5, 10 } ∧
  STATE = { 0, 5, 10 }
END

In the eventual implementation of the system components, there will be no direct reference to **COINS** or **STATE**. Instead, tests $cc \in$ **COINS** will become disjunctions $cc = 5 \lor cc = 10$, for instance.

The **Coin_slot** machine is as follows:

MACHINE **Coin_slot**
SEES **Vend_data**
VARIABLES
  cstate, current_coin
INVARIANT
  cstate ∈ **CSTATE** ∧
  current_coin ∈ **COINS**
INITIALISATION
  cstate := coin_absent ||
  current_coin :∈ **COINS**
OPERATIONS
  give_change(cc) $\widehat{=}$
      PRE cc ∈ **COINS**
      THEN
          cstate := coin_absent
      END;

  coin ⟵ accept_coin $\widehat{=}$
      ANY cc
      WHERE cc ∈ **COINS**
      THEN
          current_coin := cc ||
          cstate := coin_present ||
          coin := cc
      END

END

cstate records whether a coin is present in the slot or not. accept_coin informs the remainder of the system about the particular coin which has been most recently entered by the user.

There are three proof obligations for internal consistency of this machine, all of which are automatically provable (by Version 3.0 of the B-Core (UK) B Toolkit).

Dispenser is:

```
MACHINE Dispenser
SEES Vend_data
VARIABLES
  dstate, given
INVARIANT
  dstate ∈ DSTATE ∧
  given ∈ ℕ
INITIALISATION
  dstate := unstocked ||
  given := 0
OPERATIONS
  restock ≙
    dstate := stocked;

  give_drink ≙
    PRE dstate = stocked
    THEN
      dstate :∈ DSTATE ||
      given := given + 1
    END

END
```

There are 4 internal consistency proof obligations, each of which is provable automatically.

The **BasicController** has the form:

```
MACHINE BasicController
SEES Vend_data
INCLUDES Dispenser, Coin_slot
PROMOTES restock, accept_coin
VARIABLES
  state      / *   The current change held by the
                     machine * /
INVARIANT
  state ∈ STATE
INITIALISATION
  state := 0
OPERATIONS
  accept_10 ≙
    BEGIN
      IF state = 0
      THEN
        state := 10
      ELSE
```

```
            state  :=  0
        END ||

        IF state  =  5
        THEN
          give_drink
        ELSE
          IF state  =  10
          THEN
               give_drink || give_change(5)
          END
        END
      END;

accept_5  ≙
    BEGIN
        state  :=  (state + 5) mod 15 ||
        IF state = 10
        THEN
             give_drink
        END
    END

END
```

Notice that the preconditions of **give_drink** are not ensured by the **accept_10** or **accept_5** operations. This error is identified by the following unprovable proof obligations:

$$state = 5 \;\Rightarrow\; dstate = stocked$$

and

$$state = 10 \;\Rightarrow\; dstate = stocked$$

for **accept_10**, and

$$state = 10 \;\Rightarrow\; dstate = stocked$$

for **accept_5**.

It is possible to claim that these omissions are acceptable, because we expect to provide an operation **give_drink** without a precondition in the eventual implementation: such an implementation will simply provide a helpful error message to the user if there is no drink in stock (but the vending machine will, nonetheless, swallow their coins).

In a fully formal development, we should instead check that **dstate = stocked** before invoking **give_drink**. This test would be implemented in refinements of **BasicController** by invoking a suitable enquiry operation on **Dispenser**.

Animation of **BasicController** can be used to explore the specified behaviour in the main scenarios of use of the system:

- trying to get a drink by entering sufficient coins when there are no available drinks;
- obtaining a drink when there is sufficient stock by entering exact change;
- obtaining a drink and change by entering more money than necessary.

An example of the third case is:

```
Initialising ...

Nondeterminacy

    current_coinx? 5
=====================================
        State display for BasicController.mch

    Current State

        current_coin  5
        cstate  coin_absent
        given  0
        dstate  unstocked
        state  0
=====================================
Operation?
> accept_10

    Current State

        current_coin  5
        cstate  coin_absent
        given  0
        dstate  unstocked
        state  10
=====================================
Operation?
> restock

    Current State

        current_coin  5
        cstate  coin_absent
        given  0
        dstate  stocked
        state  10
=====================================
Operation?
> accept_10
```

Nondeterminacy

    dstatex?: {stocked,unstocked}
>stocked

  Current State

    current_coin 5
    cstate coin_absent
    given 1
    dstate stocked
    state 0

Notice that the state of all included components is also shown, together with changes on the state of these components resulting from invocations of their operations from **BasicController**.

The controller itself is then formed from **BasicController**:

MACHINE **Controller**
INCLUDES **BasicController**
SEES **Vend_data**
PROMOTES **restock**
OPERATIONS
    enter_coin $\hat{=}$
        ANY cc
        WHERE cc $\in$ COINS
        THEN
            IF cc = 5
            THEN
                accept_5
            ELSE
                accept_10
            END
        END

END

The unprovable obligations from **BasicController** also appear as unprovable obligations for **Controller**.

5.3.2   Refinement

In refining this system towards code we have adopted the continuity of structure approach: if **A** SEES **B** at the specification level then a refinement or implementation of **A** also SEES **B**. INCLUDES becomes IMPORTS at implementation stages. Library machines providing scalar data structures are used to implement the data of the system.

Thus, for **Coin_slot**, we have:

IMPLEMENTATION **Coin_slot_2**
REFINES
   Coin_slot
IMPORTS
   Coin_Nvar(10), Coin_Vvar(CSTATE)
SEES **Vend_data, basic_io**
INVARIANT
   current_coin = **Coin_Nvar** $\wedge$
   cstate = **Coin_Vvar**
INITIALISATION
   Coin_STO_VAR(coin_absent)
OPERATIONS

  give_change(cc) $\widehat{=}$
     IF cc = 5 $\vee$ cc = 10
     THEN
       Coin_STO_VAR(coin_absent);
       PUT_STR("Your change is : ");
       PUT_NBR(cc)
     END;

  coin $\longleftarrow$ accept_coin $\widehat{=}$
     VAR cc
     IN
       cc $\longleftarrow$ **GET_PROMPT_NBR**("Enter coin : (5 or 10) ",10);
       IF (cc $\neq$ 5 $\wedge$ cc $\neq$ 10)
       THEN
         PUT_STR("Wrong denomination : assuming its a 5");
         cc := 5
       END;
       Coin_STO_VAR(coin_present);
       Coin_STO_NVAR(cc);
       coin := cc
     END

END

Notice that reference to the abstract set-valued constant **COINS** has been re-placed by implementable tests. **Coin_Nvar(10)** encapsulates an integer vari-able **Coin_Nvar** in the range 0 to 10, and operations on this. The cc $\longleftarrow$ **GET_PROMPT_NBR**(string, bound) operation gets the number cc from the input stream, prompting the user with **string**, and accepting only numbers up to **bound**.

Refinement proof obligation is performed, resulting in 17 obligations, of which 10 are automatically proved. The initialisation obligation

   $0 \in$ **COINS**

is clearly false – this notifies us that we should have included a
Coin_STO_NVAR(5) or **Coin_STO_NVAR**(10) statement in the concrete
initialisation.

Refinement of **Dispenser** is carried out in two stages. In the first stage
we introduce a variable which records the actual level of stock held by the
dispenser:

REFINEMENT **Dispenser_1**
REFINES
    Dispenser
SEES **Vend_data**
VARIABLES
    drinks, given1
INVARIANT
    drinks $\in$ $\mathbb{N}$ $\land$
    ((**drinks** = 0) $\equiv$ (**dstate** = **unstocked**)) $\land$
    given1 = **given**
INITIALISATION
    drinks := 0 || **given1** := 0
OPERATIONS

  restock $\hat{=}$
    BEGIN
        drinks := **drinks** + 10
    END;

  give_drink $\hat{=}$
    PRE **drinks** > 0
    THEN
        drinks := **drinks** − 1 ||
        given1 := **given1** + 1
    END

END

We have chosen an arbitrary number 10 of new drinks to be added when a
restock is performed. The invariant also implies that **dstate** = **stocked** is
equivalent to **drinks** > 0: writing this equivalence explicitly in the invariant
may assist in discharging proof obligations (although it will also give rise to
new obligations). An alternative is to use an assertion, as discussed in Section
3.4.1. Thus the original and refined specifications of **give_drink** have logically
equivalent preconditions under the refinement relation.

In turn, this refinement is implemented by:

IMPLEMENTATION **Dispenser_2**
REFINES
    Dispenser_1
IMPORTS
    basic_io, Dispenser_Nvar(10000),
    Given_Nvar(10000)

SEES
    BooLTYPE, Vend_data
INVARIANT
    Dispenser_Nvar = drinks ∧
    Given_Nvar = given1
OPERATIONS

restock ≙
    BEGIN
        Dispenser_ADD_NVAR(10);
        PUT_STR("Restocking ")
    END;

give_drink ≙
    VAR bb
    IN
        bb ⟵ Dispenser_LEQ_NVAR(0);
        IF bb = TRUE
        THEN
            PUT_STR("Out of stock − − Sorry")
        ELSE
            PUT_STR("Here is your drink");
            Given_INC_NVAR;
            Dispenser_DEC_NVAR
        END
    END

END

The **drinks** variable is implemented by the variable **Dispenser_Nvar** encapsulated in the **Dispenser_Nvar** machine, and **given** is implemented by the variable **Given_Nvar** encapsulated in the **Given_Nvar** machine.

The first unprovable obligation

Dispenser_Nvar\$2 + 10 ≤ 10000

for **restock** indicates that we should have placed the bound 10000 on **drinks** in the earlier development stage. In the present toolsets for the B method all numeric types are finite, and if a fully formal and proved development is required, then suitable bounds for numeric values must be identified at the abstract specification level. This requirement can lead to un-natural specifications, and is usually relaxed if a less formal development path is sufficient, as is the case here.

The proof obligations for **give_drink** concern the differences between the actions which are taken in the implementation from those taken in the refinement when **drinks** = 0. Since the refinement operation is preconditioned by **drinks** > 0, the implementation is allowed to carry out any state transition in this case, and so it can be proved correct (in this case, by using proof by contradiction).

5.3.3   Implementation

The implementation of **BasicController** has the form:

```
IMPLEMENTATION BasicController_1
REFINES BasicController
IMPORTS
    Controller_Nvar(30),  Coin_slot,  Dispenser
SEES Vend_data
PROMOTES restock, accept_coin
INVARIANT
    Controller_Nvar  =  state
OPERATIONS

  accept_10  ≙
    VAR oldstate
    IN
        oldstate  ⟵  Controller_VAL_NVAR;
        IF oldstate  =  0
        THEN
            Controller_STO_NVAR(10)
        ELSE
            Controller_STO_NVAR(0)
        END;

        IF oldstate  =  5
        THEN
            give_drink
        ELSE
            IF oldstate  =  10
            THEN
                give_drink;
                give_change(5)
            END
        END
    END;

  accept_5  ≙
    VAR oldstate
    IN
        oldstate  ⟵  Controller_VAL_NVAR;
        Controller_ADD_NVAR(5);
        Controller_MOD_NVAR(15);
        IF oldstate  =  10
        THEN
            give_drink
        END
    END

END
```

We have selected a bounded natural number variable **Controller_Nvar** with maximum value 30 to represent the amount of stored change. As at earlier development stages, we still have the problem that the embedded calls to the **Dispenser** may violate the precondition of the **give_drink** operation: this has been dealt with in practice by making the implementation of **give_drink** completely robust.

Finally, **Controller** is directly implemented:

```
IMPLEMENTATION Controller_1
REFINES Controller
IMPORTS BasicController
SEES Vend_data
PROMOTES restock    / * restock is used to implement itself  * /
OPERATIONS

    enter_coin  ≘
        VAR cc
        IN
            cc  ⟵  accept_coin;
            IF cc = 5
            THEN
                accept_5
            ELSE
                accept_10
            END
        END

END
```

An advantage of splitting the controller of the system into **Controller** and **BasicController** is that the definition of the top-level operation **enter_coin** has been simplified: the code of the conditional branches has been replaced by operation calls. As a result, the refinement proof for **enter_coin** is simplified, as it makes use of the specifications of **accept_5** and **accept_10**, rather than their implementations.

To complete the development, we also need to provide an implementation of **Vend_data**. This is the trivial implementation

```
IMPLEMENTATION Vend_data_1
REFINES
    Vend_data
END
```

Some statistics about the development are as follows (in lines of code). Notice the growth in size and complexity of the system from specification to implementation and code, and the contribution to the overall system size made by the library modules.

Development stage	New modules	Library/Interface modules
Specification	164	1340
Implementation	191	–
Code	306	1672

Exercises

(1) Suitable for term project. Investigate further techniques for the specification and development of reactive systems using B. What extensions could be added to the language to make it more suitable for this domain? Alternatively, investigate how it could be combined with a suitable formalism for reactive systems, such as CSP [36].

(2) Suitable for term project. Investigate test case generation from B specifications. This could build on existing techniques for Z (see the Z User Meeting proceedings for relevant papers).

Chapter 6

Conclusions

At present, by far the largest use of formal methods in industry is in the specification of software components, rather than in later development stages. Further, when we take into consideration the lack of methodological support for refinement of such specifications it is clear that many "formal developments" are nothing more than "formally *contrived* developments". The result is that implementations, quite often, behave in a manner that is non-congruent with respect to their specifications. This causes many problems for the users and eventual maintainers of such systems. The B method avoids these problems because it allows developers to develop systems in a rigorous/verifiable way.

Another problem associated with the use of most so called formal development methods, is their lack of support for requirements modelling. It is now generally accepted that bad designs and implementations arise, not only from imprecisely stated requirements, but also from inadequately understood requirements (on the behalf of the system developers). In this book we have shown how ideas from object-oriented analysis can be used to model requirements so that formal specification can be more easily facilitated. This mapping from analysis to specification means that a client can more easily validate such specifications.

The B method has been built around the need to support proof in a practical manner, and the present tool support for the method is one of the most advanced in this respect for any formal method. An equally important aspect is the capability to 'execute' formal specifications. Execution (or animation) is useful from two standpoints:

1. internal validation (for the developer) that their design decisions satisfy the behaviour and functionality of the previous design phases and ultimately the specification;
2. external validation (for the client/customer) that the development corresponds to the intended product.

The importance of early validation cannot be over-emphasised. It enables early resolution of perceived problems before such problems become too expensive to remedy. The B method via the concept of animation facilitates the validation of specifications.

There are two main approaches to the formal development of code: (1) *invent and verify* [60] (2) *program transformation* [57]. The invent and verify approach places emphasis on a developer to conjecture refinement steps (i.e. data or procedural refinements) and to subsequently prove the correctness of these steps. The main tasks involved in this approach are to:

- identify refinement steps;
- prove the correctness of refinements.

An advantage of the invent and verify approach is that the developer is allowed as much freedom as necessary in choosing appropriate refinements. This in turn can lead to expressive developments largely controlled by the developer. A disadvantage of this approach is the burden of proof imposed on the developer. The more creative a developer is, in choosing refinement steps, the greater the likelihood of more complex refinement proofs. In most cases of non-trivial development proof becomes infeasible, due to the management overhead of orchestrating proof, e.g. axiomatisation of mathematical properties and creation of tactics.

The program transformation approach places emphasis on automated (computer assisted) refinement steps. The basis of this assistance comes in the form of transformation rules which are applied to patterns of a development in order to produce a provably correct refinement (i.e. by the replacement of another pattern). The main tasks involved in this approach are:

- produce reusable transformation rules;
- prove the correctness of each transformation rule.

The above tasks must be completed and results integrated into a development tool, prior to using the approach. Some advantages of adopting this approach include reduction of the burden, on behalf of a developer, in deciding which data/algorithmic refinement to undertake, and elimination of refinement proofs. The former can be achieved via the use of intelligent selection techniques which determine applicable rules that might be applied at any stage of development. The latter advantage follows from the fact that the rules have already been proved to be correct.

A disadvantage for a developer, using a transformation system, is the lack of freedom afforded concerning the choice of appropriate refinement steps. That is, a developer might be able to think of a more intuitive way of producing a refinement than they are allowed to use via the system.

The B method allows both the invent and verify and the program transformation approach to be accommodated during a development. In this way the best of both worlds can be achieved.

Both approaches contribute positive and negative effects on issues related to maintainability and efficiency. Thus, an implementation might be more maintainable on the basis that it reflects the structure of a specification. Alternatively a transformation system can be used to record development steps and then to subsequently "replay" some of these steps for a modified development.

If we contrast what may be termed as traditional software development with that of the B approach, we see that the latter has some immediate advantages:

- the B method (with its supporting tools) enables the creation of rapid-evolutionary prototypes. These animatable specifications can be tested to see whether early designs are conformant with the domain requirements. Any deficiencies can be rectified immediately, without incurring unnecessary costs later on in the development. Due to the highly modular way systems can be constructed in AMN, the effects of change can be localised. That is, if it is known that only a certain aspect of the specification is incorrect, due to the structuring facilities, only those parts affected need be re-verified. This saves needless repetition of work and ultimately saves time and money. It is clear that, using traditional techniques, much analysis would have to be undertaken in order to prove that changes have local effects. The orchestration of this analysis would undoubtedly require some form of manual maintenance which only serves to increase the cost of developments;
- the B method does not deal specifically with issues concerning the most efficient way of implementing algorithms. It does however, provide efficient implementations for those specifications whose data structures can be mapped into its library machines, which are written according to the method;
- formal proof can be provided for all of the development. Moreover due to the nature of abstract machines it is possible to re-use large parts of AMN developments in other developments. The basis of this re-use derives from the ability of abstract machines to encapsulate data and operation definitions. It is, therefore, possible for a machine to be implemented in a completely different manner to its specification or preceding refinements, and provided the required services are satisfied this new machine is a refinement of the old.

Like many formal methods, the B method lacks a notion of real numbers. As such it is not possible to directly express such numbers and moreover to reason about specifications containing them. This is not a severe limitation but it does make modelling of many numerical applications difficult.

Many of the complex safety critical systems not only involve the use of real numbers, but exhibit various forms of concurrency. This is another issue not presently covered by the B method. Some initial ideas are described in the paper [43].

Many writers of texts on formal development methods fail to remember that most software engineers are not accomplished formal methods specialists. They do not attempt to show how their method relates to other notations/methods. In this book the relation of AMN to object-oriented concepts has been detailed. Within this framework it is possible to use object-oriented analysis and map these directly on to abstract machines. The benefit of this approach is that it encourages structured composite specifications/designs and leads to reusable developments. As a result proof is simplified, as proof can be conducted on a compositional basis. The close relationship between Z and B implies that those developers, familiar with Z, can use the Z notation as a specification language and then proceed to translate into AMN where it is possible to use tool support to produce running code.

Other information on B can be found in references [1, 2, 10, 11, 17, 34, 37, 42, 48] and via the web page http://www.tees.ac.uk/bresource/b.html. A UK-based mailing list exists for B issues. To join it, mail the message body: subscribe b-talk to b-talk-request@tees.ac.uk. The B User Group also has a mailing list. To join it, mail the message subscribe bug to listserv@estas1.inrets.fr. Its FAQ can be obtained from ftp:// ftp.inrets.fr/ESTAS/BUG/Admin/FAQ. B issues are also discussed on the comp.specification newsgroup.

Bibliography

[1] J R Abrial, *A Refinement Case Study (Using the Abstract Machine Notation)*, Proceedings of 4th Refinement Workshop, J M Morris and R C Shaw (Editors), Workshops in Computing, Springer Verlag, 1991.

[2] J R Abrial, **The B Book: Assigning Programs to Meaning**, Cambridge University Press, 1995, to appear.

[3] M Ben-Ari, **Mathematical Logic for Computer Science**, Prentice Hall, 1993.

[4] P Bernard, G Laffitte, *The French Population Census for 1990*, Z User Meeting 1995, Springer-Verlag LNCS Vol. 967, 1995, pp. 334–352.

[5] J Bicarregui, D Clutterbuck, G Finnie, H Haughton, K Lano, H Lesan, W Marsh, B Matthews, M Moulding, A Newton, B Ritchie, T Rushton, P Scharbach, *Formal Methods into Practice: Case Studies in the Application of the B Method*, BUT Project internal report, 1995.

[6] J Bicarregui, B Ritchie, *Invariants, Frames and Postconditions: A Comparison of the VDM and B notations*, IEEE Transactions On Software Engineering, 21(2) 1995, pp. 79–89.

[7] P Bieber, N Boulahia-Cuppens, T Lehmann, E van Wickeren, *Abstract Machines for Communication Security*, Proc. of IEEE Workshop on Foundations of Computer Security VI, IEEE Press, 1993.

[8] P Bieber, N Boulahia-Cuppens, *Formal Development of Authentication Protocols*, Proc. of BCS-FACS Sixth Refinement Workshop, Springer-Verlag, 1994.

[9] J Bowen, J Nicholls (Eds), **Z User Meeting, 1992**, Springer-Verlag Workshops in Computing, 1993.

[10] J Bowen, V Stavridou, *Safety-critical systems, formal methods and standards*, Software Engineering Journal, July 1993, pages 189 – 209.

[11] P Chapront, *Vital Coded Processor and Safety Related Software Design*, in: H H Frey (Editor), Safety of Computer Control Systems 1992 (SAFECOMP '92), Computer Systems in Safety Critical Applications, Proc IFAC Symp. Switzerland, 29–30 October 1992 (Pergamon Press, 1992), pages 141 – 145.

[12] D Coleman, F Hayes, S Bear, *Introducing Objectcharts or How to Use Statecharts in Object-Oriented Design*, IEEE Transactions on Software Engineering, Vol. 18, No. 1, January 1992.

[13] D Coleman, F Hayes, *Coherent Models for Object-Oriented Analysis*, Proceedings OOPSLA '91, 1991.

[14] D Coleman, P Arnold, S Bodoff, C Dollin, H Gilchrist, F Hayes, and P Jeremaes. **Object-oriented Development: The Fusion Method.** Prentice Hall Object-oriented Series, 1994.

[15] B P Collins, J E Nicholls, and I H Sørensen. Introducing formal methods: The CICS experience with Z. Technical report, Programming Research Group, Oxford University, 1988.

[16] S Cook and J Daniels. **Designing Object Systems: Object-Oriented Modelling with Syntropy**. Prentice Hall, Sept 1994.

[17] C DaSilva, B Dehbonei, F Mejia, *Formal Specification in the Development of Industrial Applications: The Subway Speed Control Mechanism*, **FORTE '91**, pages 207 – 221, 1991.

[18] B Dehbonei, F Mejia, *Verification of Proofs for the B Formal Development Process*, ACM SIGPLAN Notices, Vol. 28, No. 11, 1993, pp. 16–21.

[19] E Dijkstra, **A Discipline of Programming**, Prentice Hall, Englewood Cliffs, NJ, 1976.

[20] A Diller, R Docherty, *Z and Abstract Machine Notation: A Comparison*, Proc. of Z Users Workshop, J. Bowen (Ed.), 1994.

[21] C Draper, *Practical Experiences of Z and SSADM*, Z User Meeting, Springer-Verlag Workshops in Computing, 1992.

[22] R Duke, P King, G Rose, G Smith, *The Object-Z Specification Language*, 91-1 (Version 1), University of Queensland, Department of Computer Science, Software Verification Research Centre, May 1991.

[23] E Durr, A Duursma, N Plat (Eds), VDM^{++} Language Reference Manual, AFRODITE project document AFRO/CG/ED/LRM/V9.1, CAP Gemini Innovation, May 1994.

[24] E Durr, E Dusink, The role of VDM^{++} in the development of a real-time tracking and tracing system. In Proceedings of **FME '93**, eds. J. Woodcock and P. Larsen, LNCS, Springer-Verlag, 1993, pp. 64–72.

[25] M Eva, **SSADM Version 4: A User's Guide**, McGraw Hill International Series in Software Engineering, 1992.

[26] A Evans, *Position Paper*, Formal Specification and Object Orientation Workshop, Logica London, November 1992.

[27] J Fiadeiro, T Maibaum, *Sometimes "Tomorrow" is "Sometime"*, in *Temporal Logic*, D. M. Gabbay and H. J. Ohlbach (editors), LNAI 827, Springer-Verlag 1994, 48–66.

[28] C Fidge, *Proof Obligations for Real-Time Refinement, Proceedings of 6th Refinement Workshop*, Springer-Verlag Workshops in Computing, 1994.

[29] R Fink, S Oppert, P Collinson, G Cooke, S Dhanjal, H Lesan, R Shaw. *Data Management in Clinical Laboratory Information Systems*, Directions in Safety-critical Systems, Springer-Verlag, 1993.

[30] R France. *Semantically Extended Data Flow Diagrams: A Formal Specification Tool*, IEEE Transactions on Software Engineering, Vol. 18, No. 4, April 1992.

[31] D Harel. *Statecharts: A visual formalism for complex systems*, Science of Computer Programming 8 (1987), 231 - 274.

[32] J Hares. **SSADM for the Advanced Practitioner**, Wiley, 1990.

[33] H Haughton. Specification of communication protocols using formal methods. *Information and Software Technology*, 1992.

[34] H Haughton, K Lano. *Testing and Safety analysis of AM specifications*, in Proceedings of the 6th Refinement Workshop, City University, London January '94, Springer-Verlag Workshops in Computing, 1994.

[35] J V Hill. **Microprocessor Based Protection Systems**, Elsevier 1991.

[36] C A R Hoare. **Communicating Sequential Processes**, Prentice Hall, 1985.

[37] J Hoare. The use of B in CICS. In J Bowen and M Hinchey, editors, **Applications of Formal Methods**. Prentice Hall, 1995.

[38] J A Goguen, T Winkler, *Introducing OBJ3*, SRI International, Computer Science Lab, SRI-CSL-88-9, August, 1988.

[39] D Gries. **The Science of Programming**. Prentice Hall, 1986.

[40] C B Jones. **Systematic Software Construction using VDM**. Prentice Hall, 1990.

[41] K Lano, *Method Case Study: Invoice System*, BUT Project Document BUT/LLOYDS/KL/14/V1, 1992.

[42] K Lano, H Haughton, *Improving the Process of Specification and Refinement in B AMN*, Proceedings of 6th Refinement Workshop, D Till (Ed.), Springer-Verlag Workshops in Computing, 1994.

[43] K Lano, J Dick, *Concurrent Specification in B AMN*, Dept. of Computing, Imperial College, 1995.

[44] K Lano, *B User Trials Code Generation Course*, BUT Project Document BUT/LLOYDS/KL/79/V1, October 1993.

[45] K Lano, *The Specification of a Real Time System in Z*, REDO project document 2487-TN-PRG-1015, December 1991.

[46] K Lano, *Reactive System Specification and Refinement*, Proceedings of TAPSOFT '95, Springer-Verlag LNCS, 1995.

[47] K Lano, H Haughton, *Formal Development in B Abstract Machine Notation*, Information and Software Technology, Vol. 37, No. 5–6, May–June, 1995, pp 303–316.

[48] M K O Lee, P N Scharbach and I H Sørensen, *Engineering Real Software Using Formal Methods*, Proceedings of 4th Refinement Workshop, J M Morris and R C Shaw (Editors), Workshops in Computing, Springer Verlag, 1991.

[49] S Mellor and P Ward. **Structured Development for Real-time Systems (3 Volumes)**. Yourdon Press, 1985.

[50] S M Merad, *Adding Formalism to Object-oriented analysis*, KBSL Conference on Requirements and Design Analysis for Object-Oriented Environments, 1992.

[51] B Meyer. **Object-Oriented Software Construction**. Prentice Hall, 1988.

[52] Ministry of Defence. *Draft Interim Defence Standard 00-55*, April 1991.

[53] Ministry of Defence, *Hazard Analysis and Safety Classification of the Computer and Programmable Electronic System Elements of Defence Equipment. Interim Defence Standard 00-56*, April 1991.

[54] E F Moore, *Gedanken-experiments on Sequential Machines*, in Automata Studies, Princetown University Press, Princetown N.J., 1956.

[55] C Morgan, **Programming from Specifications**, Prentice Hall, 1990.

[56] F Polack, M Whiston, *Formal Methods and System Analysis*, Proceedings of Methods Integration Conference, Springer-Verlag 1992.

[57] PROgram Development by SPECification and TRAnsformation Volume 1 Methodology PROSPECTRA Report M.1.1S3-R-55.3 March 1990

[58] D R Pyle, M Josephs, *Enriching a Structured Method with Z*, Oxford University Programming Research Group, 1991.

[59] D R Pyle, M Josephs, *Entity-Relationship Models Expressed in Z: A Synthesis of Structured and Formal Methods*, Oxford University Programming Research Group, 1991.

[60] The RAISE Language Group, **The RAISE SPECIFICATION LANGUAGE**, Prentice Hall, 1992.

[61] B Ritchie, J Bicarregui and H Haughton, *Experiences in Using the AMN in a GKS Study*, in **FME'94** : Industrial Benefits of Formal Methods, Lecture Notes in Computer Science, Vol. 873, Springer Verlag, 1994, pp. 93–104.

[62] J Rumbaugh, M Blaha, W Premerlani, F Eddy, W Lorensen, **Object-Oriented Modelling and Design**, Englewood Cliffs, NJ, Prentice Hall Ltd., 1991.

[63] J Spivey, **The Z Reference Manual**, 2nd Edition, Prentice Hall, 1992.

[64] A C Storey, H Haughton, *A Strategy for the Production of Verifiable Code Using the B Method*, in **FME'94 : Industrial Benefits of Formal Methods**, Lecture Notes in Computer Science, Vol. 873, Springer Verlag, 1994, pp. 346–365.

[65] H Waeselynck, J-L Boulanger, *The Role of Testing in the B Formal Development Process*, Proc. 6th International Symposium on software Reliability Engineering (ISSRE'95), Toulouse, 1995.

[66] IEC/TC65A(Secretariat)123, *Functional Safety of Electrical / Electronic / Programmable Electronic Systems: Generic Aspects. Part 1 : General Requirements*, International Electrotechnical Commission, 1992.

Exercise Solutions

A.1 Exercises 1

(1)

1. $\text{mx} \longleftarrow \text{MAX\_VAL}(\text{nn}) \;\widehat{=}$
    PRE $\text{nn} \in \mathbb{N}$
    THEN
        IF $\text{nn} > \text{val}$
        THEN
            $\text{mx} := \text{nn}$
        ELSE
            $\text{mx} := \text{val}$
        END
    END

2. $\text{bb} \longleftarrow \text{is\_member}(\text{xx}) \;\widehat{=}$
    PRE $\text{xx} \in \mathbb{N}$
    THEN
        IF $\text{xx} \in \text{ss}$
        THEN $\text{bb} := \text{TRUE}$
        ELSE $\text{bb} := \text{FALSE}$
        END
    END

3. $\text{bb} \longleftarrow \text{try\_add}(\text{xx}) \;\widehat{=}$
    PRE $\text{xx} \in \text{ss}$
    THEN
        CHOICE
            $\text{ss} := \text{ss} \cup \{\, \text{xx} \,\}$ ||
            $\text{bb} := \text{TRUE}$
        OR
            $\text{bb} := \text{FALSE}$
        END
    END

(2)

```
MACHINE Scalar(maxval)
CONSTRAINTS maxval > 0
SEES BooL_TYPE
VARIABLES
    val
INVARIANT
    val ∈ ℕ ∧ val ≤ maxval
INITIALISATION
    val := 0
OPERATIONS

ok ⟵ replace(xx) ≙
    PRE xx ∈ ℕ
    THEN
      IF xx ≤ maxval
      THEN
            val := xx ||
            ok := TRUE
      ELSE
            ok := FALSE
      END
    END ;

vv ⟵ value ≙
    vv := val;

ok ⟵ increment(xx) ≙
    PRE xx ∈ ℕ
    THEN
            IF xx + val ≤ maxval
            THEN
                val := val + xx ||
                ok := TRUE
            ELSE
                ok := FALSE
            END
    END ;

ok ⟵ decrement(xx) ≙
    PRE xx ∈ ℕ
    THEN
      IF val ≥ xx
      THEN
        val := val − xx ||
        ok := TRUE
      ELSE
        ok := FALSE
      END
    END ;
```

$$\text{mx} \longleftarrow \text{max\_val(nn)} \ \hat{=}$$
  PRE **nn** $\in \ \mathbb{N}$
  THEN
      IF **nn** $>$ **val**
      THEN
          mx $:=$ **nn**
      ELSE
          mx $:=$ **val**
      END
  END

END

(3)

  [PRE **x** > 0 THEN **y** $:=$ **y/x** END]**(y** > 1)

is **x** $> 0 \land$ **y/x** > 1, ie, **x** $> 0 \land$ **y** $>$ **x**.

  [CHOICE **ss** $:=$ **ss** $\cup \{$**xx**$\}$ $\|$ **bb** $:=$ **TRUE**
  OR **bb** $:=$ **FALSE** END]**(xx** $\in$ **ss**)

is **xx** $\in$ **ss** $\cup \{$**xx**$\} \land$ **xx** $\in$ **ss**, ie, **xx** $\in$ **ss**. Thus we cannot guarantee that **xx** $\in$ **ss** after the operation unless it is already true before it executes, because of the non-determinism.

  [**x** $:=$ **a** $+ 1 \|$ **y** $:=$ **x** $+$ **a**]**(x** $=$ **new_x** $\land$ **y** $=$ **new_y**)

is **a** $+ 1 =$ **new_x** $\land$ **x** $+$ **a** $=$ **new_y**

  [**x** $:=$ **a** $+ 1$; **y** $:=$ **x** $+$ **a**]**(x** $=$ **new_x** $\land$ **y** $=$ **new_y**)

is **a** $+ 1 =$ **new_x** $\land 2$**a** $+ 1 =$ **new_y**

  [ANY **vv** WHERE **vv** $\in \mathbb{N} \land$ **vv** $>$ **xx** THEN **xx** $:=$ **vv** END]**(xx** $\in$ **ss**)

is $\forall$**vv**.**(vv** $>$ **xx** $\land$ **vv** $\in \mathbb{N} \Rightarrow$ **vv** $\in$ **ss**).

  [**ww** $:=$ **vv** $+ 1$]**(ww** $=$ **vv**)

is just **vv** $+ 1 =$ **vv**. Notice that if a variable **vv** does not occur on the LHS of an assignment in S, then **vv** $=$ **val** $\Rightarrow$ [S]**(vv** $=$ **val**).

(4) Obligations 1 and 2 are trivially true (there are no parameters or constants). Obligation 3 is:

  $\exists$ **ss**.(**ss** $\in \ \mathbb{F}(\mathbb{N})$)

which clearly holds. Obligation 4 is:

$$\varnothing \in \mathbb{F}(\mathbb{N})$$

which clearly holds. Obligation 5 for **choose** is trivially true since this operation does not change the state. Obligation 5 for **add** is:

$$ss \in \mathbb{F}(\mathbb{N}) \wedge xx \in \mathbb{N} \Rightarrow$$
$$ss \cup \{ xx \} \in \mathbb{F}(\mathbb{N})$$

which is clearly true.

Thus the machine is internally consistent. However: **fis(choose)** is

$$\neg \, [\text{ANY } vv \text{ WHERE } vv \in ss \text{ THEN } xx := vv \text{ END}]\textbf{false}$$

which is

$$\neg \, \forall vv.(vv \in ss \Rightarrow \textbf{false})$$

ie:

$$\exists vv.(vv \in ss)$$

This is *not* guaranteed by the operation precondition or the machine invariant, so we can't refine this to code. A precondition of $ss \neq \varnothing$ should be added.

fis(add) is **true**.

A.2 Exercises 2

(1) Suitable machines are:

```
MACHINE Person(maxper)
SETS
    STRING;
    PERSON;
    GENDER = { female, male }
VARIABLES
    persons, age, address, gender, date_of_birth
INVARIANT
    persons ⊆ PERSON ∧
    age ∈ persons → 0 .. 200 ∧
    address ∈ persons → STRING ∧
    gender ∈ persons → GENDER ∧
    date_of_birth ∈ persons → ℕ
INITIALISATION
    persons, age, address, gender, date_of_birth := ∅, ∅,
                                                     ∅, ∅, ∅
```

```
OPERATIONS
    pp  ⟵  create_person(addr, gen, dob)  ≙
            PRE persons ≠ PERSON ∧
                    addr ∈ STRING ∧
                    gen ∈ GENDER ∧
                    dob ∈ 0..200
            THEN
                ANY oo, ss
                WHERE oo ∈ PERSON − persons ∧
                            ss ∈ STRING
                THEN
                    persons := persons ∪ { oo } ||
                    age(oo) := 0 ||
                    address(oo) := ss ||
                    gender(oo) := gen ||
                    date_of_birth(oo) := dob ||
                    pp := oo
                END
            END;

    birthday(pp)  ≙
            PRE pp ∈ persons ∧
                age(pp) < 200
            THEN
                age(pp) := age(pp) + 1
            END


END
```

The disadvantage with this type of model is that we cannot directly assert that gender(pp) is constant throughout the lifetime of a particular person pp, in contrast to the model which represents just a single person instance.

```
MACHINE Patient(maxper)
EXTENDS Person(maxper)
VARIABLES
    body_mass, temperature
DEFINITIONS
    patients == dom(temperature)
INVARIANT
    body_mass ∈ persons ⇸ ℕ ∧
    temperature ∈ persons ⇸ seq(ℕ) ∧
    dom(body_mass) = dom(temperature)
INITIALISATION
    body_mass, temperature := ∅, ∅
OPERATIONS
    define_readings(pp, bm)  ≙
            PRE pp ∈ persons ∧ bm ∈ ℕ
            THEN
                temperature(pp) := [ ] ||
                body_mass(pp) := bm
```

```
        END;

add_reading(pp, tmp)  ≙
    PRE tmp ∈ ℕ ∧
        pp ∈ patients
    THEN
        temperature(pp)  :=  temperature(pp)  ⌢  [tmp]
    END;

diff  ⟵  get_difference(pp)  ≙
    PRE pp ∈ patients ∧
        size(temperature(pp))  >  1
    THEN
        LET ll
        BE ll  =  size(temperature(pp))
        IN
            diff  :=  temperature(pp)(ll)  −  temperature(pp)(ll − 1)
        END
    END

END
```

Notice that **patients** can be a strict subset of **persons**, as is to be expected in the case of a 'proper' subtype – ie, there are people who are not patients.

(2)

1. **vv1, vv2, ww1, uu1** are the visible variables in **DD**. **cc2** is the only visible constant (**cc1** is not visible because of the rule that SEES is intransitive). The externally visible operations are **set** and **redo** – the other two operations are not externally usable because INCLUDES is used to access **BB** in **DD**;

2. Again, **vv1, vv2, ww1, uu1** and **cc2** are the data items that can be used internally. All the previously defined operations can be used internally in **DD**: **set, gtr** and **correct**;

3. Only variables declared in a machine can be updated directly in operations declared in it – only **uu1** has this property.

(3)

1. **fis(S)** for **S** being the definition of **create_book** is

    $$ii \in \mathbb{N} \wedge aut \in \mathbf{STRING} \Rightarrow \mathbf{fis}(S_1)$$

    where S_1 is the ANY statement.
    fis(S_1) is

    $$\neg \, [S_1]\mathbf{false}$$

which is

$$\neg\, \forall\, oo.(oo \in BOOK - books \Rightarrow false)$$

ie:

$$\exists\, oo.(oo \in BOOK - books)$$

The termination condition is

$$ii \in \mathbb{N} \land aut \in STRING \land trm(S_1)$$

and $trm(S_1)$ is **true**.

2. The definition is suspect because its feasibility condition is not **true** – thus it cannot be refined to executable code. A way of ensuring feasibility is to strengthen the precondition to ensure $fis(S_1)$, ie, to rewrite the operation as

```
cb  ⟵  create_book(ii, aut)  ≙
    PRE ii ∈ ℕ ∧ aut ∈ STRING ∧
        BOOK ≠ books
    THEN
        ANY oo
        WHERE oo ∈ BOOK − books
        THEN
            books := books ∪ { oo } ||
            cb := oo ||
            author(oo) := aut ||
            isbn(oo) := ii
        END
    END ;
```

An alternative would be to use a conditional reporting an error if the condition $fis(S_1)$ is not met:

```
cb, ok  ⟵  create_book(ii, aut)  ≙
    PRE ii ∈ ℕ ∧ aut ∈ STRING
    THEN
        IF BOOK ≠ books
        THEN
            ANY oo
            WHERE oo ∈ BOOK − books
            THEN
                books := books ∪ { oo } ||
                ok := TRUE ||
                cb := oo ||
                author(oo) := aut ||
                isbn(oo) := ii
            END
```

```
            ELSE
                ok  :=  FALSE
            END
        END
```

3. **change_author** is simply:

```
    change_author(bk, newaut)  ≙
        PRE bk ∈ books ∧ newaut ∈ STRING
        THEN
            author(bk)  :=  newaut
        END
```

search is:

```
    bk  ⟵  search(ii)  ≙
        PRE ii ∈ ℕ ∧
            ∃ oo.(oo ∈ books ∧ isbn(oo) = ii)
        THEN
            ANY oo
            WHERE oo ∈ books ∧ isbn(oo) = ii
            THEN
                bk := oo
            END
        END
```

Notice that we need to precondition the operation by the feasibility constraint of the ANY statement to ensure feasibility. Also note that the operation is non-deterministic if there are two books with the same ISBN – either may be returned by **search**.

(4) The invariant needs to be strengthened by the fact that **aa.yy** = **bb.yy** (indeed these values are constants). The condition **aa.xx** ≤ **bb.xx** would certainly not hold if we could apply **aa.up** independently of **bb.up**, which would be the case if EXTENDS were used instead of INCLUDES.

A.3 Exercises 3

(1) A suitable refinement is:

```
REFINEMENT SortSet_1
REFINES SortSet
SEES BooL_TYPE
CONSTANTS
    is_ordered
```

PROPERTIES
   is_ordered $\in$ $\mathbb{P}(\text{seq}(\mathbb{N}))$ $\wedge$
   $\forall$ ss.(ss $\in$ seq($\mathbb{N}$) $\Rightarrow$
      (ss $\in$ is_ordered $\equiv$
      $\forall$ (ii, jj).(ii $\in$ dom(ss) $\wedge$
               jj $\in$ dom(ss) $\wedge$
               ii $<$ jj $\Rightarrow$
                  ss(ii) $<$ ss(jj))))

VARIABLES sq
INVARIANT
   sq $\in$ is_ordered $\wedge$
   ss $=$ ran(sq)
INITIALISATION
   sq $:=$ [ ]
OPERATIONS
  xx $\longleftarrow$ choose $\widehat{=}$
     PRE sq $\neq$ [ ]
     THEN
       xx $:=$ sq(1)
     END;

  remove(xx) $\widehat{=}$
     PRE xx $\in$ $\mathbb{N}$
     THEN
       ANY newsq
       WHERE
         newsq $\in$ is_ordered $\wedge$
         ran(newsq) $=$ ran(sq) $-$ { xx }
       THEN
        sq $:=$ newsq
       END
     END;

  add(xx) $\widehat{=}$
     PRE xx $\in$ $\mathbb{N}$
     THEN
       ANY newsq
       WHERE newsq $\in$ is_ordered $\wedge$
         ran(newsq) $=$ ran(sq) $\cup$ { xx }
       THEN
        sq $:=$ newsq
       END
     END;

  bb $\longleftarrow$ is_empty $\widehat{=}$
     IF sq $=$ [ ]
     THEN
       bb $:=$ TRUE
     ELSE
       bb $:=$ FALSE

END

END

The "non-emptiness of joint state" obligation is clearly true – there is a set (the empty set) for which there is an ordered sequence whose range is this set. The initialisations establish the refinement relation because

$$[sq := []]\neg [ss := \varnothing]\neg R$$

where **R** is the refinement relation ss = ran(sq).

The concrete **choose** operation returns results which are consistent with those specified for the abstract version of the operation, because:

$$R \wedge sq \neq [] \Rightarrow$$
$$[xx := sq(1)]\neg [xx' :\in ss]\neg (R \wedge xx' = xx)$$

since the consequent here is implied by:

$$\exists xx'.(xx' \in ss \wedge xx' = sq(1))$$

The obligation for **remove** has the form:

$$R \wedge xx \in \mathbb{N} \Rightarrow$$
$$\forall newsq.(newsq \in is\_ordered \wedge$$
$$ran(newsq) = ran(sq) - \{xx\} \Rightarrow$$
$$\neg [ss := ss - \{xx\}]\neg R)$$

which is clear because any such **newsq** has ran(**newsq**) = ss − {**xx**} by construction.

Similarly for **add**. The obligation

$$sq = [] \equiv ss = \varnothing$$

for **is_empty** follows from the refinement relation.

(2) The following is a suitable refinement:

REFINEMENT **Dispenser_1**
REFINES **Dispenser**
VARIABLES
   drinks
INVARIANT
   drinks $\in \mathbb{N} \wedge$
   (**drinks** = 0 $\equiv$ **dstate** = **unstocked**)
INITIALISATION
   drinks := 0
OPERATIONS
   restock $\widehat{=}$

```
          BEGIN
             drinks  :=  drinks  +  10
          END ;

     give_drink  ≙
          PRE  drinks  >  0
          THEN
                  drinks  :=  drinks  −  1
          END

  END
```

The refinement obligations are again direct to prove. Non-emptiness of the joint state is shown by taking **dstate** = **unstocked** and **drinks** = 0.

The initialisations establish the refinement relation **R**: **drinks** = 0 ≡ **dstate** = **unstocked** because they respectively set **drinks** to 0 and **dstate** to **unstocked**.

The **restock** operation has the obligation:

R ⇒
$$[\textbf{drinks} := \textbf{drinks} + 10]\neg\,[\textbf{dstate} := \textbf{stocked}]\neg\,\textbf{R}$$

which is obviously true.

The obligation for **give_drink** is

R ∧ **dstate** = **stocked** ⇒
$$(\textbf{drinks} > 0) \wedge [\textbf{drinks} := \textbf{drinks} - 1]\neg$$
$$[\textbf{dstate} :\in \textbf{DSTATE}]\neg\,\textbf{R}$$

which is immediate.

Properties of Weakest Preconditions

Dijkstra [19] formulated a number of "healthiness" conditions for the weakest precondition operator. Some of these, such as the "law of the excluded miracle" (that for no S does [S]false) are specific to conventional programming languages, and, it has been argued, do not need to hold for specification languages [55]. However, the following are more basic, and have important consequences for definitions of refinement in particular:

(Monotonicity):

$(P \Rightarrow Q) \Rightarrow$
$\qquad ([S]P \Rightarrow [S]Q)$

(Distributivity of Conjunction):
$[S](P \wedge Q) \equiv [S]P \wedge [S]Q$

These can be proved by structural induction over the given constructs. One law which fails to hold is the distributivity of *disjunction*:

$[S](P \vee Q) \equiv ([S]P \vee [S]Q)$

Intuitively, this is because of non-determinism: we may have that, from a given state, every execution of S leads to a state satisfying *either* P or Q, without it being the case that every execution of S leads to a state satisfying (say) P, simply because there are at least two distinct post-states which could arise from a single pre-state.

A simple counter-example to the law is given by the substitution S:

$x := 1 \;[\!]\; x := 2$

which has:

$[S](x = 1 \vee x = 2) \equiv$
$\qquad [x := 1](x = 1 \vee x = 2) \wedge [x := 2](x = 1 \vee x = 2) \equiv$
$\qquad \text{true} \wedge \text{true}$

but:

$$[S](x = 1) \vee [S](x = 2) \equiv$$
$$([x := 1](x = 1) \wedge [x := 2](x = 1)) \vee$$
$$([x := 1](x = 2) \wedge [x := 2](x = 2)) \equiv$$
false $\vee$ **false**

However, this law is true for all substitutions not containing [] or @ other than in the form of an IF-THEN-ELSE command.

Similarly, note that if we had included a construct of 'program conjunction' [55]:

$$[S_1 \sqcap S_2]P \equiv [S_1]P \vee [S_2]P$$

then the distribution of conjunction would also fail.

Just as $[S]P$ describes the set of states from which *every* accepted execution of S leads to termination in a state satisfying P, $\neg [S] \neg P$ describes the set of states from which *there exists* an accepted execution of S which leads to non-termination, or to termination in a state satisfying P. These two predicate constructions are "dual" rather in the way that universal and existential quantification in classical logic, or possibility and necessity in temporal logic are.

The construction $\neg [S] \neg P$ frequently arises in the context of refinement and feasibility.

Note that this construct is also monotonic:

$$(P \Rightarrow Q) \Rightarrow$$
$$(\neg [S] \neg P \Rightarrow \neg [S] \neg Q)$$

We have the following theorem, which shows that every generalised substitution which corresponds directly to executable code is feasible:

Theorem
If S is a substitution built entirely from assignment, **skip**, sequencing, IF THEN ELSE, and VAR (with an immediate initialisation), then

$$[S]P \equiv \neg [S] \neg P$$

for any predicate P.

Proof
By structural induction on S. The cases of assignment and **skip** are trivial. If S is IF **E** THEN S1 ELSE S2 END where S1 and S2 satisfy the theorem, then:

$$[S]P \equiv (E \wedge [S1]P) \vee (\neg E \wedge [S2]P)$$
$$\equiv \neg ((E \wedge [S1] \neg P) \vee (\neg E \wedge [S2] \neg P))$$
$$\equiv \neg [S] \neg P$$

For sequencing:

$$[S1; \; S2]P \equiv [S1][S2]P$$
$$\equiv [S1]\neg \, [S2]\neg \, P$$
$$\equiv \neg \, [S1]\neg \, \neg \, [S2]\neg \, P$$
$$\equiv \neg \, [S1; \; S2]\neg \, P$$

if S1 and S2 satisfy the hypothesis of the theorem. For VAR:

$$[\text{VAR } \mathbf{v} \text{ IN } \mathbf{v} := e; \; S \text{ END}]P$$
$$\equiv \forall \mathbf{v} \bullet ([S]P)[e/\mathbf{v}]$$
$$\equiv ([S]P)[e/\mathbf{v}]$$
$$\equiv (\neg \, [S]\neg \, (P))[e/\mathbf{v}]$$
$$\equiv \neg \, [\text{VAR } \mathbf{v} \text{ IN } \mathbf{v} := e; \; S \text{ END}]\neg \, P$$

under the assumption that the result holds for **S**.

Intuitively this theorem holds because for such code-like statements **S**, there is a *unique* state transformation associated with a generalised substitution. Thus $[S]P$ and $\neg \, [S]\neg \, P$ mean the same.

B.1   Termination and Feasibility

For every generalised substitution **S** we can define two predicates, **trm(S)** and **fis(S)**, called the *termination* and *feasibility* conditions for **S**, respectively.

In the following we will use the following definitions:

$$\mathbf{trm(S)} \equiv [S]\mathbf{true}$$

That is, in this set of states, every execution of **S** that is accepted by the computer is guaranteed to terminate (in a state satisfying **true**). The parenthesised condition is vacuous and can be dropped.

$$\mathbf{fis(S)} \equiv \neg \, [S]\mathbf{false}$$

That is, the feasibility of a substitution is taken to be the (predicate defining the) set of pre-states in which it is possible to feasibly execute, and either to not terminate or to terminate in a state satisfying **true**.

Examples of these predicates are:

$$\mathbf{fis(P ==> x := e)} \equiv \mathbf{P} \qquad\qquad \mathbf{trm(P ==> x := e)} \equiv \mathbf{true}$$
$$\mathbf{fis(P \mid x := e)} \equiv \mathbf{true} \qquad\qquad \mathbf{trm(P \mid x := e)} \equiv \mathbf{P}$$
$$\mathbf{fis(\text{IF } E \text{ THEN } S_1 \text{ ELSE } S_2 \text{ END})} \equiv (\mathbf{E} \Rightarrow \mathbf{fis(S_1)}) \wedge (\neg \, \mathbf{E} \Rightarrow \mathbf{fis(S_2)})$$

In general they have the definitions:

$\mathbf{fis(x := e)}$	$\equiv$ $\mathbf{true}$	$\mathbf{trm(x := e)}$	$\equiv$ $\mathbf{true}$
$\mathbf{fis(P ==> S)}$	$\equiv$ $\mathbf{P} \wedge \mathbf{fis(S)}$	$\mathbf{trm(P ==> S)}$	$\equiv$ $\mathbf{P} \Rightarrow \mathbf{trm(S)}$
$\mathbf{fis(P \mid S)}$	$\equiv$ $\mathbf{P} \Rightarrow \mathbf{fis(S)}$	$\mathbf{trm(P \mid S)}$	$\equiv$ $\mathbf{P} \wedge \mathbf{trm(S)}$
$\mathbf{fis(@v.S)}$	$\equiv$ $\exists \, v.\mathbf{fis(S)}$	$\mathbf{trm(@v.S)}$	$\equiv$ $\forall \, v.\mathbf{trm(S)}$
$\mathbf{fis(S_1 [] S_2)}$	$\equiv$ $\mathbf{fis(S_1)} \vee \mathbf{fis(S_2)}$	$\mathbf{trm(S_1 [] S_2)}$	$\equiv$ $\mathbf{trm(S_1)} \wedge \mathbf{trm(S_2)}$

Notice the strong duality between the definition of **trm** and that of **fis**. We have the following instructive identities on generalised substitutions:

$$(\mathbf{trm(S)} \mid \mathbf{S}) = \mathbf{S}$$
$$(\mathbf{fis(S)} ==> \mathbf{S}) = \mathbf{S}$$

The first identity implies that when we come to prove an abstract machine internally consistent, the obligation

$$\mathbf{P} \wedge \mathbf{I} \Rightarrow [\mathbf{S}]\mathbf{I}$$

for each operation definition **S** will also imply that, within the machine invariant **I**, operations of other machines invoked from within **S** are always invoked within their preconditions. This follows since

$$[\mathbf{op}]\mathbf{J} \equiv [\mathbf{trm(op)} \mid \mathbf{op}]\mathbf{J}$$

for each operation call **op**, and therefore

$$[\mathbf{op}]\mathbf{J} \Rightarrow \mathbf{trm(op)}$$

Feasibility proofs are not performed as part of internal consistency, but, in a number of steps, as part of refinement.

The two concepts are in a sense orthogonal: it is possible to define completely terminating but completely infeasible substitutions:

$$\mathbf{false} ==> \mathbf{skip}$$

and completely feasible but completely non-terminating substitutions:

$$\mathbf{false} \mid \mathbf{skip}$$

or

WHILE **true** DO **skip** INVARIANT **false** VARIANT 0 END

In general we have the weak connection:

$$[\mathbf{S}]\mathbf{P} \Rightarrow \mathbf{trm(S)}$$
$$\neg\,[\mathbf{S}]\mathbf{P} \Rightarrow \mathbf{fis(S)}$$

for any **P** and **S**.

Notice however that

$$\neg\,\mathbf{fis(S)} \Rightarrow \mathbf{trm(S)}$$

since

$$[\mathbf{S}]\mathbf{false} \Rightarrow [\mathbf{S}]\mathbf{true}$$

for any **S**: we can make sense of this by regarding non-termination as *chaotic* behaviour (informally it may produce any result at any time or fail to terminate altogether). An infeasible execution however is not chaotic: it has no possible result.

B.2   Set-theoretic Semantics

At first sight, there appears to be a significant gap between the set-theoretic foundation for the basic mathematical notation of B AMN, and the weakest-precondition semantics for generalised substitutions. However each generalised substitution S can be regarded as defining a relation on a suitable set. A pair of states will be in this relation if and only if there is an accepted execution of S starting from the first element of the pair, which either fails to terminate, or which terminates in the second.

More precisely, let s represent the cartesian product of the types of the variables **x** involved in S. Then we define:

$$\textbf{rel}(S) \ = \ \{\textbf{x}, \textbf{x}' \mid \textbf{x} \in s \wedge \textbf{x}' \in s \wedge \neg\,[S]\neg\,(\textbf{x} = \textbf{x}')\}$$

We have the following examples:

$$\textbf{rel}(\textbf{false} ==> \textbf{skip}) \ = \ \varnothing$$
$$\textbf{rel}(\textbf{x} := \textbf{x} + 1) \ = \ \{\textbf{m}, \textbf{n} \mid \textbf{m} \in \mathbb{N} \wedge \textbf{n} \in \mathbb{N} \wedge \textbf{n} = \textbf{m} + 1\}$$
$$\textbf{rel}(\textbf{x} :\in \mathbb{N}) \ = \ \mathbb{N} \times \mathbb{N}$$
$$\textbf{rel}(\textbf{false} \mid \textbf{skip}) \ = \ \mathbb{N} \times \mathbb{N}$$

The last two examples show that the relation **rel** is not sufficient to distinguish semantically distinct substitutions. The intuition behind the behaviour of **rel** is as follows. If S does not possess a feasible execution from a value $\textbf{x} \in s$ then **x** simply does not appear in the domain of **rel**(S): there is no actual execution path from this point. However, if **x** is a feasible starting point from execution, then either one of the executions from this point is non-terminating, and **rel** includes the completely chaotic and unpredictable behaviour

$$\{\textbf{x}\} \times s$$

or every execution is terminating, and the set of states in which execution terminates, say **r**, is associated with **x**:

$$\{\textbf{x}\} \times \textbf{r} \subseteq \textbf{rel}(S)$$

and

$$\textbf{rel}(S)[\{\textbf{x}\}] \ = \ \textbf{r}$$

Returning to the last two examples above, however, we see that modelling non-termination by chaotic behaviour is ambiguous if we actually wanted to specify such behaviour. $\textbf{x} :\in \mathbb{N}$, unlike **false** | **skip**, is specifying a state transition which has to be implemented by a terminating computation.

We, therefore, define a specific set which is the set of elements from which termination is guaranteed:

$$\textbf{pre}(S) \ = \ \{\textbf{x} \mid \textbf{x} \in s \wedge [S]\textbf{true}\}$$

Figure B.1 gives an example of the relational equivalent of the generalised substitution S:

$$(x > 0) ==> ((x > 1) \mid x := 2)$$

Notice that

$$trm(S) \equiv (x > 0 \Rightarrow x > 1)$$

so that:

$$pre(S) = \{0\} \cup \{x \mid x \in \mathbb{N} \land x > 1\}$$

As expected, the domain of infeasibility is a subset of the domain of terminating behaviour.

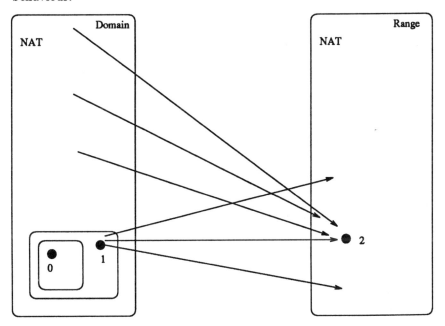

Figure B.1: Pictorial Representation of Substitution

B.3 Refinement

Refinement in B AMN is defined in terms of properties of generalised substitutions. In the case of *procedural* refinement, we have the simple definition "S_2 refines S_1":

$$pre(S_1) \subseteq pre(S_2) \ \land$$
$$rel(S_2) \subseteq rel(S_1)$$

which can be shown to be equivalent to the meta-logical version:

$$(S_1 \sqsubseteq S_2) \equiv$$
$$\forall P \bullet [S_1]P \Rightarrow [S_2]P$$

That is, any property P which S_1 can establish can be established under weaker conditions by S_2.

Refinement, according to this definition, implies that the precondition of a generalised substitution may become weaker (so that the operation will be more robust in accepting a wider range of inputs), and that, within the original precondition, the behaviour of the operation is more deterministic:

$$(S_1 \sqsubseteq S_2) \Rightarrow$$
$$(\mathbf{trm}(S_1) \Rightarrow \mathbf{trm}(S_2))$$

Examples:

$$(x > 0 \mid x := x + 1) \sqsubseteq x := x + 1$$
$$S_1 [] S_2 \sqsubseteq S_1$$
$$S_1 \sqsubseteq (G ==> S_1)$$

In terms of satisfaction of contracts, the weakening of the precondition from a substitution S to a refinement T means that T will be well-behaved over a wider range of starting states than S. In addition, the strengthening of the postcondition means that within the original precondition of S, T has behaviour which meets the contract expressed by S, and hence also obeys any contract that S obeys.

A more surprising consequence of the definition of refinement is that:

$$(S_1 \sqsubseteq S_2) \Rightarrow$$
$$(\mathbf{fis}(S_2) \Rightarrow \mathbf{fis}(S_1))$$

that is, the more refined a substitution becomes, the smaller its domain of feasible behaviour!

In terms of the relational model of generalised substitutions, we can see that this means that the set

$$\mathbf{dom}(S) = \{x \mid x \in s \land \neg [S]\mathbf{false}\}$$

becomes smaller during refinement. Intuitively, this is because refinement is concerned with making the behaviour of a substitution more 'predictable' or less non-deterministic: and the behaviour is actually most predictable in the places where the operation is infeasible: at these points there is no behaviour.

However, all executable code S has

$$\mathbf{fis}(S) \equiv \mathbf{true}$$

so that, for an operation to be eventually executable, it must be feasible at the most abstract level: guards should therefore appear only in the form of ANY or

IF statements, or in SELECT statements where at least one guard condition is always true, rather than as naked **G** ==> **S** statements. Animation provides some warning of infeasibility, and, as we show in Section 2.5, proofs of relative feasibility are a component of refinement.

A very significant property of the relation $\sqsubseteq$, and of its more complex counterpart for data refinement, is that each of the generalised substitution constructs is monotonic with respect to this (pre-order) relation. That is, if $S_1 \sqsubseteq S_2$, then:

$$S_1 [\!] S \quad \sqsubseteq \quad S_2 [\!] S$$
$$P \mid S_1 \quad \sqsubseteq \quad P \mid S_2$$
$$P ==> S_1 \quad \sqsubseteq \quad P ==> S_2$$

and so forth, for each generalised substitution combinator.

This means that if we have an operation **op** defined in terms of another, **op1**, say:

$$op(xx1, xx2) \ \widehat{=}$$
> BEGIN
>> . . . .
>> $rr1 \ \longleftarrow \ op1(ee1)$
>> . . . .
> END

then a refinement of **op1** will automatically lead to a refinement of **op**. In particular, **op** may be defined in an IMPLEMENTATION, and **op1** in a machine **M** imported by this implementation. In this case **op1** is actually implemented by an operation (in code) which is a refinement of the (visible) formal specification of the abstract operation given in **M**. Thus any guarantee about the behaviour of **op** which we make on the basis of the definition in **M** of **op1** will be true about the actual code of **op** (which invokes the code implementation of **op1**).

B.4 Well-formedness Obligations

Each expression which may give undefined results should be contained in a scope where a suitable precondition which ensures its correctness is asserted. For example, the expression $v = f(x)$ requires that $x \in dom(f)$ has been established in a containing scope. In an invariant we could write:

$$x \in dom(f) \ \Rightarrow \ v = f(x)$$

whilst in a substitution we must use a suitable precondition or selection clause to assert this well-formedness requirement:

> PRE $x \in dom(f)$
> THEN
>> $... \ v = f(x) \ ...$
> END

Such well-formedness obligations should, in principle, be expressed as part of the proof obligations of a machine. For example, the full semantics of a (normalised) assignment would be:

$$[x := e]P \equiv \mathcal{W}_M(e) \wedge P[e/x]$$

where $\mathcal{W}_M(e)$ expresses the conditions for e to be well-formed in the current machine **M**.

These conditions can be given by the following definitions (assuming that all expressions are well-typed):

1. $\mathcal{W}_M(n) \equiv$ **false** if **n** is a literal numeric value and is not a natural number in $0 .. 2^{31} - 2$;
2. $\mathcal{W}_M(n) \equiv$ **true** if **n** is a literal numeric value and is a natural number in $0 .. 2^{31} - 2$;
3. $\mathcal{W}_M(v) \equiv v \in 0 .. 2^{31} - 2$ if **v** is a machine variable or local operation variable of numeric type;
4. $\mathcal{W}_M(f(a)) \equiv \mathcal{W}_M(f) \wedge \mathcal{W}_M(a) \wedge a \in dom(f)$;
5. $\mathcal{W}_M(a \ Op \ b) \equiv \mathcal{W}_M(a) \wedge \mathcal{W}_M(b) \wedge (a \ Op \ b) \in 0 .. 2^{31} - 2$ where **Op** is a binary operator on numeric arguments;
6. $\mathcal{W}_M(Op \ a) \equiv \mathcal{W}_M(a) \wedge (Op \ a) \in 0 .. 2^{31} - 2$ for each unary arithmetic operator **Op**.

For a list $e = (e_1, \ldots, e_n)$ of expressions, $\mathcal{W}_M(e) = \mathcal{W}_M(e_1) \wedge \ldots \wedge \mathcal{W}_M(e_n)$.

Then every generalised substitution has these additional conditions as extra preconditions in its definition: IF **E** THEN S_1 ELSE S_2 END has additional precondition $\mathcal{W}_M(E)$, likewise for SELECT, PRE, ANY and WHILE.

B.5   Normal Forms

For B AMN substitutions **S** there is a standard "normal form" with the structure

```
PRE  P
THEN
     ANY  w
     WHERE  Q
     THEN
          S1
     END
END
```

in which **S** can always be equivalently expressed. When an operation **m** of a B machine is written it is assumed at least that all preconditions of the definition **S** of **m** have been gathered together into an initial precondition **P** as in the normal form. This **P** is then used as the operation precondition by the B Toolkit in generating its proof obligations.

If such a normalisation were not performed by the specification writer then the toolkit would still attempt to use the outermost precondition as the "operation precondition". As a result, an operation defined by

```
PRE P
THEN
    PRE P1
    THEN
        S1
    END
END
```

would generate an internal consistency obligation of the form

$$\textbf{Inv} \wedge \textbf{P} \ \Rightarrow \ \textbf{P1}$$

"The operation precondition **P** must establish the internal operation precondition **P1** under the machine invariant." If this obligation can be proved then the separation of **P** and **P1** is in a sense redundant; if it cannot then the operation is not well-defined in cases where **P** holds and **P1** fails to hold.

B.6 Rules for ||

A set of properties for the || operator which mean that it can usually be eliminated from substitutions are as follows:

$$
\begin{aligned}
\textbf{S} \ || \ \textsc{skip} \ &= \ \textbf{S} \\
\textbf{S} \ || \ (\textbf{P} \ | \ \textbf{T}) \ &= \ \textbf{P} \ | \ (\textbf{S} \ || \ \textbf{T}) \\
\textbf{S} \ || \ (\textbf{T} [] \textbf{U}) \ &= \ (\textbf{S} \ || \ \textbf{T}) [] (\textbf{S} \ || \ \textbf{U}) \\
\textbf{S} \ || \ (\textbf{P} ==> \textbf{T}) \ &= \ \textbf{P} ==> (\textbf{S} \ || \ \textbf{T}) \\
\textbf{S} \ || \ @\textbf{z}.\textbf{T} \ &= \ @\textbf{z}.(\textbf{S} \ || \ \textbf{T})
\end{aligned}
$$

In the fourth case $\textbf{trm}(\textbf{S}) \equiv \textbf{true}$ is needed, and in the fifth **z** is not free in **S**. || can be defined using **pre** and **rel** introduced above:

$$
\begin{aligned}
\textbf{pre}(\textbf{S} \ || \ \textbf{T}) \ &= \ \textbf{pre}(\textbf{S}) \times \textbf{pre}(\textbf{T}) \\
\textbf{rel}(\textbf{S} \ || \ \textbf{T}) \ &= \ \textbf{rel}(\textbf{S}) \ || \ \textbf{rel}(\textbf{T})
\end{aligned}
$$

where the last || is the parallel product of the two relations.

B.7 Definition of :=

The definition of substitution is given by structural induction over formulae, where **v**, **w** represent lists of identifiers, **x** and **y** are single identifiers, **E**, **F**, **G** are general expressions, and φ and ϕ are general formulae:

1. $[\mathbf{x} := \mathbf{E}](\varphi \wedge \phi)$ is $[\mathbf{x} := \mathbf{E}]\varphi \ \wedge \ [\mathbf{x} := \mathbf{E}]\phi$, and similarly for $\Rightarrow$, $\vee$ and $\equiv$;

2. $[\mathbf{x} := \mathbf{E}]\neg \varphi$ is $\neg ([\mathbf{x} := \mathbf{E}]\varphi)$;

3. $[\mathbf{x} := \mathbf{E}]\forall \mathbf{v}.\varphi$ is $\forall \mathbf{w}.([\mathbf{x} := \mathbf{E}]\varphi')$ where any variables in $\mathbf{v}$ which occur free in $\mathbf{x}$ or $\mathbf{E}$ are renamed to new variables not occurring in these formulae or in $\mathbf{v}$ or φ, and systematically replaced in both $\mathbf{v}$ and φ to produce $\mathbf{w}$ and φ'. Similarly for $\exists$;

4. $[\mathbf{x} := \mathbf{E}]\mathbf{x}$ is $\mathbf{E}$;

5. $[\mathbf{x} := \mathbf{E}]\mathbf{F}$ is $\mathbf{F}$ if $\mathbf{x}$ is not free in $\mathbf{F}$;

6. $[\mathbf{x} := \mathbf{E}](\mathbf{F}, \mathbf{G})$ is $([\mathbf{x} := \mathbf{E}]\mathbf{F}, [\mathbf{x} := \mathbf{E}]\mathbf{G})$;

7. $[\mathbf{w}, \mathbf{x} := \mathbf{E}, \mathbf{F}]\varphi$ is $[\mathbf{y} := \mathbf{F}][\mathbf{w} := \mathbf{E}][\mathbf{x} := \mathbf{y}]\varphi$ where $\mathbf{y}$ is a new identifier not free in $\mathbf{w}$, $\mathbf{x}$, $\mathbf{E}$, $\mathbf{F}$ or φ;

8. $[\mathbf{x} := \mathbf{E}](\mathbf{F} = \mathbf{G})$ is $[\mathbf{x} := \mathbf{E}]\mathbf{F} \ = \ [\mathbf{x} := \mathbf{E}]\mathbf{G}$ and similarly for other binary expression constructors;

9. $[\mathbf{x} := \mathbf{E}]\mathbb{F}(\mathbf{F})$ is $\mathbb{F}([\mathbf{x} := \mathbf{E}]\mathbf{F})$ and similarly for other unary expression constructors;

10. $[\mathbf{x} := \mathbf{E}]\{\mathbf{v} \mid \varphi\}$ is $\{\mathbf{w} \mid [\mathbf{x} := \mathbf{E}]\varphi'\}$ where $\mathbf{w}$ and φ' are as in case 3 above for quantifiers.

For example:

$$[\mathbf{x} := \mathbf{y} + 5]\{\mathbf{y} \mid \mathbf{y} \in \mathbb{N} \wedge \mathbf{y} \geq \mathbf{x}\}$$

is

$$\{\mathbf{z} \mid \mathbf{z} \in \mathbb{N} \wedge \mathbf{z} \geq \mathbf{y} + 5\}$$

by rules 10, 4, 5 and 8. Likewise

$$[\mathbf{x} := \mathbf{y} + 5]\forall \mathbf{y}.(\mathbf{y} \in \mathbb{N} \ \Rightarrow \ \mathbf{x} \geq \mathbf{y})$$

is

$$\forall \mathbf{z}.(\mathbf{z} \in \mathbb{N} \ \Rightarrow \ \mathbf{y} + 5 \geq \mathbf{z})$$

Proof Techniques

This chapter will introduce some proof techniques that can be used to manually or automatically support proof in B. They are based upon the Gentzen *sequent calculus* [3], and are also similar to the techniques currently provided by automated support tools for B.

Let U and V be (possibly empty) sequences of formulae in the predicate calculus language of set theory used for B. A step in a formal proof typically has the form

$$U \longrightarrow V$$

which is termed a *sequent*. Intuitively it states that the conjunction of the formulae in U implies the disjunction of the formulae in V:

$$\vdash U_1 \wedge \ldots \wedge U_n \Rightarrow V_1 \vee \ldots \vee V_m$$

V is the *succedent* of the sequent, U the *antecedent*.

Notice that the order of a formula within U or V does not affect the meaning of the sequent, nor do duplicates in either U or V. Thus we have some simple structural rules:

$$\frac{U \longrightarrow S, A, B, T}{U \longrightarrow S, B, A, T}$$

for any lists U, S, T of formulae, and formulae A and B, and:

$$\frac{U \longrightarrow S, A, A, T}{U \longrightarrow S, A, T}$$

for any formula A. Similar rules hold for the antecedent.

Likewise, a sequent can always be weakened:

$$\frac{U \longrightarrow V}{U, A \longrightarrow V, B}$$

These are examples of *inference rules*, which identify how a set of *hypothesis* sequents (above the horizontal line) can be used to infer a single *conclusion* sequent (below the line).

In practical reasoning we usually work backwards from the conclusion to possible hypotheses which could be useful starting points for further proof steps. The aim of these steps is to reduce the sequent to be proved to the form of an *axiom*:

$$S, A, T \longrightarrow X, A, Y$$

That is, any sequent with a formula that occurs both in the antecedent and the succedent. Once such a sequent has been produced, the proof branch on which it occurs can be closed.

Each logical connective has two proof rules: one to introduce it into the antecedent, and another to introduce it into the succedent. They are named $C \longrightarrow$ for the rule introducing C into the antecedent, and $\longrightarrow C$ for the rule introducing C into the succedent. For propositional connectives the rules are:

$$\frac{U, A, B \longrightarrow V}{U, A \wedge B \longrightarrow V}$$

$$\frac{U \longrightarrow V, A \qquad U \longrightarrow V, B}{U \longrightarrow V, A \wedge B}$$

$$\frac{U \longrightarrow V, A, B}{U \longrightarrow V, A \vee B}$$

$$\frac{U, A \longrightarrow V \qquad U, A \longrightarrow V}{U, A \vee B \longrightarrow V}$$

Notice the strong duality between these two sets of rules.

$$\frac{U, A \longrightarrow V, B}{U \longrightarrow V, A \Rightarrow B}$$

$$\frac{U \longrightarrow V, A \qquad U, B \longrightarrow V}{U, A \Rightarrow B \longrightarrow V}$$

$$\frac{U, A \longrightarrow V}{U \longrightarrow V, \neg A}$$

$$U \longrightarrow V, A$$
$$\overline{U, \neg A \longrightarrow V}$$

A proof of a sequent **S** within the propositional sequent calculus is then a tree of sequents with root **S**, each topmost "leaf" sequent being an axiom, and each inner sequent being derived from its immediate ancestors by one of the above rules of inference.

We will usually apply structural rules without explicitly writing down the proof steps. Notice that we only need to search for proofs involving *subformulae* of the desired conclusion, in a pure propositional calculus.

Some simple examples of proofs or partial proofs are:

$$A \longrightarrow A$$
$$\overline{\longrightarrow A, \neg A}$$
$$\overline{\longrightarrow A \vee \neg A}$$

and

$$\longrightarrow A, \neg A \qquad B, B \Rightarrow \neg A \longrightarrow \neg A$$
$$\overline{A \Rightarrow B, B \Rightarrow \neg A \longrightarrow \neg A}$$

$\longrightarrow\Rightarrow$ corresponds to the **DED** or deduction rule built into the B-Tool, and $\longrightarrow\wedge$ to the **AND** rule. In general, an inference rule acts like a rewrite rule, allowing us to replace one proof requirement by a set of simpler ones.

The sequent calculus can be extended to predicate (quantifier) formulae by the rules:

$$U \longrightarrow V, A(a), \exists x.A(x)$$
$$\overline{U \longrightarrow V, \exists x.A(x)}$$

$$U, A(z) \longrightarrow V$$
$$\overline{U, \exists x.A(x) \longrightarrow V}$$

for $\exists$, where in the last rule z does not occur elsewhere in the sequent. Intuitively this is because the hypothesis then becomes independent of the details of the variable z, and states that **V** holds if **U** does, provided there is some (arbitrary) value that satisfies **A**. In the first rule a must be free for **x** in **A**, that is, no variables free in a are quantified in any scope enclosing the places where it is substituted for **x**.

The rules for $\forall$ are dual to these:

$$U, \forall x.A(x), A(a) \longrightarrow V$$
$$\overline{U, \forall x.A(x) \longrightarrow V}$$

$$\frac{\mathbf{U} \longrightarrow \mathbf{A(z)}, \mathbf{V}}{\mathbf{U} \longrightarrow \forall \mathbf{x}.\mathbf{A(x)}, \mathbf{V}}$$

Where $\mathbf{z}$ is not free in $\mathbf{U}$ and $\mathbf{V}$ in the last rule. Again, $\mathbf{a}$ must be free for $\mathbf{x}$ in $\mathbf{A}$ in the first rule.

$\longrightarrow \forall$ corresponds to the B-Tool inference **GEN**.

Proofs involving quantifiers require care in the application of these rules in the correct order. A well-known "difficult" proof is the following:

$$\frac{\longrightarrow \forall \mathbf{x}.\varphi(\mathbf{x}), \exists \mathbf{x}.(\varphi(\mathbf{x}) \Rightarrow \psi) \qquad \psi \longrightarrow \exists \mathbf{x}.(\varphi(\mathbf{x}) \Rightarrow \psi)}{\forall \mathbf{x}.\varphi(\mathbf{x}) \Rightarrow \psi \longrightarrow \exists \mathbf{x}.(\varphi(\mathbf{x}) \Rightarrow \psi)}$$

where $\mathbf{x}$ is not free in ψ.

The two hypotheses can be separately proved as follows:

$$\frac{\dfrac{\varphi(\mathbf{a}) \longrightarrow \varphi(\mathbf{a}), \psi, \Pi}{\longrightarrow \varphi(\mathbf{a}), \varphi(\mathbf{a}) \Rightarrow \psi, \Pi}}{\longrightarrow \varphi(\mathbf{a}), \Pi}$$

by using $\longrightarrow \exists$, where $\mathbf{a}$ is not free in Π, which is the formula $\exists \mathbf{x}.(\varphi(\mathbf{x}) \Rightarrow \psi)$.

$$\frac{\dfrac{\psi, \varphi(0) \longrightarrow \psi, \Pi}{\psi \longrightarrow \varphi(0) \Rightarrow \psi, \Pi}}{\psi \longrightarrow \Pi}$$

by the same rule.

Additional axioms and inference techniques are needed for reasoning about set theoretic terms and natural numbers. For example, induction principles for natural numbers, sequences and finite sets are:

$$\varphi(0), \forall \mathbf{n}.(\mathbf{n} \in \mathbb{N} \wedge \varphi(\mathbf{n}) \Rightarrow \varphi(\mathbf{n}+1)) \longrightarrow \forall \mathbf{n}.(\mathbf{n} \in \mathbb{N} \Rightarrow \varphi(\mathbf{n}))$$

$$\varphi(\varnothing),$$
$$\forall \mathbf{s}, \mathbf{x}.(\mathbf{s} \in \mathbb{F}(\mathbf{T}) \wedge \mathbf{x} \in \mathbf{T} \wedge \varphi(\mathbf{s}) \Rightarrow \varphi(\mathbf{s} \cup \{\mathbf{x}\})) \longrightarrow$$
$$\forall \mathbf{s}.(\mathbf{s} \in \mathbb{F}(\mathbf{T}) \Rightarrow \varphi(\mathbf{s}))$$

$$\varphi([]),$$
$$\forall \mathbf{s}, \mathbf{x}.(\mathbf{s} \in \mathrm{seq}(\mathbf{T}) \wedge \mathbf{x} \in \mathbf{T} \wedge \varphi(\mathbf{s}) \Rightarrow \varphi(\mathbf{s} \frown [\mathbf{x}])) \longrightarrow$$
$$\forall \mathbf{s}.(\mathbf{s} \in \mathrm{seq}(\mathbf{T}) \Rightarrow \varphi(\mathbf{s}))$$

Elementary axioms about sequences, sets and numbers are also assumed. For example:

$$\longrightarrow \varnothing = \mathrm{ran}([])$$

This is also written as a rewrite rule $\text{ran}([]) == \varnothing$ intended to be used in a left-to-right direction to replace the LHS by the RHS in sequents.

Axioms and inferences for equality are frequently used:

$$x = y \longrightarrow y = x$$
$$\longrightarrow x = x$$
$$x = y, \varphi(x) \longrightarrow \varphi(y)$$

Where the substitution of y for x in φ does not cause free variables of y to come within the scope of quantifiers on themselves in $\varphi(y)$.

A simple example of reasoning using equality is the following, which is typical of a simple refinement proof obligation:

$$\frac{ss = \text{ran}(sq), sq = [] \longrightarrow ss = \text{ran}([])}{ss = \text{ran}(sq), sq = [] \longrightarrow ss = \varnothing}$$

The first line is an equality axiom, and the second follows from the first since we are allowed to rewrite l by r in any sequent if we have a known rewrite rule $l == r$.

Index

232